THE SUNDAY GAME 2010

THE SUNDAY GAME 2010

RTÉ

Gill & Macmillan

Gill & Macmillan Ltd
Hume Avenue, Park West, Dublin 12
with associated companies throughout the world
www.gillmacmillan.ie

978 07171 4790 8

Print origination and design by Outburst Design
Printed and bound in Italy by L.E.G.O SpA

This book is typeset in Trade Gothic 9pt on 11pt.

The paper used in this book comes from the wood pulp of managed forests.
For every tree felled, at least one tree is planted, thereby renewing natural resources.

A CIP catalogue record for this book is available from the British Library.

1 3 5 4 2

This book is dedicated to Mícheál Ó Muircheartaigh in recognition of his outstanding contribution to broadcasting with RTÉ and his long and passionate association with our national games.

CONTENTS THE SUNDAY GAME

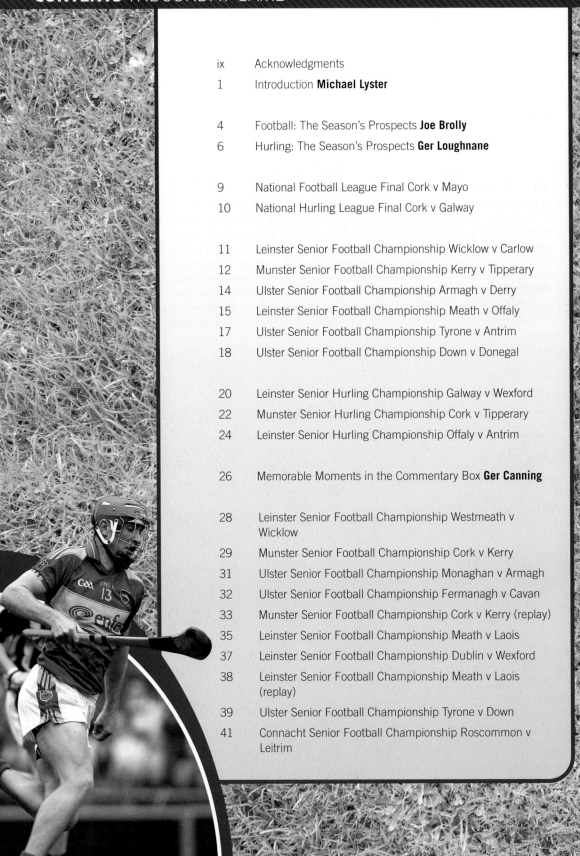

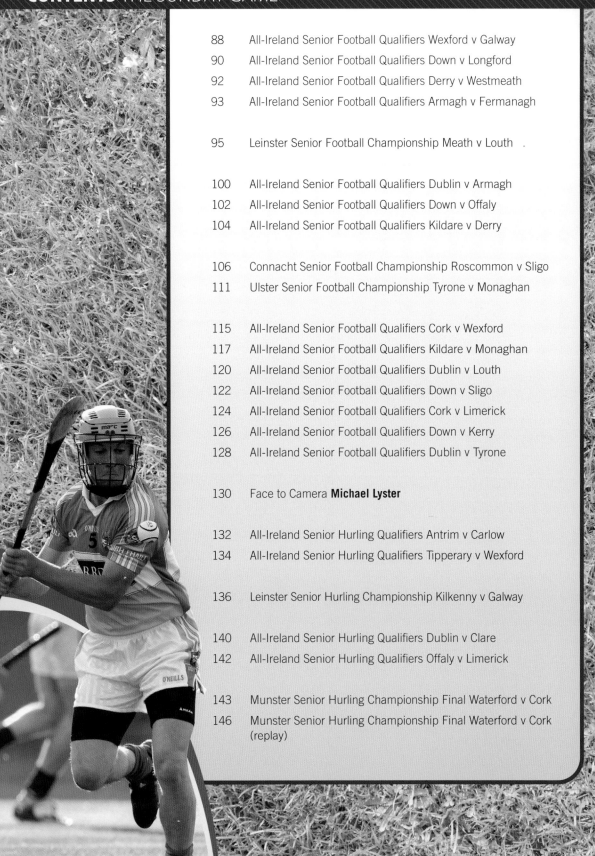

CONTENTS THE SUNDAY GAME

Thanks to all of the contributors and
to the staff of RTÉ Sport's GAA coverage for their
hard work and commitment in getting this book written.

MICHAEL LYSTER

For over thirty years *The Sunday Game* has been bringing you all the highs and lows of the Gaelic football and hurling championships. I suppose we're like passengers on a great rollercoaster ride. We watch the drama unfold and in turn deliver the best coverage and analysis of the championship throughout the summer.

There's always plenty of action to keep us busy in the studio as we react to what's happening on the field of play. The challenge for us is to adequately reflect the major talking points of each game we cover during the championship season. We watch out for things like what player is moving position? Who is switching with whom? Who is playing an extra midfielder or a sweeper? Where was that pass intended to go? Who is niggling? Who is fouling? What is happening off the ball and why is the umpire trying to get the referee's attention? Why are the crowd on Hill 16 suddenly cat-calling when there is no obvious incident on the field? Even with multiple cameras you sometimes don't have enough eyes to watch the modern GAA games.

You couldn't script drama like Joe Sheridan's Leinster Championship-winning goal, Benny Coulter's semi-final goal for Down, the could-it-really-happen moment when Lar Corbett of Tipperary fired the ball into the net past PJ Ryan after ten minutes of the All-Ireland hurling final or the high octane end-to-end action of the Munster hurling final and All-Ireland hurling quarter-finals.

In almost every game you're guaranteed one or two crucial incidents that will turn the entire summer for a county. Like when Ciaran Lyng's stoppage-time winner sent Galway out of the championship or when Kalum King's fingertips prevented Kildare from reaching the All-Ireland final. Every

championship is littered with tales of missed opportunity, and of the collective heartache suffered as counties bow out along the perilous route to championship glory.

This year was no different and come September Tipperary, Wexford, Cork and Dublin had collected the all-important trophies. Along the way they, and their opponents, left us with many enduring memories. Memories of a county team that gained some mid-summer momentum from an unpromising start; memories of that split-second decision that ultimately lead to the achievement of their dreams, as Tipperary did so spectacularly in hurling and Dublin and Kildare nearly did in football.

We were uplifted by the unforgettable joy on Cork faces in coming back to the scene of their many defeats to capture their first All-Ireland in twenty years. And if there is anything that resembles consensus in *The Sunday Game* studio (as if) we had something close to it this year: that Cork were overdue their All-Ireland success.

We also had, for the entire run of the hurling championship, the mouth-watering prospect of Kilkenny taking five in a row, something that has never been achieved in hurling history, only to have it snatched away by a blue and gold blitzkrieg on the first Sunday in September.

Neutrals traditionally dislike habitual winners and prefer to see change at the top. Though Tipperary are worthy and popular winners you couldn't help but feel sorry for

Kilkenny as they fell short when history beckoned. They have given us immense pleasure throughout the years and I suspect it will be a long time before we will see anyone capable of matching Kilkenny's 21 championship matches without defeat.

As always, when the final whistle sounds the talking begins, and this year we had lots of talking to do on *The Sunday Game*. Living rooms and social gatherings the length and breadth of the country are extensions of our studio. On *The Sunday Game* our aim is to instigate, invigorate and share in the nation's discussion. And to add to the day's talking points with some meaningful after-match comment from players, managers and, of course, our panel. Everybody who tunes in on a championship Sunday has a stake in the proceedings. It may be to support the county of their birth or temporary allegiance, or hoping to see a good match between two evenly matched teams, to witness a dramatic incident, or simply to be able to say they were there, that they watched as history was made. It is a compelling draw, as true today as when *The Sunday Game* first trundled their cameras into a GAA ground for the 1979 Munster hurling final between Cork and Limerick.

The 2010 championship provided plenty of topics for debate. Meath's Leinster championship win with a goal that was clearly not a goal. Down's All-Ireland semi-final victory with a goal that was not a goal. The hurling quarter-final between Galway and Tipperary was a match that thoroughly deserved to be described by that usually over-used word epic. For the first time in championship history none of the provincial champions made it to the All-Ireland semi-final, which was a talking point in itself.

You couldn't blink during a summer of incident: Tony Browne's last minute goal which set up another chapter in the on-going championship saga between Cork and Waterford. Offaly's excellence in a thrilling Leinster semi-final against a Galway side who were strongly fancied to be there or thereabouts come September. Sligo taking the scalp of the big two in Connacht before falling at the final hurdle to a young Roscommon side. The ever-intriguing neighbouring battle of Kerry and Cork. Dublin's surprise win over Clare and Antrim's subsequent surprise victory over favourites Dublin. The list goes on, the moments too numerous to recount, the heroic efforts of the players impossible to put in to words.

But that's the task that faced our commentators Ger Canning, Darragh Maloney, Marty Morrissey and Micheal Ó Sé each week as they followed the action. Back in the studio we then scratched our heads and tried to make sense of it all.

I am not sure we succeeded, but we had great fun trying.

Be it with our hurling panellists Ger Loughnane, Cyril Farrell and Tomás Mulcahy or the football team of Joe Brolly, Colm O'Rourke and Pat Spillane the discussions were often heated and the arguments seldom resolved Joe, who predicted a win for Down, is still expecting the third half of the football final to begin so he can convince us that he was right all along!

Obviously the players and managers are crucial to the enjoyment of the championship and to the programme; the analysts, commentators and reporters add another layer to the complex tapestry that makes a championship event. And then of course there are the fans, they give the championship, and by extension *The Sunday Game*, its great sense of colour and excitement.

The flags, the colours and the banter are what makes these championship days special. There's also the thrill of seeing your neighbour, your postman or your teacher playing for your county. Unlike so many other sporting codes, the super stars within the GAA are local, they have a connection with the community and that community shows its appreciation and admiration by turning up, week in week out, to cheer for their side.

The ethos of GAA hasn't changed throughout its long and successful existence. The traditions continue to be passed on to younger generations, and in growing numbers.

The viewership for the football final in 2010 was the highest in five years, an average of 900,000* viewers watched the match with a peak audience of over a million (1.064 million**) in the final minutes. That is on top of the 81,604 who attended the football and 81,765 at the hurling final.

At its heart, the GAA is still a community organisation built on local allegiances and based on altruism and service to the greater good. Without the volunteers who give their free time to look after young players, and who take part in fund-raising for facilities and outdoor activities it wouldn't exist. We try to reflect that on *The Sunday Game* and to pay tribute to those countless volunteers.

The GAA has long cherished its status as 'more than a sporting organisation'. For many of us *The Sunday Game* is more than a sports show. Over the decades it has become a place to share emotion; the elation of victory or the despair of defeat, the anger of being on the receiving end of a controversial call or the relief of having come through those close contentious moments.

Our analysts and panellists have become a channel for our rapidly evolving popular culture. Behind the camera a full team of people are working hard to complete the package. A package that complements the games with statistical analysis and strong expert opinion throughout the season

There is always a sense of sadness when the lights go down on *The Sunday Game* every September for another year but this book, looking back on the year and the great moments it provided, will help fill the wait until next May. Roll on 2011, the opening bars of Jägerlatein (*The Sunday Game* theme tune) another championship, and another season of *The Sunday Game*.

Source: Nielsen TV Audience Measurement
*Actual match average 15:29-17:02, Live + VOSDAL
** One-minute peak viewership, Live + VOSDAL

JOE BROLLY

Galway better not doze off in the city that never sleeps. It is a curious anomaly that there is no back door for the losers of this annual transatlantic fixture, presumably because no one has ever contemplated the possibility of New York actually winning. This year they are training hard and have picked up a few very good players. Complacency can be fatal, particularly in the narrow confines of a blazing hot Gaelic Park. Galway will survive, but their ambitions will be confined to the province, where I expect a three-horse race. Joe Kernan was hired to win an All-Ireland, but this will not happen, no matter how many trophies he smashes against the wall.

Mayo, meanwhile, will not recover from the shattering blow dealt them by Cork in the league final. The repeated public beatings they have taken at HQ have created a psychological fear deep in their bones. To win, you must first believe. Not even Nelson Mandela could cure their problem now.

This brings me to Sligo who, for all their shortcomings, do genuinely trust themselves. Apart from a stutter in their first league game against Antrim in Belfast, they were imperious in Division 3. Fit, strong, well motivated and carrying no baggage, they could easily upset Connacht's biggish two.

In Ulster, the main question is whether Tyrone are pretending to be bad, or really are. It is stretching it to think their woeful showing in the league was Mickey Harte's greatest con trick. For their do or die league finale against the Dubs at home, I expected them to flex their muscle. Instead the Dubs gave them a hiding. Most of their great team are gone or on the wane and the resultant loss of chemistry is permanent. 'Brian Dooher is back in training' just doesn't mean that much any more. Yet, they could win Ulster, on the basis that even in their weakened state, they remain experts in the art of winning. Antrim first, followed by Down or Donegal, will not scare them. Once in the final, who would bet against them?

Derry might have a big day or two if Eoin Bradley and the forwards go mad, but with no established number 3, 6, 8 or 11, we do not have the strong spine required for a sustained championship run.

The Fermanagh experiment is extinct; Cavan are afraid of their own shadow and Donegal will flip flop about as usual, entirely dependent on their nineteen-year-old wunderkind Michael Murphy. Why they persist in a short hand-passing game when Kieran Donaghy's heir apparent is on the edge of their square is beyond me. James McCartan has taught Down to defend as a group, but simply doesn't have the players to go much further.

Armagh, meanwhile, might make a challenge on the basis that they have prototypical players at full-back (Donaghy), centre-back (McKeever), midfield (Toner) and full forward (McDonnell/Clarke). Yet they are not as good as they looked in the Division 2 final and their overwhelmingly defensive game-plan is not suited to the big days in Croke Park.

Monaghan are the real dark horse in Ulster. Seamus McEnaney has always brought war, save for last year when they lost their confidence in the face of widespread criticisms of their style and collapsed against Derry in the qualifiers in truly abject fashion. But their battling league campaign confirms they are again ready to rumble. Crucially, Conor McManus is now providing proper support to Thomas Freeman up front. Since he was a child, Conor has been described by Monaghan people as 'a great bit of stuff'. He is now mature enough to show it on the big stage.

The Dubs are the most interesting team in this championship. Pat Gilroy has finally abolished their 30-year passion for all-out attack coupled with defending like the Italian army. At last, they have an arse in their trousers. Against Tyrone, their biggest game of the league against a team that has inflicted so much harm on them in the millennium, the Dubs started with only four of last year's championship team and a brand new full-back line. They proceeded to out-Tyrone them, shutting them out, turning them over, then counter-attacking with precision. That performance confirmed that the days of glorious failure are gone. They are 2010's dark horse.

As for Kildare, they blew their big chance last year. As Fermanagh under Malachy O'Rourke have shown, you can only punch above your weight for so long before something gives, and it is already starting to give for McGeeney's men.

Meath are unchanged, remaining at a level below the top tier, yet still able to scare the pants off anyone. A rollicking good Leinster championship beckons, with the Dubs winning their sixth in a row, this time without the high fives and public self-loving. This year it will be a mere stepping stone. Anyone who takes a different view will not be on Pat Gilroy's panel long.

The championship is an annual testament to the power of optimism. Teams like Wicklow, Antrim, Sligo and Monaghan will have their fun. Marty Morrissey will have the odd near heart attack at a last minute goal from Benny Coulter or a fabulous high catch by the Leitrim midfielder. We will pore over the chances of every team in minute detail. But in the end, 2010 boils down to Cork and Kerry. Cork's casual, regular annihilations of good

Divison 1 teams is an ominous warning. They are now feared in a way that no other team is. But after three years, the pressure is firmly on them to deliver, which means delivering against the Kingdom. They may swat the others like flies, but can they conquer their biggest fear? Kerry are certainly diminished.

Their game-changer last year was Tommy Walsh, but to Conor Counihan's relief, the young Dolph Lundgren is now ram-raiding his way through the Antipodes. Their second most influential player was Tadhg Kennelly, who might soon be Tommy's agent. Finally, Darragh Ó Sé, the man who annually hung the kryptonite round Nicholas Murphy's neck, is gone. Compensation comes however in the form of a refreshed and super fit Donaghy, Gaelic football's most influential player. And they are still the Kingdom, sporting the country's best forward division and second smartest manager. Like Tyrone, they are experts in the art of winning big championship matches.

There are two big challenges for Cork. Firstly, Conor Counihan must prove that he can compete with Jack O'Connor on the line, an area where he was comprehensively trumped last year. Secondly, the Cork players must break Kerry's psychological hold over them. No better man to lead that charge than Paul Kerrigan, . whose father, Jimmy, was part of the rebel forces that buried Kerry's last great empire. The new rebellion is finally ready. 2010 will make or break it.

September Postscript
There is nothing more dangerous than May predictions, written before a ball has been kicked in anger. On the plus column, Tyrone did indeed win Ulster and the biggest prize was beyond the old legs of Dooher. Sligo should have won Connacht, but having put the big two to the sword, they forgot about Roscommon. The Dubs probably were 'the most interesting team in the championship' and but for a few moments of indiscipline might have won it outright. And Cork are in fact the champions, even though they avoided the Kingdom and in the end did their best to blow it. And New York nearly did Galway over!

On the other hand, I was wrong about Kildare (even if the Louth debacle initially confirmed my view) and like Kerry, didn't foresee the Down revolution. I really must start getting this crystal ball serviced more regularly...

GER LOUGHNANE

Every hurling season starts with an air of expectation, speculation and optimism for the contending counties. This year however is extra special as the hurlers of Kilkenny set out on the road to immortality, the elusive five in a row, a feat never before accomplished in the 126 year history of the GAA.

Kerry came closest in football in 1982 when a last gasp goal by Seamus Darby from Offaly denied them their place in history, something that still haunts many Kerry football people today. It's an ironic twist of fate that the team that beat them and the man who scored the goal are now as famous as football's greatest ever team. If any county can knock out Kilkenny in the final stages of the championship this year immortality awaits them in just the same way.

So who are the challengers? Tipperary must be in pole position following their near miss against the champions in last year's epic All-Ireland final. Rarely have so many players on the same team played to the absolute maximum of their ability and still ended up losing. Failure to take gilt-edged goal chances, erratic refereeing and some poor sideline decision making undid them. If they have learned from these mistakes and if they manage to get as far as a semi-final or final against the same opposition the desire for redemption might get them over the line. On the way they need to unearth two wing-forwards capable of gaining possession for their own puck-outs, and a hardworking midfield partner for Shane McGrath. This year they must go all the way and get the reward that they deserve for their work over the past three years.

Next comes Galway; an ordinary team with an extraordinary player in the brilliant Joe Canning. It is a measure of his genius that without him Galway would not be viewed as contenders, not to mention potential champions. His level of skill, his vision, his strength and his big-match temperament set him apart as the greatest forward of the modern era. Galway are the league champions but it is their consistency so far this year that has encouraged

their followers. The combination of a settled goalkeeper and full-back line, a half-back line which will be better when John Lee gains full fitness, an exciting and creative midfield by Ger Farragher and David Bourke, and a forward line that combines pace, power and skill to complement the genius of Canning looks ideal to unhinge Kilkenny. They might get two chances to do so, in the Leinster Final and then the All-Ireland – if they are good enough.

Cork come next thanks to their strong tradition and ability to produce their best form when it's most needed. Their big problem is that they are almost totally reliant on the stars from the first half of the last decade. In the last five years only three players of real quality have emerged: Eoin Cadogan, Shane O'Neill and Pat Horgan. Despite this they can never be underestimated. Should they win their championship clash on 30 May against Tipperary in Páirc Uí Chaoimh they will most likely face Waterford in the Munster final in another episode in the long-running history of epic games between these two counties over the past ten years.

What a pity Waterford haven't won at least one All-Ireland in that time. But all is not lost. Davy Fitzgerald has steadied the ship since he arrived there in controversial circumstances three seasons ago and through careful planning they are now set for one more assault on hurling's summit. For many of Waterford's great players this will be their final climb, but even if they fail, hurling's future in the county is secure as fantastic work has been done at underage level leading to great success at school and county level. Waterford will remain a real hurling force.

Of the rest Clare will

not be a force for the next four years as, due to retirements and internal turmoil, Ger O'Loughlin is left with a young team lacking in power and field leaders.

Limerick hurling should be declared a disaster area by GAA hurling powers. All power should be temporarily removed from their officers and the board should be run by Croke Park for the next three years. Limerick is important to hurling given the few genuine hurling counties we have. The collateral damage caused by the dispute will take years to repair and while it is not the end of hurling in Limerick it does signal the end of Limerick as a genuine force for the foreseeable future.

For once the Leinster championship is more interesting and more competitive than its long-dominant Munster neighbour. Galway's participation has brought new life to the province and Wexford, fresh from their promotion to Division 1, will have a right go at lowering them in Nowlan Park on 29 May. It's a tricky game

for Galway as Wexford have a core of very experienced players and will play with freedom as they are not expected to win.

Laois, Carlow and Antrim will also hope for a good run in the qualifiers but Carlow and Laois in particular are making great strides in trying to bridge the gap between second and top tier. The first big day out in Leinster will be in Croke Park on 20 June when, most likely, Offaly play Galway and Kilkenny play Dublin.

Offaly have been touted as an up and coming team for the past five years but their progress has been mostly in the wrong direction. Over the years they have done well to upset fancied Galway teams but this is unlikely to happen this year.

Dublin got to the Leinster finals last year by beating a very poor Wexford side in the semi-final but they performed well against Kilkenny in the Leinster final, the game not over until Martin Comerford scored a Kilkenny goal towards the end.

Kilkenny will be on their guard as they know that Dublin's up-and-at'-em all-action style will demand their full concentration and commitment. Kilkenny are the team holding all the aces. Noel Hickey and

Clare's Darach Honan celebrates a goal

'Cha' Fitz are back giving the back line and midfield a more solid and balanced look and no other county has so many top-class forwards to choose from. Their hunger for success will not be a problem as Kilkenny players are born with an insatiable desire to win in every game and in every competition.

So, here are my predictions for championship 2010:

MUNSTER

First Round: Tipperary to beat Cork
Semi-finals: Waterford to beat Clare and Tipp to beat Limerick
Final: Tipp to beat Waterford

LEINSTER

First Round: Galway to beat Wexford
Dublin to beat Laois
Offaly to beat Antrim
Semi-Finals: Galway to beat Offaly
Kilkenny to beat Dublin

Quarter Finals: Cork, Galway, Waterford, Dublin
Semi- Finals Winners: Tipperary, Kilkenny
Final: Kilkenny to beat Tipperary for five in row.

There will be shocks, controversies, dull games and epic games but for one team in 2010 immortality beckons!

September Postscript

Long-term sports predicting is a bit like long-term weather forecasting, you have a fair idea of what is likely to happen, but it's only as the time gets closer and you can read the signs that you have a better grasp of the likely outcome. Many people had predicted a Tipperary v Kilkenny All-Ireland Hurling final but few would have forecast the route that Tipp would follow.

But, in the lead up to the final, it was easy to see the storm clouds gathering over Kilkenny. Injuries to Henry Shefflin and John Tennyson were bad enough, but worse still was the circus that ensued. When a team's training session gets more publicity than any of their previous championship matches you know immediately that the team is in trouble.

Playing these two brilliant players when they were crippled with cruciate injuries was like driving a car at full speed with the nuts loose in one wheel. It was only a matter of time before it came off. This is the main reason why, in the days leading up to the final, I was certain Tipp would win. Anyway, even with a fully fit team Kilkenny would not have beaten Tipp this year and were extremely lucky to do so last year.

The highlights of the year for me were Cork's victory over Tipp in late May, Waterford's replay win under lights in Thurles in the Munster final and the Tipp v Galway quarter-final. The game of the year was the final, with Tipperary completely dominating the great Kilkenny team to become the worthiest of champions and open up new possibilities for many other teams for next year. Roll on 2011.

Limerick's Cathal Mullane with Tommy Walsh of Kilkenny

Division 1 Final

CORK 1-17 0-12 **MAYO**

25 April 2010

Cork recorded a comprehensive victory over Mayo in the Allianz National Football League Division 1 final in front of 27,005 spectators at Croke Park.

The superb finishing of Donncha O'Connor illuminated the game. His five points sent the Rebels in with a 0-09 to 0-05 advantage, with three of Mayo's scores coming from Conor Mortimer as they rued three missed goal chances in the opening period.

Mayo were never able to augment the excellent finishing of Mortimer, who tallied six points.

Meanwhile, the Rebels scored at will, with Daniel Goulding banging in a 63rd-minute goal to establish a personal tally of 1-05.

The reigning Division 2 champions efficiently and stylishly saw off the challenge of Mayo to lift the New Ireland Cup, recording a resounding victory which will ease them gently into serious preparations for the Munster Championship.

Mayo's long-ball strategy crafted three goal chances in as many minutes midway through the first half.

But Aidan O'Shea punched Kevin McLoughlin's delivery against the crossbar, Mark Ronaldson blazed his opportunity wide, and Jamie O'Sullivan denied O'Shea with a superb block.

Cork had already moved 0-04 to 0-01 ahead by that stage, with Patrick Kelly getting the pick of their well-crafted scores.

And, unfazed by the close shaves at the back, they continued to pick off points from distance, with O'Connor blasting over a couple of huge efforts.

Alan Dillon and Conor Mortimer converted frees to close the gap, but Dillon's creativity failed to inspire his fellow attackers to find the range, until Mortimer became the first Mayo attacker to score from play in the 31st minute.

O'Connor added another couple off both feet, and by the halfway stage, the Rebels had established a 0-09 to 0-05 advantage.

Mortimer nailed on another couple of scores, but Daniel Goulding and Alan O'Connor knocked over points to maintain a safe distance between the sides, with Mayo goalkeeper David Clarke forced to stretch to deflect O'Connor's fisted effort over the bar.

The introduction of Ronan McGarrity lifted Mayo, and they pulled back scores through Mortimer and Andy Moran, but Cork were scoring at will, and they put the outcome beyond all doubt in the 63rd minute when Ciaran Sheehan picked out Goulding with a perfectly timed pass, and the corner-forward slotted the ball past Clarke for a personal tally of 1-05.

Mayo scored the last three points of the game, but it mattered little, even when Andy Moran's deflected shot was pushed round a post by Cork goalkeeper Patrick O'Shea.

CORK: P O'Shea; R Carey, M Shields, E Cotter; N O'Leary (0-01), P Kissane, J O'Sullivan; A O'Connor (0-01), A Walsh (0-01); F Goold, D O'Connor (0-05), P Kelly (0-01); D Goulding (1-05), C Sheehan (0-02), P Kerrigan (0-01)
Subs: N Murphy for F Goold; D Kavanagh for A Walsh; C O'Neill for D O'Connor; J Hayes for D Goulding; G Spillane for M Shields

MAYO: D Clarke; C Barrett, G Cafferkey, L O'Malley; D Vaughan, T Howley, K McLoughlin; T Parsons, S O'Shea (0-02); A Moran (0-01), A Dillon (0-03), T Mortimer; C Mortimer (0-06), A O'Shea, M Ronaldson
Subs: R McGarrity for M Ronaldson; A Kilcoyne for T Mortimer; A Freeman for Parsons; B Moran for T Mortimer; P Harte for A O'Shea

REFEREE: P Hughes (Armagh)

Division 1 Final

GALWAY 2-22 | 1-17 **CORK**

2 May 2010

Full-back and captain Shane Kavanagh led by example as Galway won their first National Hurling League Division 1 title since 2004, with a 2-22 to 1-17 victory over Cork at Semple Stadium.

The crowd may have been 3000 less than last year's final attendance, but the 14,200 paying customers were treated to a thrilling game of championship intensity, particularly in the first half.

It did not take long for the fireworks to ignite, with Damien Hayes bulging the back of the Cork net with just a minute and 15 seconds gone on the clock.

The Portumna clubman cut in from the right corner, rounding Sean Óg Ó hAilpín before pushing his side into a 1-00 to 0-00 lead with an angled shot.

Both sides were clinical in front of the posts during a keenly-contested opening half, with Ben O'Connor's impressive sideline cuts, allied to John Gardiner's excellent long-range efforts, delighting the Rebels' supporters.

A first Andy Smith point edged Galway into a 1-03 to 0-04 lead after 16 minutes following good work by Hayes and Ger Farragher, but Cork's creative juices were beginning to flow.

Scores from Michael Cussen and Gardiner ensured the sides were level for the first time after 18 minutes, but Galway quickly responded.

Farragher was immense for the Tribesmen throughout this contest and his quick brace of points edged Galway 1-05 to 0-06 in front.

But Cork, hoping to seal a football-hurling league double, bounced back with a superb kicked goal from Cathal Naughton, after Ben O'Connor had done the groundwork.

That strike put Cork ahead for the first time, but their joy was short-lived.

Joe Canning, one of the most dangerous forwards in the country, used his strength to firstly brush off corner-back Brian Murphy before rounding the inexperienced Eoin Dillon to fire a rasping shot past goalkeeper Dónal Óg Cusack.

Armed with a 2-05 to 1-06 buffer, John McIntyre's men would not relinquish the lead for the remainder of the game.

No more than three points separated the sides over the next twelve minutes, before Farragher's fifth point of the final opened a four-point lead at the break at 2-12 to 1-11.

Joe Canning continued to prove his worth in the second half, landing a superb point within 30 seconds of the restart.

Despite Cork scoring three of the next four points, Galway proved to be top dogs in the second half, with Kavanagh and Ollie Canning starring in defence.

The Connacht side, winners of the Walsh Cup in February, hit three points in succession as Joe Canning, Smith and Iarla Tannian added well-taken scores.

Pat Horgan, Kieran 'Fraggy' Murphy, Cathal Naughton and substitute Jerry O'Connor did their utmost to keep the Rebels in touch.

Galway could afford to strike twelve second-half wides, while at the opposite end goalkeeper Colm Callanan produced some excellent saves.

He batted a stinging penalty effort from Horgan over the crossbar, and was assured under pressure from Cork's twin towers, Aisake Ó hAilpín and Michael Cussen.

Cork desperately needed a goal but they could not find a way past a stubborn and hard-working Galway defence, with substitute Joe Gantley firing over the insurance points for the new league champions.

GALWAY: C Callanan; D Joyce, S Kavanagh, O Canning; D Barry, T Óg Regan, D Collins; G Farragher (0-06), D Burke (0-01); A Harte (0-03), C Donnellan (0-01), A Smith (0-02); D Hayes (1-01), J Canning (1-05), I Tannian (0-01)
Subs: J Gantley (0-02) for I Tannian; K Hynes for A Smith; N Callahan for D Burke

CORK: D Óg Cusack; S O'Neill, E Dillon, B Murphy; J Gardiner (0-03), R Curran (0-01), S Óg Ó hAilpín; T Kenny, L McLoughlin; M Cussen (0-02), K Murphy (0-02), C Naughton (1-01), B O'Connor (0-04), A Ó hAilpín, P Horgan (0-03)
Subs: J O'Connor (0-01) for L McLoughlin; M Walsh for S Óg Ó hAilpín; P O'Sullivan for K Murphy

REFEREE: J Owens (Wexford)

WICKLOW 3-13 0-12 CARLOW
16 May 2010

A hat-trick of goals saw Wicklow clear the Leinster Championship's first hurdle as they overcame Carlow at O'Moore Park.

Wicklow had Nicky Mernagh sent off in first half injury-time but a Paul Earls goal ensured a 1-06 to 0-06 lead for them at the break.

Carlow lost midfielders Brendan Murphy (straight red) and Thomas Walsh (second yellow) in the closing 35 minutes, and their provincial hopes were ended by further goals from Wicklow's Leighton Glynn and JP Dalton.

After a pulsating encounter that saw referee Gearóid Ó Conamha award three red cards and 16 yellows, the reward for Mick O'Dwyer's men is a quarter-final clash with Westmeath on 6 June.

Carlow dominated possession in the opening half, but were unable to make it count on the scoreboard as they registered seven wides inside the opening 21 minutes.

Wicklow were more clinical: centre-forward Tony Hannon fired over two of his side's first three points and Leighton Glynn was also on target as the Garden County built a 0-03 to 0-00 lead.

Carlow were left exposed defensively, while the expected midfield dominance by former Aussie Rules hopeful Brendan Murphy and ex-Wicklow player Thomas Walsh failed to materialise in the opening quarter.

Luke Dempsey's charges had registered four wides before Murphy landed Carlow's opening point to cut the deficit to two points.

The Rathvilly clubman soon added a second, and a Simon Rea free levelled this local derby for the first time in the 18th minute.

But Wicklow took control with Earls' 33rd-minute goal putting them in the driving seat.

There was some excellent play by Hannon and defender Patrick McWalter in the lead-up to the goal which saw the St Patrick's clubman shake off a defender before knocking the ball beyond the reach of goalkeeper James Clarke.

The strike gave Wicklow a 1-06 to 0-04 advantage but they were on the back foot in injury-time, with the dismissal of Mernagh and two Rea points leaving a goal between the sides at the break.

There was nothing pedestrian about the second-half display of either side, with Wicklow's numerical disadvantage failing to show.

McWalter bagged another Wicklow point within 40 seconds of the restart, with scores from Hannon and Glynn giving O'Dwyer's side a 1-10 to 0-07 lead by the 45th minute.

Carlow pressed hard, with Murphy beginning to exert his authority on proceedings, although Wicklow goalkeeper Mervyn Travers denied him in the 58th minute.

The Barrowsiders were reduced to 14 men when Murphy saw red with eight-and-a-half minutes remaining. They tried hard to pick up the pieces but were dealt a huge blow with two sucker-punch goals in a six-minute spell.

Wicklow captain Glynn found the net after an excellent long ball in from midfielder JP Dalton. Glynn outpaced both Padraig Murphy and Benny Kavanagh before beating Clarke from close range.

Dalton turned scorer as he completed Wicklow's hat-trick in the 68th minute, nipping the ball past Clarke to put his side 3-11 to 0-09 in front.

Carlow rallied in the closing stages with scores from substitute Daniel St Ledger and defender Alan Curran. But it was too late for Dempsey's side to stage a recovery and Wicklow progressed through to the last eight.

WICKLOW: M Travers; S Kelly, D O'hAnnaidh, A Byrne; P McWalter (0-01), B McGrath, D Hayden; J Stafford, D Jackman; L Glynn (1-04), T Hannon (0-06), N Mernagh; D Odlum, S Furlong (0-02), P Earls (1-00)
Subs: JP Dalton (1-00) for D Jackman; S Canavan for P McWalter; P Dalton for D Odlum

CARLOW: J Clarke; P Murphy, L Murphy, B Kavanagh; A Curran (0-03), J Hayden, P McElligott; B Murphy (0-03), T Walsh; S Gannon, D Foley, M Carpenter; S Rea (0-04), J Murphy, J Kavanagh.
Subs: S Redmond for L Murphy; JJ Smith (0-01) for D Foley; D St Ledger (0-01) for J Murphy; P Cashin for J Hayden

REFEREE: G Ó Conamha (Galway)

Thomas Walsh of Carlow

11

KERRY 2-18 2-06 TIPPERARY
16 May 2010

Kieran Donaghy pulled the strings for All-Ireland champions Kerry as they passed this early summer examination against Tipperary, running out 12-point winners.

The 4,965-strong Thurles crowd had hopes of an upset as Tipperary ended the first half just 0-08 to 1-04 in arrears. But, turning with the wind, the Kingdom hit their stride in the second period to cruise through to a semi-final showdown with Munster title holders Cork.

The visitors hit the front after a minute and 20 seconds, Donaghy turning inside two defenders to land the opening point.

But Tipperary levelled with a '45' from Barry Grogan and took a seventh-minute lead when Philip Austin beat Brendan Kealy with a measured finish.

Hugh Coghlan played the ball through for the pacy centre-forward to evade Tom O'Sullivan's challenge and crack a rasping right-footed shot to the bottom-left corner of the net.

Peter Acheson landed a point soon after but Kerry were back level at 1-02 to 0-05 by the quarter-hour mark.

Colm Cooper and Paul Galvin got Kerry back on terms, but they should have been in front. Brian Sheehan had a 14th-minute goal disallowed for an illegal hand-pass from Donaghy, a decision that may well have gone for Kerry on another day.

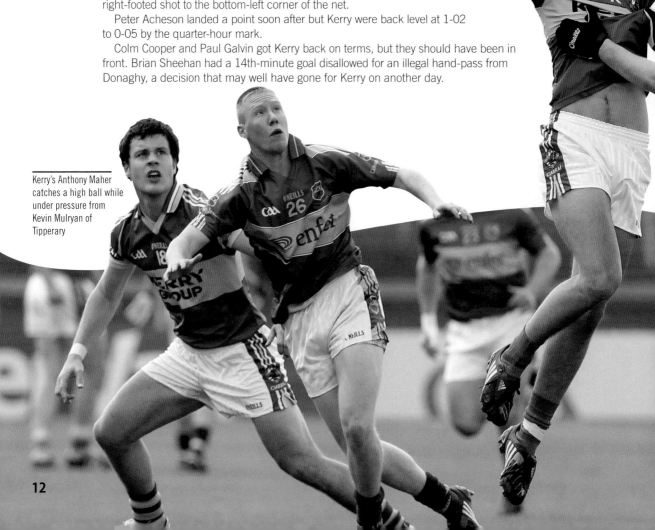

Kerry's Anthony Maher catches a high ball while under pressure from Kevin Mulryan of Tipperary

The sides were level for a third time as Sheehan cancelled out a George Hannigan effort from play, and despite coming under increasing pressure, Tipp were able to hold their own.

Their goalkeeper, Paul Fitzgerald, blocked a goal-bound effort from Donaghy and the Tralee giant had two wides in quick succession as the Tipp rearguard did their job in frustrating Kerry's fluent forwards.

Cooper watched a point attempt bounce back off the post, and the Premier County went back in front when a strong burst in from the left from Austin set up a Brian Mulvihill point.

Kerry were rewarded for their persistence in the closing stages of the half as pointed efforts from Sheehan and Galvin put them ahead 0-08 to 1-04.

In the second half Sheehan hit the woodwork with a point attempt, and Cooper traded points with Grogan as Jack O'Connor's charges kept ahead. Donaghy, as a target man, played a key role in most of Kerry's advance. After Declan O'Sullivan had fisted over and Grogan pointed at the other end, Kerry's full-forward showed his worth when tapping down a high ball for the hard-working

Donnacha Walsh to slot over.

Sheehan added a free and then collected his first goal. The Tipp defence was caught out in the 47th minute as Tomás Ó Sé and Mike McCarthy raided forward; the latter's point attempt failed to find the target but Donaghy scooped the ball over for Sheehan to slip a low shot to the net for a 1-12 to 1-06 score line.

Tipp were unfortunate not to close the gap as Austin went wide from a kickable free and Kealy had to be on his toes to block a snap shot from Acheson.

They did manage to whittle Kerry's lead down to three points when the Kerry net-minder was beaten to a high ball by Grogan for Tipp's second goal in the 52nd minute.

Sheehan and Seamus Scanlon cancelled out the goal and then a terrific catch from Donaghy set up a point for substitute Barry John Keane who quickly added his second point as increasing amounts of space appeared in the Tipp defence.

Five minutes from the finish, another top-drawer catch and feed by Donaghy teed up Sheehan for a drilled finish to the bottom left corner of Paul Fitzgerald's net.

Cooper added Kerry's final point in injury-time.

Tipperary have a long wait until the first round of the All-Ireland qualifiers and their search for a first Munster Championship win since 2003 goes on.

TIPPERARY: P Fitzgerald; P Codd, N Curran, C McDonald; C Aylward, R Costigan, C McGrath; K Mulryan, G Hannigan (0-01); P Acheson (0-01), P Austin (1-00), H Coghlan; S Carey, B Grogan (1-03), B Mulvihill (0-01)

Subs: B Fox for H Coghlan; B Fox for B Mulvihill; B Coen for S Carey; J Cagney for P Austin; B Jones for C Aylward; A Morrissey for C McGrath

KERRY: B Kealy; M Ó Sé, T Griffin, T O'Sullivan; T Ó Sé, M McCarthy, K Young; S Scanlon(0-01), M Quirke; P Galvin (0-02), Declan O'Sullivan (0-01), D Walsh (0-01); C Cooper (0-05), K Donaghy (0-01), B Sheehan (2-05)

Subs: P Reidy for T O'Sullivan; Darran O'Sullivan for P Galvin; A Maher for M Quirke; A O'Connell for K Young; BJ Keane (0-02) for Declan O'Sullivan

REFEREE: D Coldrick (Meath)

13

ARMAGH **1-10** **1-07** DERRY

16 May 2010

Armagh inflicted a first Celtic Park championship defeat on Derry since 1994 to set up a first-round Ulster Senior Football Championship meeting with Monaghan.

A drama-packed second half saw the game take two decisive twists in favour of Paddy O'Rourke's side.

Firstly, influential Derry attacker Eoin Bradley was sent off, and almost immediately, Orchard substitute Jamie Clarke pounced for a match-winning goal.

In front of a crowd of 10,242, Armagh almost got in for a goal in the opening minute when Brian Mallon went one-on-one with Barry Gillis, but the Derry goalkeeper pulled off a brilliant save to deny the Tír na nÓg man.

It was point-for-point all the way throughout the opening 22 minutes, with the Oak Leafers pulling away with frees from Paddy Bradley and Mark Lynch, only to be pegged back by Aaron Kernan and Steven McDonnell.

A tense contest burst to life in the 30th minute when Paddy Bradley grabbed a goal. Patsy Bradley beat James Lavery to possession in midfield, before Lynch and Fergal Doherty combined for the latter to pick the former All-Star attacker out at the far post. Bradley still had plenty to do, diving at full stretch to punch past Paul Hearty.

That was the signal for McDonnell to show his class yet again. He fired over four points late in the half, two of them from exceptionally difficult frees, to level the scores and send the sides in at the break deadlocked at 1-05 to 0-08.

Charlie Vernon displayed tremendous strength to hold off Fergal Doherty as he powered through to shoot Armagh in front for the first time two minutes into the second half.

Derry suffered a double blow at the beginning of the final quarter. First Eoin Bradley picked up a second booking after hauling Aaron Kernan to the ground.

Less than two minutes later, the Orchard men forged ahead with a goal from substitute Jamie Clarke. The Crossmaglen youngster collected McDonnell's cross from the left to shoot deftly past Gillis for a 1-10 to 1-06 lead.

Derry managed just two points in the second half against a solid Armagh defence in which Kieran Toner, Brendan Donaghy and Ciaran McKeever were outstanding.

Derry were thrown a lifeline five minutes from the end when they were awarded a penalty after Finnian Moriarty charged into Paddy Bradley, but Gerard O'Kane's kick was superbly saved by Hearty.

DERRY: B Gillis; B Óg McAlary, K McGuckin, D McBride; G O'Kane, B McGuigan, M Bateson; F Doherty, Patsy Bradley; SL McGoldrick, M Lynch (0-4) D Mullan; Paddy Bradley (1-02), E Bradley (0-01), R Wilkinson
Subs: B McGoldrick for B McGuigan; J Kielt for R Wilkinson; M Craig for M Bateson; J Diver for F Doherty; E Muldoon for SL McGoldrick

ARMAGH: P Hearty; A Mallon, K Toner, B Donaghy; P Duffy, C McKeever, F Moriarty; C Vernon (0-01), J Lavery; M Mackin, A Kernan (0-03), G Swift; B Mallon, S McDonnell (0-05), R Henderson (0-01)
Subs: V Martin for J Lavery; J Clarke (1-00) for R Henderson; M McNamee for M Mackin

REFEREE: M Deegan (Laois)

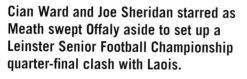

MEATH 1-20 2-07 OFFALY
23 May 2010

Cian Ward and Joe Sheridan starred as Meath swept Offaly aside to set up a Leinster Senior Football Championship quarter-final clash with Laois.

Ward and Sheridan were in blistering form for the Royals, who led by 0-11 to 2-03 at half-time in Portlaoise. Brian Connor and Ken Casey netted Offaly's goals.

But with Offaly midfielder John Coughlan shown a straight red card in the 39th minute, Meath dominated for the remainder and Sheridan's 68th-minute goal sealed it.

Offaly began the game brightly and exerted most of the early pressure, with Niall Darby firing over the opening score in the second minute.

Meath were soon off the mark and although Niall McNamee levelled in the tenth minute for Offaly, the Faithful County failed to score in the next 11 minutes as Eamonn O'Brien's pre-match favourites marched into an ominous 0-07 to 0-02 lead.

Free-taker Cian Ward was Meath's sharpest player in the opening quarter, but Offaly bounced back thanks to a 21st-minute goal from Brian Connor.

Offaly's Ciaran McManus and Anthony Moyles of Meath

15

The championship debutant cut the deficit to two points thanks to a well-executed goal which involved both Niall McNamee and Niall Darby.

Meath added a trio of points – with the impressive Shane O'Rourke, Cian Ward and defender Gary O'Brien all on target – to claim a 0-10 to 1-02 advantage with six minutes remaining in the opening half.

However, Offaly grabbed a timely second goal. McNamee was again involved as he caught a long-range delivery from Conor McManus and fed Ken Casey to finish to the net.

McNamee got the better of Eoghan Harrington as he raided through to set up a one-on-one with the Meath goalkeeper. Paddy O'Rourke saved the Offaly forward's initial effort and just as the ball rebounded to McNamee, referee Derek Fahy blew for half-time, much to the disgust of the Offaly players. Veteran midfielder McManus was yellow carded for his protests.

It summed up what had been a stop-start opening period, peppered by the referee's whistle and with the controversial hand-pass rule once again causing problems.

As the second half started, Offaly hit the ground running as goal scorer Casey landed the first point inside 50 seconds of the restart. But this was as close as Tom Cribbin's men could get to last year's beaten All-Ireland semi-finalists.

Offaly's chances grew bleak when they lost Coughlan to a red card, awarded for an apparent elbow to the head of Meath full-back Anthony Moyles.

Meath used their numerical advantage to press on, with Ward slotting over his fifth point, and Offaly's woes continued to mount as Darby sent his fourth effort wide of the posts.

Offaly's wides tally now stood at eight, but with Casey taking over the free-taking duties he provided the Faithful County with a glimmer of hope. The St Brigid's clubman cut the deficit to two points with a 46th-minute free.

However, Meath blazed into a 0-16 to 2-05 lead by the end of the third quarter as Cian Ward, Shane O'Rourke and Nigel Crawford added points.

The extra man added to the Royals' growing confidence and endeavour and further points followed from top scorer Ward and O'Rourke as the game took on a one-sided nature.

The Meath management could afford to take off both O'Rourke and Ward in the closing ten minutes, and the death knell was sounded for Offaly when Sheridan, who had a first-half effort ruled out, slipped home a deserved late goal.

MEATH: P O'Rourke; C O'Connor, A Moyles, E Harrington; G O'Brien (0-01), M Burke, C King; N Crawford (0-01), M Ward; S Kenny, J Sheridan (1-03), G Reilly; C Ward (0-08), S O'Rourke (0-04), S Bray (0-02)
Subs: P Byrne for G Reilly; B Farrell (0-01) for C Ward; C Gillespie for M Ward; B Meade for S O'Rourke

OFFALY: A Mulhall; S Sullivan, S Brady, P Sullivan; C Kiely, R Dalton, K Slattery; C McManus, J Coughlan; N Darby (0-02), B Connor (1-00), S Ryan; K Casey (1-02), J Reynolds (0-01), N McNamee (0-01)
Subs: A Sullivan (0-01) for N Darby; A Lynam for S Ryan; B Geraghty for C McManus; R Brady for B Connor; S Lonergan for C Kiely

REFEREE: D Fahy (Longford)

TYRONE 2-14 1-13 ANTRIM

23 May 2010

Tyrone got the better of Antrim in front of 18,159 spectators at Casement Park to book their place in the Ulster Senior Football Championship semi-finals.

For 45 minutes the Red Hands re-created the sort of intensity and passion that carried them to three All-Ireland titles in the past decade, but had to dig deep to hold off a resurgent Saffron side in the end.

Nine points behind at one stage, Liam Bradley's men battled their way back into the game with a Kevin Niblock goal, but Tyrone had too much guile and experience to be caught.

They go forward to a last-four meeting, while Antrim head into the qualifiers yet again, and a prospect of another adventure to equal that of 2009.

Kevin Hughes got in for Tyrone's first goal after eight minutes, taking Owen Mulligan's return pass to finish first-time past John Finucane.

By the 14th minute, they led by 1-03 to 0-01, with Stephen O'Neill and the Cavanagh brothers, Sean and Colm, all hitting the target.

Paddy Cunningham narrowed the gap, but the Saffrons were repeatedly running into walls of Tyrone defenders as they tried to craft scoring opportunities.

Mickey Harte's men were able to break from defence with searing pace, and it was full-back Justin McMahon who drove forward to score in the 23rd minute, and centre-back Ryan McMenamin who was in support for Brian Dooher to make it 1-06 to 0-03 three minutes later.

A superb point from substitute CJ McGourty raised Antrim spirits but in the 29th minute Tyrone struck for another goal.

Mulligan dispossessed Colin Brady 25 metres out, and there was only one thing on his mind as he set off, finishing with a stinging shot past Finucane.

Tyrone led by 2-06 to 0-05 at the break, and continued to look the part in the early stages of the second half.

Sean Cavanagh, Hughes, O'Neill and wing-back Philip Jordan all hit the target as the gap grew to nine points.

But the dynamic of the game changed dramatically as Antrim appeared to adapt better to the soaring temperature, and the Red Hand challenge visibly wilted.

Tony Scullion led by example when he shrugged off two tackles to forge his way through for a point, and further scores followed from Cunningham and CJ McGourty, who by now had been joined by his older brother Kevin in the Antrim side.

In the 56th minute the game was right back in the melting pot when CJ McGourty sent Kevin McGourty in for a goal, and Cunningham's fifth point left just a goal between the sides.

But the experienced Red Hands were able to win frees on the breakaway, which Martin Penrose and Sean Cavanagh converted to see them safely through.

ANTRIM: J Finucane; C Brady, A Douglas, K O'Boyle; T Scullion (0-01), J Crozier, S Kelly; B Herron, A Gallagher; T O'Neill, K Niblock (1-01), J Loughrey; P Cunningham (0-05), M McCann (0-01), T McCann (0-01)
Subs: CJ McGourty (0-04) for S Kelly; G O'Boyle for T O'Neill; K McGourty for B Herron; K Brady for T McCann

TYRONE: P McConnell; M Swift, Justin McMahon (0-01), D Carlin; D Harte, R McMenamin, P Jordan (0-01); K Hughes (1-01), C Cavanagh (0-01); B Dooher (0-01), S Cavanagh (0-03), Joe McMahon; M Penrose (0-02), S O'Neill (0-03), O Mulligan (1-00)
Subs: P Harte for B Dooher; Sean O'Neill for R McMenamin; C McCarron for D Harte; T McGuigan (0-01) for K Hughes; B McGuigan for O Mulligan

REFEREE: P McEnaney (Monaghan)

DOWN 1-15 2-10 DONEGAL

30 May 2010

Benny Coulter inspired Down to an extra-time win over Donegal in the Ulster Football Championship at Ballybofey.

The veteran attacker turned in a vintage performance, hitting a 1-04 tally, including the killer goal deep into extra-time.

Now, James McCartan, in his first year as Down manager, takes his side to meet provincial champions Tyrone in the Ulster semi-final.

But for Donegal, it's another foray into the qualifiers and a summer of uncertainty.

Dermot Molloy celebrated his first championship appearance with a sublime Donegal goal on 12 minutes, firing a rocket past Brendan McVeigh after Michael Murphy had fielded Barry Monaghan's delivery.

Down, after a slow start, finally got moving with purpose, and after Benny Coulter had shot their opening score, they registered further points from John Clarke and a Mark Poland free.

But they were rocked back on their heels again by a second Donegal goal in the 19th minute.

Murphy and Molloy were involved again, and when the latter's shot for a point came off a post, an unmarked Conal Dunne collected to shoot past McVeigh.

With Marty Clarke gradually emerging as an effective playmaker, Down rallied again, and, after Clarke got his name on the scoresheet, Daniel Hughes squeezed over a brilliant score from a tight angle.

With James Colgan protecting his full-back line, Donegal struggled to get the ball to danger man Murphy, and Down's more direct style saw them get further scores from Poland and Hughes.

However, Molloy brought his tally to 1-03 with two frees, and the home side led by 2-03 to 0-07 at the break.

Substitute Adrian Hanlon had just eased John Joe Doherty's side into a three-point lead when McCartan gambled on sending Dan Gordon to full-forward, with Coulter dropping deep, and the switch worked a treat.

Coulter played a one-two with Brendan McArdle to shoot a superb equalising score, and landed another beauty from distance after David Walsh had edged Donegal back in front.

But it was goalkeeper Paul Durcan who emerged as Donegal's hero, pulling off a stunning save as Gordon got a fist to Clarke's sideline ball.

Clarke hit what appeared to be the winner from the resultant '45', but Rory Kavanagh sent the tie to added time with a stoppage-time leveller, tying it up at 2-07 to 0-13.

Down moved two points clear with another Coulter special and a fourth for Hughes to go into the second period of extra-time ahead by 0-15 to 2-07.

And when Coulter got on the end of a move involving Hughes and Clarke to drill home a goal four minutes from the end, it was all over for John Joe Doherty's men.

Donegal's Michael Murphy with Conor Maginn of Down

DONEGAL: P Durcan; F McGlynn, N McGee, K Lacey; M Maguire, K Cassidy, B Dunnion; B Monaghan, N Gallagher; R Kavanagh (0-01), C Toye, D Walsh (0-01); D Molloy (1-03), M Murphy (0-01), C Dunne (1-00)
Subs: A Hanlon (0-01) for C Toye; A Thompson for B Monaghan; M McHugh (0-01) for N Gallagher; C McFadden (0-01) for D Molloy; N Gallagher for A Thompson; P McGrath for F McGlynn; E Wade (0-01) for M Maguire

DOWN: B McVeigh; B McArdle, D Rooney, D Rafferty; K McKernan, J Colgan, C Garvey; D Gordon, K King; D Hughes (0-04), M Poland (0-03), P McComiskey; B Coulter (1-04), J Clarke (0-01), M Clarke (0-03)
Subs: C Maginn for J Clarke; P Fitzpatrick for P McComiskey; D O'Hagan for K McKernan; C Laverty for M Poland; R Murtagh for C Garvey

REFEREE: J McQuillan (Cavan)

19

GALWAY 2-22 1-14 WEXFORD
29 May 2010

Ger Farragher topped the scoresheet with 13 points as Galway beat Wexford at Nowlan Park to make it through to the quarter-finals of the Leinster Hurling Championship.

The Tribesmen held a 1-09 to 0-06 interval lead thanks to Joe Canning's injury-time goal, with team captain Diarmuid Lyng keeping his Wexford side in touch.

Tomás Waters' 55th-minute goal brought Wexford to life. But despite the efforts of Lyng (0-11), a Kevin Hynes goal steadied Galway.

Wexford's woes were summed up in the closing stages when David Redmond and Lyng were both sent off.

This was a game which could have been characterised by missed opportunities and dismissals – Galway also had half-forward Andy Smith dismissed in the 54th minute – but ultimately some excellent scoring shone through on a dull evening in Kilkenny.

Farragher and Lyng were coolness personified for most of this encounter, with both players showing some enviable accuracy in front of the target.

Castlegar clubman Farragher was in terrific form as he struck six early points to nudge Galway into a 0-07 to 0-03 lead by the 26th minute.

Lyng and Harry Kehoe claimed Wexford's opening scores, and with Keith Rossiter doing an excellent man-marking job on Joe Canning, the Portumna ace was confined to just one point in the opening 35 minutes.

However, the ever-dangerous Canning made the breakthrough in first-half injury-time. After being fouled by Rossiter the 21-year-old stepped up to smack the resulting 20-metre free to the back of the Wexford net and give his side a six-point lead at the break.

Even still, Galway manager John McIntyre will have been disappointed with his side's wides tally of 11 over the opening 35 minutes.

Galway added four wides to their tally as Wexford were able to close the deficit with Lyng continuing to slot placed balls between the uprights.

Just a goal separated the sides at 1-12 to 0-12, 13 minutes into the second half; but then the Tribesmen seized the initiative with three unanswered points.

Farragher, Damien Hayes and Joe Canning added points to give them a six-point buffer as the game entered the final quarter.

Galway were now reaping rewards in attack, with Joe Canning operating at right half-forward and Hayes switched to full-forward.

Smith received a straight red card for an elbow-led challenge on Wexford midfielder Colm Farrell. Lyng lobbed the resultant free towards the square and substitute Waters tapped it in to the back of the net to leave just three points between the sides. But that was as

Galway's Andy Smith, with support from Joe Gantley, gathers possession while under pressure from Darren Stamp of Wexford

close as Wexford would get in the closing stages.

McIntyre's men simply turned on the turbo switch in the closing 15 minutes, with Farragher to the fore in terms of scoring. He collected his tenth point in the 57th minute, before substitute Kevin Hynes scored his first championship goal.

Hynes was only on the pitch for two minutes when he took a great pass from Damien Hayes and got the better of Wexford goalkeeper Noel

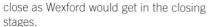

Carton from close range.

Lyng kept his side battling away with some well-taken scores, but Galway were now firing over from all angles as Aidan Harte, David Burke, Farragher and substitute Aonghus Callanan all tagged on points.

There was no way back for Wexford who missed out on a goal when full-forward Stephen Banville failed to ripple the net following an excellent catch.

The Model men's frustrations were obvious as substitute Redmond received his second yellow card for a foul on the excellent Hayes, and Lyng also walked late on for a poorly-timed challenge on David Burke.

GALWAY: C Callanan; D Joyce, S Kavanagh, O Canning; D Barry, T Óg Regan, D Collins; G Farragher (0-13), D Burke (0-01); D Hayes (0-02), C Donnellan, A Smith (0-01); A Harte (0-01), J Canning (1-03), J Gantley
Subs: I Tannian for C Donnellan; K Hynes (1-00) for J Gantley; A Callanan (0-01) for A Harte; J Lee for T Óg Regan; A Cullinane for D Collins

WEXFORD: N Carton; L Prendergast, K Rossiter, C Kenny; R Kehoe, D Stamp, M Travers; H Kehoe (0-01), C Farrell; M Jacob, E Quigley (0-01), D Lyng (0-11); R Jacob (0-01), S Banville, P Atkinson
Subs: D Redmond for M Travers; T Waters (1-00) for R Kehoe; P Morris for M Jacob

REFEREE: J Sexton (Cork)

21

CORK 3-15 | 0-14 TIPPERARY

30 May 2010

Tipperary surrendered their Munster Senior Hurling Championship title in alarming fashion as Cork signalled their championship intent with a ten-point dismissal of their great rivals at Páirc Uí Chaoimh.

Pat Horgan and Aisake Ó hAilpín starred, along with the entire Rebels defence, as Denis Walsh's men comfortably qualified for a semi-final against Limerick.

The Rebels' game-plan stopped Tipperary in their tracks and allowed players like target man Aisake Ó hAilpín, dual star Eoin Cadogan, and goalkeeper Dónal Óg Cusack – who produced a stunning second-half save – to rise to the occasion.

Tipperary lined out as selected and took a 0-02 to 0-00 lead after eight minutes.

Lar Corbett and Eoin Kelly split the Cork posts for those opening points, before Ben O'Connor got Cork off the mark. Seamus Callanan replied with a neat catch and point, and Tipp goalkeeper Brendan Cummins reacted well to deny Ó hAilpín a goal.

O'Connor doubled his and Cork's tally from a free, and the game's first real twist arrived in the 13th minute. The on-fire Ó hAilpín collected possession on the edge of the square and booted the ball to the net, only for referee Barry Kelly to call play back for a penalty, awarded for a foul by Pádraic Maher.

Corner-forward Pat Horgan stepped up to fire the sliotar to the net and O'Connor's third point punished Maher, who

was struggling to cope with the long-limbed Ó hAilpín, as Cork forged ahead.

Corbett and Kelly closed the gap to 1-03 to 0-05 by the 21st minute, but Ó hAilpín was proving a real handful to deal with and the Na Piarsaigh clubman created enough chaos for the alert Horgan to smack home his second goal into the roof of the net.

John Gardiner and John O'Brien traded points as the end-to-end nature of the contest continued, and Tipp had the better of the half's closing stages as pointed efforts from Kelly, O'Brien and Brendan Maher sandwiched a lone score from Cork's excellent midfielder Cathal Naughton.

That left just two points between them at the break, and Tipp were poised to mount a serious challenge as another Kelly free made it a one-point game as the second half kick-started into gear.

However, Liam Sheedy's charges could only score four more points – all but one from placed balls – as Cork used their experience, guile, power and pace to stretch away from the defending champions.

Full-forward Ó hAilpín added his name to the scoresheet; Niall McCarthy struck a quick brace of points – with Sean Óg Ó hAilpín involved in the second – and Gardiner converted a '65' to edge Cork four points clear.

Tipp looked to be struggling as the younger Ó hAilpín threatened again in front of Cummins and a typically well-executed point from Ben O'Connor kept the Rebels on track, delighting the majority of the 36,827 attendance.

Two more Kelly scores reduced the arrears to four with 20 minutes remaining, but Cork's dominance in defence and midfield bore further fruit as they strung together 1-03 without reply to put the result beyond any doubt.

Ben O'Connor and Horgan put their names to the points and right on the hour mark Jerry O'Connor passed for the unmarked Ó hAilpín to round Cummins and slot home to an empty net.

Tipperary were being overwhelmed and Cork stopper Cusack showed his class when flinging himself to the left to save a difficult, bouncing effort from Kelly.

With Cadogan and his defensive colleagues sewing up the much-vaunted Tipp attack, late points from Kelly and substitute Timmy Hammersley mattered little as Cork, with Naughton and substitute Paudie O'Sullivan adding the clinching scores, sealed a runaway victory.

Cork's Aisake Ó hAilpín is tackled by Paul Curran and Pádraic Maher of Tipperary

CORK: D Óg Cusack; S O'Neill, E Cadogan, B Murphy; J Gardiner (0-02), R Curran, S Óg Ó hAilpín; T Kenny, C Naughton (0-02); B O'Connor (0-05), J O'Connor, N McCarthy (0-02); K Murphy, A Ó hAilpín (1-01), P Horgan (2-02)
SUBS: M Cussen for N McCarthy; P O'Sullivan (0-01) for P Horgan; L McLoughlin for T Kenny

TIPPERARY: B Cummins; P Stapleton, P Maher, P Curran; D Fanning, C O'Mahony, M Cahill; B Maher (0-01), S McGrath; N McGrath, S Callanan (0-01), J O'Brien (0-02), E Kelly (0-07), B O'Meara, L Corbett (0-02)
SUBS: S Hennessy for B O'Meara; G Ryan for C O'Mahony; T Hammersley (0-01) for N McGrath; J Brennan for J O'Brien; C O'Brien for S McGrath

REFEREE: B Kelly (Westmeath)

OFFALY 2-26 | 3-16 ANTRIM
30 May 2010

Antrim's quest for a first championship win over Offaly since 1989 ended in extra-time heartbreak as they lost the quarter-final tussle at Parnell Park.

It was all about the Saffrons for the vast majority of the game as Offaly seemed stunned by the sheer work ethic and skill of Dinny Cahill's charges.

However, Offaly stole a march on the northerners in extra-time thanks to a Rory Hanniffy goal. Substitutes Odhran Kealey and Ger Healion also chipped in with vital points.

Antrim looked odds-on for a shock victory deep in the second half of normal time when Shane McNaughton's fifth point of the afternoon put two between the sides.

However, a late Dylan Hayden point and a last-gasp Shane Dooley score levelled the tie for Offaly and ensured extra-time.

The super-charged Saffrons hit the ground running to claim a 1-02 to 0-00 lead after just six minutes, leaving Offaly shell-shocked. Full-forward Neil McManus was in superb form, getting this blockbuster off the ground with a second-minute point.

Johnny Campbell pointed a long-range free soon after, with the majestic McManus' powerfully-struck sixth minute goal, teed up by McNaughton, edging Antrim into a five-point lead.

But Offaly responded in impressive fashion, hitting the next six points with top scorer Shane Dooley in sparkling form.

Indeed, Offaly's first goal arrived from the stick of Dooley to push the Faithfuls 1-06 to 1-02 ahead by the end of the first quarter.

Antrim stayed in touch, however, and were the better side before the break. Goals from Colm McFall and Karl McKeegan, inside an action-packed three-minute spell, sent the Saffrons in at half-time 3-09 to 1-12 in front.

McFall finished to the net in the 32nd minute, after Thomas McCann's initial effort had come back off the post. For Antrim's third goal, McKeegan ended a good team move by rasping a superb strike to the back

of the Offaly net.

Offaly manager Joe Dooley opted to replace his goalkeeper Brian Mullins on the restart, with James Dempsey introduced, but Antrim extended their lead thanks to scores from Karl Stewart and Neil McAuley.

Joe Bergin had the ball in the Antrim net in the 42nd minute, but the Seir Kieran clubman was denied a much-needed goal when referee Anthony Stapleton and his umpires adjudged that he was in the square.

Offaly needed to catch a break and Antrim goalkeeper Gareth Magee was not about to give it to them. He produced a terrific save in the 46th minute to block out Rory Hanniffy's effort.

Shane Dooley grabbed a point back for Offaly, bringing his tally to 1-05, but Offaly were reduced to 14 men shortly afterwards.

Wing-forward Derek Molloy was sent to the line, earning his second yellow card for a wild swing on Antrim midfielder Karl Stewart.

Despite Stewart claiming the next score, which propelled his side into a 3-12 to 1-13 lead, Offaly dug deep to register four unanswered points – all from the talismanic Dooley.

Dooley's string of scores ensured the deficit was cut to the minimum, but Antrim kept ahead thanks to scores from McNaughton and Kieran McGourty.

Indeed, Antrim were unlucky not to extend their lead even further, as Joey Scullion was thwarted by Offaly goalkeeper James Dempsey in the 65th minute. Substitute Liam Watson also misfired on three occasions in the closing six minutes.

Antrim led by 3-15 to 1-19 a minute into injury-time, with McNaughton rifling over, but Hayden and Dooley pulled Offaly back from the jaws of defeat with two nerveless efforts.

Antrim were second best in extra-time, however, and Offaly showed renewed energy after Hanniffy netted to give his side a lead they would not relinquish.

Joe Dooley's charges led by 2-23 to 3-15 at half-time in extra-time, and despite the efforts of Brian McFall for Antrim, subsequent scores from Kealey and Healion confirmed a hard-fought seven-point success for Offaly which sets them up for a crack at Galway.

OFFALY: B Mullins; D Franks, P Cleary, M Verney; J Rigney, D Kenny, D Morkan; R Hanniffy (1-01) K Brady (0-03); D Currams, J Brady, D Molloy (0-01); B Carroll (0-03), J Bergin (0-03), S Dooley
SUBS: J Dempsey for Mullins; B Murphy for Currams; G Healion (0-01) for B Carroll; C Parlon for Brady; D Hayden for Brady; B Carroll for Molloy; O Kealey (0-02) for Parlon; S Egan for Verney; S Kelly for Murphy

ANTRIM: G Magee; K McGourty (0-01), C Donnelly, A Graffin; N McAuley (0-01), J Campbell (0-02), C Herron; P Shiels, K Stewart (0-02); E McCloskey, T McCann, J Scullion; S McNaughton (0-05), N McManus (1-04), K McKeegan (1-00)
SUBS: C McFall (1-00) for McCloskey; L Watson for McCann; S McCrory for Shiels; B McFall (0-01) for Stewart; McCloskey for C McFall; Stewart for McCloskey

REFEREE: A Stapleton (Laois)

Antrim's Ciaran Herron and Derek Molloy with Rory Hanniffy, Offaly

25

GER CANNING

On the day of a match the TV commentator is expected to make his way to the dressing room doors an hour before throw-in. We knock gently, wait patiently and pray for a sympathetic response. 'Can you tell me if there are any changes?' we ask of the man on the door. Getting the correct information can depend on the status of the man protecting the doorway. Mostly we leave reassured, but not always!

'Dummy teams' may be an imaginative way of hoodwinking the opposition, but the last thing a journalist wants is to be an unwitting participant in a scam.

The Cork football team which was to have started the 2009 All-Ireland final included Ray Carey at right corner-back. We knew he wouldn't play because of injury, but the information forthcoming an hour before the game was hazy. The uncertainty affected Cork far more than our viewers (or Kerry, for that matter). The matter was cleared up once we saw Cork in the team parade.

But even the parade is not always a reliable guide as we saw in 1997 when Clare lined up for the hurling final against Tipperary with Fergal Hegarty in their ranks. By the time the match got underway, Fergal was 'on the bench', while Niall Gilligan took his place on the pitch. Ger Loughnane was mischievously playing a game!

Few teams are immune to this practice but occasionally there are extenuating circumstances such as when Monaghan played Armagh this year in Casement Park. Their goalkeeper, Shane Duffy, failed a fitness check and the reserve goalkeeper was informed that he wasn't being considered and left the panel. By the time Monaghan arrived at the ground forty-five minutes before the start, rumours were flying but the dressing room door was firmly closed.

By 1.30 there was still no opening that door, but there were a lot of raised voices inside. We were beginning to panic as deadlines were passing.

Finally, close to 1.45, captain Vinnie Corey led his men out. One by one, Seamus McEnaney, the manager, gave each player a farewell greeting, 'you're gonna be needed today'.

We followed him down the corridor.

'Any changes, Seamus?'

'Owen Lennon for Shane Duffy.'

'Who's in goal?'

'Darren Hughes.'

The full-back was switching positions. We had our information. Time to tell the public.

Among the greatest moments from my recall are the four matches that Dublin and Meath played in 1991. It was a drama of epic proportions, finally decided by a Kevin Foley goal for Meath in the fourth game.

The other great rivalry at that time was the one between Cork and Meath, which developed into bitterness after a series of highly-charged matches. Cork's victory in the 1990 final over Meath resulted in the Rebels winning the double. Mind you, the hurling final against Galway that year was a far better sporting contest than the tetchy football equivalent.

The 1990s were a golden age for hurling. 'Live' TV coverage came in from 1995, and Clare were the new darlings of the viewing public. Wexford and Offaly were also triumphant in this decade, while Kilkenny and Cork were never too far away from a McCarthy

Cup win. Technology was advancing and upwards of 18 cameras were used for the top matches. Viewing numbers increased accordingly. All of this was most reassuring. Surely nothing could possibly go wrong? But alas, sometimes it did. Remember Tuam Stadium?

Galway were pitting their wits against neighbours Mayo in a Connacht championship match. The programme was going fine until about ten minutes into the second half. I was commentating with Tony Davis, a man of very calm demeanour; suddenly the pictures on our monitors went blank. I indicated to Tony not to say anything, just in case the sound (if not the picture) was still being transmitted to our Sunday afternoon audience. With the bright sunlight streaming into our little box it was difficult to detect, but I thought I could make out a tiny red light suggesting a selective break in the system.

We continued to talk about the match as best we could, and about seven minutes later our pictures were restored to normality. We learned that while we had experienced a break-up locally, the viewers at home continued to receive uninterrupted coverage of the match.

Later we discovered what had happened. The outside broadcast truck was positioned about 40 metres behind one of the goals with its miles of cable running out to the cameras and the sound system. On this particular day, a couple of spectators wondered to themselves what it was they were standing on. There was a junction box connecting two very long red cables whose function puzzled them greatly. They unscrewed the connectors and Tony and I were thrown into confusion.

But it could have been worse – what might have happened had we carried on a conversation about the game's participants in a carefree way and not respected the convention of broadcasting – always mind your 'ps' and 'qs'! Whether it's Tuam, Taiwan, or Timbuktu, the message drummed into me at an early stage was to always assume that the microphones are live.

Commentary positions for broadcasting sport vary. Croke Park is state-of-the-art, its only slight blemish being that it's set a little too high in the sky. One level below would be perfect. Thurles is one of the best, while Páirc Uí Chaoimh, although cramped, still gives ideal sight-lines. The vast majority of commentary boxes that I work in are the size of an enlarged telephone box, so the first thing I request is to have the glass in front taken out, which can make the technical experts somewhat uneasy.

While they were rebuilding Croke Park, the positions we used as broadcast bases varied from a double-decker bus parked on the sideline of what is now the Hogan Stand to a wobbly structure covered by a tarpaulin. For the Tipperary v Wexford 2001 semi-final the volume of rainwater over our heads was such that a colleague prodded the soaking material with a stick, thereby ditching a vast amount in front of us, but not before the wind swept it back into our faces and on to our notes...and microphones...and monitors!

Even the newest press box in the country, the completely glassed-in facility at Healy Park in Omagh, has its problems. Last year I did a night match there between Tyrone and Galway which was played in torrential rain.

Here we were inside the glass, unable to see because of the lashing rain OUTSIDE, while the local officials spent the night trying to remove the condensation from INSIDE the glass.

But these are minor distractions compared to the sheer pleasure of watching hurling and football. Nothing in world sport can ever rival an All-Ireland final.

True, there have been years when finals were disappointing, but in recent times the Tyrone versus Kerry matches and the 2009 hurling final between Kilkenny and Tipperary are games that will stand the test of time against any era. Henry Shefflin, Sean Cavanagh, Darragh Ó Sé, Peter Canavan, Tommy Walsh and Eoin Kelly have thrilled us in the major matches up to now, and Joe Canning could yet be one of the greatest of all time. Aside from their genius, these young men are also some of the nicest, friendliest people you could wish to meet. True role models!

P.S.   Don't tell my bosses, but this isn't just a job, it's a joy!

WESTMEATH 0-15 | 1-11 WICKLOW

6 June 2010

A late point by Dennis Glennon gave Westmeath the narrowest of wins over Wicklow in their Leinster Football Championship quarter-final clash in Tullamore.

Westmeath did it the hard way after losing John Gaffey and David Duffy to second half red cards, with Wicklow having Leighton Glynn dismissed.

Paul Earls' 71st-minute goal levelled the tie, only for Glennon's last-gasp point to swing it for his side.

Martin Flanagan and Tony Hannon led the scoring in a scrappy first half which Westmeath edged by 0-05 to 0-04.

In the end, Westmeath did enough to pull through and claim their second successive Leinster Championship win over Mick O'Dwyer's men.

This result is a significant boost to the Lake County's flagging fortunes. They went through the recent National League losing seven games on the trot on the way to being relegated to Division 2. Brendan Hackett resigned from his managerial position and Pat Flanagan was installed as interim manager at the end of April.

Hardly the ideal build-up for this championship opener but, in warm and dry conditions, Flanagan's charges hit the ground running – moving into a 0-04 to 0-01 lead by the end of the first quarter.

Westmeath had Denis Glennon operating as a third midfielder alongside David Duffy and Paul Bannon, but Wicklow's James Stafford was cleaning up a lot of ball in that area and providing his side with the impetus.

Free-taker Hannon put O'Dwyer's side in front, yet Westmeath showed a clinical edge in their early attacks and Flanagan, team captain Michael Ennis and Paul Greville all pointed.

In defence, the Lakesiders also looked sharp, with fit-again goalkeeper Gary Connaughton setting the tone with two excellent saves. He denied Paul Earls and then went full length to stop a crisply struck Ciaran Hyland shot.

Stafford's aerial dominance helped Wicklow stay on the front foot and Darren Hayden soon picked off their only point from play in the first half. Hannon kicked the other three from placed balls, including a 48-metre effort, as Westmeath began to fall foul of referee Michael Collins.

Flanagan's second point of the afternoon was the difference between the sides at the break, and a four-point burst after the restart added to Westmeath's growing confidence. Man-of-the-match Conor Lynam took centre stage with three excellent points.

Greville, Paul Bannon and Doran Harte added scores to extend Westmeath's lead to five points with 14 minutes left on the clock, while the introduction of former All-Star Dessie Dolan also provided a boost.

Top-scorer Hannon continued to impress from placed balls and despite losing skipper Leighton Glynn to a second yellow card, they upped their game in the closing stages.

Hyland and Nicky Mernagh both pointed to cut the deficit to three and Earls found the net to leave Westmeath reeling.

But there was no early birthday present for Wicklow boss O'Dwyer – he turns 74 on 9 June – as Westmeath showed great resolve to pinch a match-winning goal.

Just when it looked like the dismissals of Gaffey and Duffy, after 60 and 62 minutes, would spoil all their good work, up popped Glennon to capitalise on a quick turnover of possession and point them into a 26 June showdown with Louth.

WESTMEATH: G Connaughton; F Boyle, D O'Donoghue, J Gaffey; M Ennis (0-01), K Martin, D Harte (0-01); D Duffy, P Bannon (0-01); J Smyth, C Lynam (0-03), A Gaughan, P Greville (0-03), M Flanagan (0-01), D Glennon (0-02)
SUBS: G Egan for Gaughan; D Dolan (0-01) for Smyth; T Warburton for Martin

WICKLOW: M Travers; C Hyland (0-01), D Ó hAnnaidh, S Kelly; A Byrne, B McGrath, D Hayden (0-01); J Stafford, JP Dalton; L Glynn, T Hannon (0-05), N Mernagh (0-01); P Dalton, S Furlong (0-02), P Earls (1-01)
SUBS: J Flynn for Travers, S Canavan for McGrath

REFEREE: M Collins (Cork)

Semi-Final

CORK 0-15 0-15 **KERRY**

6 June 2010

Arch-rivals Cork and Kerry played out a hard-fought draw in Killarney, with Colm Cooper's injury-time free sending the Munster Senior Football Championship semi-final to a replay.

Cork had the better of the counties' 20th championship encounter since 2000, but could not shake off the All-Ireland champions who scored five of the closing six points.

Kerry quickly cantered into a 0-03 to 0-00 lead, in front of a 35,782-strong crowd.

Bryan Sheehan curled a sweetly-struck free over off the ground, following an early skirmish involving Declan O'Sullivan and Michael Shields, which yielded a yellow card for the latter.

Some crisp passing from Cooper and Kieran Donaghy set up Declan O'Sullivan for Kerry's first point from play, and the 'Gooch' then created some space for his own lobbed point.

Nine minutes in and Cork needed a lift.

Slowly but surely, they got it. Daniel Goulding floated over an 11th-minute free for their opener, and Cork goalkeeper Alan Quirke gained confidence as he gathered a tricky ball under pressure from Donaghy.

The next five minutes belonged to Cork as Donncha O'Connor knocked over a free, Paddy Kelly raided through to point from a tight angle and Goulding then nudged the visitors ahead with a towering point off his left.

A Sheehan free brought the sides level for a second time, with ten minutes left in the first half, but Cork had found their rhythm and they hit three points in as many minutes to go 0-07 to 0-04 in front.

Paul Kerrigan profited from a delayed kickout from Kerry goalkeeper Brendan Kealy for the first, the rampaging Kissane then bagged his first of the afternoon and Pearse O'Neill added his name to the scoresheet in the 28th minute.

Donaghy was yellow carded as tensions began to boil over, following the awarding of a relieving free for Cork.

The game's two best forwards, Sheehan and Kerrigan, then traded scores – the Kerry skipper moving onto his right and away from the covering Graham Canty to split the posts from open play, and Kerrigan fisting over, having evaded the grasp of his marker Marc Ó Sé.

Kerry engineered a goal-scoring chance in the dying embers, and Donaghy should have at least forced a save from Quirke.

Cooper flicked the ball through for Donaghy, who played a one-two with Sheehan before drilling the ball to the left and wide, with the Cork 'keeper and his

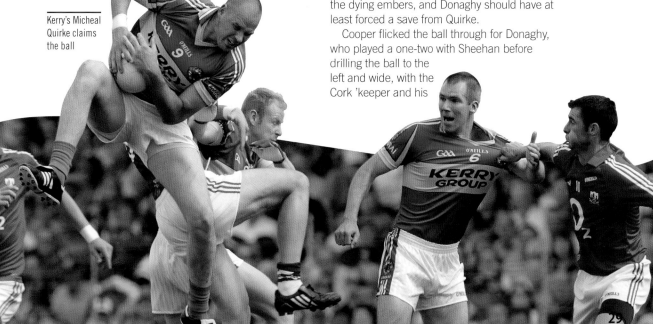

Kerry's Micheal Quirke claims the ball

defenders doing enough to put the Tralee man off.

Cooper took a heavy hit from Canty as he passed the ball through, earning the Cork captain a yellow card, and Kerry at least finished the half with a point as Sheehan cracked over another textbook free in injury-time, taking his personal haul to 0-04.

0-08 to 0-06 in arrears at the break, Kerry fell further behind as Cork burst out of the blocks for the second half.

Kerrigan cut onto his left to strike his third point from play, and after Kerry substitute Anthony Maher had been dispossessed, Alan O'Connor pointed on the turn.

A goal went a-begging for Kerry when Donnacha Walsh was put through by Donaghy.

His close-range shot was blocked by Quirke's outstretched leg but Kerry did manage to score the next three points, courtesy of efforts from Tomás Ó Sé, Sheehan and Cooper.

Defender Ó Sé went on a trademark burst forward and marked his 71st championship appearance with a brilliant point off the outside of his right boot.

Sheehan and Cooper tagged on successive frees to make it 0-10 to 0-09, only for Cork to dominate the next spell.

Getting on top in midfield, Counihan's charges found a path through to goal and Kissane needed no second asking as he kicked a sublime long-range score in the 45th minute, and followed up with a barnstorming run, two minutes later, which resulted in another top-class point.

Amid a spate of hand-passing from Cork, these were two of their best moments and when Goulding kicked another free, the gap was out to four.

After Sheehan and Donncha O'Connor had exchanged frees, Kerry manager Jack O'Connor brought on Paul Galvin and then Barry John Keane, who had impressed off the bench against Tipperary.

Kerry's Micheal Quirke with Aidan Walsh of Cork

Tomás Ó Sé, once again up in support of his forwards, flung a first-time shot over the crossbar as Kerry began to eat into Cork's advantage.

A pointed free from Cooper whittled it down to two, before Kerry net minder Kealy displayed great bravery to block Alan O'Connor's stinging shot from close range, with the ball cannoning off his face.

Kealy recovered quickly to put Aidan Walsh off, with the Cork midfielder scuffing his shot to the left and wide when one-on-one.

It was a let-off for Kerry and they built further momentum as Cooper capitalised on a poor kickout to set up Keane for a point and, with just one minute of normal time remaining, Maher jinked onto his right and then left to create enough space to draw the sides level at 0-14 apiece.

Cork showed they were capable of winning when substitute Colm O'Neill landed a lovely point off his left, scoring on the run.

But, in the second minute of injury-time, Cooper won what some felt was a dubious free on the right wing, and stepped up to convert it in impressive fashion, squaring the game up for the fourth and final time.

KERRY: B Kealy; M Ó Sé, T Griffin, T O'Sullivan; T Ó Sé (0-02), M McCarthy, K Young; S Scanlon, M Quirke; Darran O'Sullivan, Declan O'Sullivan (0-01), D Walsh; C Cooper (0-04), K Donaghy, B Sheehan (0-06)
SUBS: A Maher (0-01) for Quirke; D Moran for Scanlon; P Galvin for Darran O'Sullivan; BJ Keane (0-01) for Walsh; P Reidy for Young

CORK: A Quirke; R Carey, G Canty, J O'Sullivan; N O'Leary, M Shields, P Kissane (0-03); A O'Connor (0-01), A Walsh; P O'Neill (0-01), D O'Connor (0-02), P Kelly (0-01); D Goulding (0-03), C Sheehan, P Kerrigan (0-03)
SUBS: J Miskella for O'Leary; F Goold for D O'Connor; C O'Neill (0-01) for Goulding; D Kavanagh for A O'Connor

REFEREE: P Hughes (Armagh)

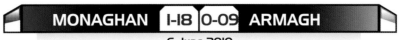

MONAGHAN 1-18 0-09 ARMAGH
6 June 2010

Monaghan scored a resounding twelve-point win over fourteen-man Armagh to book their place in the Ulster Football Championship semi-final at Casement Park.

Seamus McEnaney's side demolished the Orchard challenge in ruthless fashion in front of a crowd of 11,675.

Armagh had to play the entire second half with 14 men after Brian Mallon was sent off just before the break, and they were unable to live with a Farney side which played with passion and desire all afternoon.

The drama began even before the ball was thrown in, with Monaghan full-back Darren Hughes taking over as emergency goalkeeper following an injury to Shane Duffy and the sudden departure from the squad of reserve 'keeper Sean Gorman.

Stevie McDonnell wasted no time in displaying his legendary finishing powers, steering three delightful points between the posts in the opening 10 minutes, and forcing Monaghan manager Seamus McEnaney to shift JP Mone on to the Killeavy man.

Jamie Clarke had just eased the Orchard men into a 0-04 to 0-01 lead when Tommy Freeman silenced the Armagh supporters with a clinically finished goal, slotting low to the net past Paul Hearty from Ciaran Hanratty's perfectly timed pass.

Aaron Kernan and Paul Finlay swapped points before McDonnell's fourth had Armagh back in front, and goalkeeper Hearty denied Conor McManus an equalising point when he stretched his massive frame to pluck the ball from a foot above the crossbar.

Eoin Lennon and Dick Clerkin imposed themselves on the midfield battle for a sustained period of pressure in the final fifteen minutes of the half, and they were rewarded by some glorious points from goal scorers Finlay and McManus.

And Armagh suffered another serious blow in the 35th minute when playmaker Brian Mallon received a straight red card for striking out at Rory Woods.

Finlay's fourth point sent Monaghan in with a 1-07 to 0-06 interval lead, and Freeman stretched the advantage within thirty seconds of the restart.

Within four minutes they were eight points clear, with Finlay, Hanratty and centre-back Vinny Corey all slotting over points.

Jamie Clarke pulled back a point for Armagh, but they struggled to get any fluency into their game, until a flowing move ended with wing-back Paul Duffy unleashing a ferocious shot that stand-in 'keeper Darren Hughes did well to deflect over the bar.

Monaghan turned up the tempo again, scoring six of the game's final seven points, with Finlay driving over a couple of gems from a '45' and a sideline ball.

Dick Clerkin saluted the rapturous crowd after thumping through a couple of long-range scores, and Damien Freeman and substitute Hugh McElroy also hit the target.

Armagh reverted to route one strategy, but a series of dropping deliveries were punched away by goalkeeper Hughes, on his way to a clean sheet.

ARMAGH: P Hearty; A Mallon, B Donaghy, V Martin; P Duffy (0-01), C McKeever, F Moriarty; C Vernon, K Toner; M Mackin, A Kernan (0-01), G Swift (0-01); B Mallon, S McDonnell (0-04), J Clarke (0-02)
Subs: K Dyas for Martin; J Lavery for Mackin

MONAGHAN: D Hughes; JP Mone, D Mone, C Walshe; D Freeman (0-01), V Corey (0-01), G McQuaid; D Clerkin (0-02), E Lennon; S Gollogly, P Finlay (0-07), K Hughes; C Hanratty (0-01), C McManus (0-01), T Freeman (1-04)
Subs: R Woods for Gollogly; H McElroy (0-01) for Hanratty; F Caulfield for K Hughes; N McAdam for D Freeman

REFEREE: M Sludden (Tyrone)

31

FERMANAGH 1-13 0-13 CAVAN
12 June 2010

Fermanagh created history with a first ever championship win at Breffni Park to set up an Ulster Senior Football Championship semi-final with Monaghan.

Since reaching the Ulster final in 2008, the Erne men had endured a miserable time, winning just three games out of eighteen, and suffering successive relegations right down to Division 4 of the National Football League.

Expectation was low among their supporters, but Malachy O'Rourke's players clearly believed in their own ability, and in their capacity to lay a trap for Tommy Carr's men.

In true Erne fashion, they displayed a quite breathtaking work rate in front of a crowd of 9,677 in Cavan town.

Despite David Givney's superb display in midfield, Cavan just couldn't wrest control from their stubborn opponents, and with Seanie Johnston well held by full-back Ryan McCluskey, the home side's scoring threat was severely curtailed.

Two points each from Michael Brennan and Gareth Smith helped Cavan to a 0-08 to 0-07 interval lead, with Paul Ward hitting three Erne points.

Ryan Carson, Chris O'Brien and substitute Seamus Quigley were on target for Fermanagh in the second period, and they clinched victory with a Carson goal in the 54th minute.

Fermanagh looked lively in the opening stages, and eased ahead through Paul Ward and Ryan Carson.

They should have been four clear, but Carson and Rory Gallagher fluffed straightforward frees, and instead found themselves pegged back to 0-02 each by the 12th minute.

With Givney making a big impact in midfield, Cavan recovered from that shaky start, and points from Givney and Cian Mackey brought them level.

Full-forward Seanie Johnston was well shackled by Ryan McCluskey, but the Breffni men had others with an eye for the posts, and they led by 0-05 to 0-03 by the 22nd minute after wing-back Paul Brady, Gareth 'Nesty' Smith, the former Dublin U21 player, and Michael Brennan had all found the target.

Ward brought his tally to three, and could have had a goal with his third effort, taking the safer option when sent clear by Gallagher's lay-off.

A couple of Michael Brennan points kept Tommy Carr's men ticking over nicely, but Fermanagh finished the first half strongly and points from Chris O'Brien and Gallagher left them trailing by just one at the break, 0-08 to 0-07, with wind advantage still to come.

O'Brien and Daryl Keenan were on target to ease Fermanagh back in front, and a tight contest was swinging slowly but surely in their direction.

Cavan were restricted to breakaway attacks, and a superb Johnston effort got the lead back for them.

Fermanagh substitute Seamus Quigley lifted his side with a massive point off his first kick, but still Cavan, and Givney, refused to surrender, and the midfielder brought the sides level for the seventh time seven minutes from the end.

But there were always problems at the back for the Breffni men, and one slip too many was punished when Carson latched onto a long ball, wriggled past Eoin McGuigan and planted the ball in the bottom corner of the net.

CAVAN: F Reilly; D Sheridan, T Corr, M Cahill; P Brady (0-01), E McGuigan, A Clarke; C Galligan, D Givney (0-02); R Flanagan, G Smith (0-04), M McKeever; C Mackey (0-01), S Johnston (0-03), M Brennan (0-02)
SUBS: M Hannon for Clarke; M Reilly for Brennan; L Mulvey for McKeever

FERMANAGH: Ronan Gallagher; N Bogue, S Lyons, B Mulrone; D Ward, R McCluskey, T McElroy; J Sherry, M McGrath; D Keenan (0-01), R Carson (1-03) M Little; P Ward (0-03), Rory Gallagher (0-02), C O'Brien (0-02)
SUBS: S Quigley (0-02) for Rory Gallagher; D Kelly for D Ward; C Flaherty for Little

REFEREE: P Fox (Westmeath)

Semi-Final

KERRY | 1-15 | 1-14 | **CORK**

13 June 2010 (replay)

Reigning All-Ireland champions Kerry showed the greater composure as they overcame old foes Cork after extra-time to reach the Munster Senior Football Championship final against Limerick.

A Daniel Goulding goal had Cork 1-06 to 0-05 to the good at half-time, but Kerry, with Kieran Donaghy finding the net in the 37th minute, fought back and a late Marc Ó Sé point tied the game at 1-11 apiece.

The Kingdom won a dubious free in the closing stages of normal time, which earned Cork captain Graham Canty his second yellow card, and Colm Cooper stepped up to point the resulting free for a 1-10 to 1-10 scoreline.

An improvised overhead effort from Ciaran Sheehan nudged Cork back ahead, but Kerry swept forward to claim the levelling point in injury-time, which defender Ó Sé popped over after combining with Donaghy.

Goulding's 15th-minute goal had the Rebels 1-02 to 0-01 ahead and they continued to hold that advantage, leading by three points with 20 minutes remaining in normal time.

Paul Galvin, on as a first half substitute, covered a huge amount of ground and frustrated Cork with some vital carries in defence and attack, while Cooper's six-point tally – five from frees – was crucial in windy conditions.

Kerry had the elements to their advantage in the opening half but fell behind to two early frees from Daniel Goulding and Donncha O'Connor.

Bryan Sheehan opened Kerry's account in the ninth minute, converting a left-sided free, before O'Connor missed a kickable 12th-minute effort, coming after a forceful challenge by Pearse O'Neill on Tommy Griffin.

Kerry's Brendan Kealy was the busier of the goalkeepers. He did well to put O'Connor off as the Cork centre-forward tried to fist a high ball to the net.

But, having seemingly gathered a second high ball in on top of him, Kealy allowed Goulding to dispossess him and quickly turn to poke home off the ground for Cork's only goal. Kerry reacted smartly and Cooper

notched his first pointed free and added his only point from play soon after, with Donaghy the provider. Sheehan missed a chance to make it a one-point game, and Kerry breathed a sigh of relief when Goulding clipped a shot inches wide of Kealy's goal, with Tom O'Sullivan putting sufficient pressure on him.

Goulding was back on target, drawing a '45' over from right to left, and efforts from O'Connor and defender Michael Shields put Cork in a commanding position at 1-05 to 0-03 in the 26th minute.

Kerry ramped up the intensity when Declan O'Sullivan pointed and Paul Galvin, the 2009 Footballer of the Year, was brought on just moments later.

Tempers boiled over on the half-hour mark, as Derek Kavanagh and Canty picked up yellow cards for clashing with Cooper and Galvin respectively.

Cork missed another goal-scoring opportunity when Paudie Kissane laid the ball through on a plate for full-forward Sheehan, but the youngster's rifled right-footed shot skimmed its way over the crossbar.

The 26,486-strong crowd watched Kerry grab the half's final point through Bryan Sheehan, and Cooper should have followed it up with a goal. Donaghy plucked down a high ball and dished it off for Cooper whose placed effort slid away to the left of the target.

Cork almost engineered a goal at the start of the second half, only for Kealy to parry Alan O'Connor's punched effort. Kerry were quickly back on the attack and Donnacha Walsh's through ball allowed Cooper to create Donaghy's well-taken goal.

Gobbling up Cooper's hand-pass, Donaghy fended off Canty's challenge and his low effort beat Alan Quirke to nestle in the bottom right corner of the net.

A brace of points from Donncha O'Connor saw Cork recover to take a 1-08 to 1-05

33

advantage, and as scores followed from Bryan Sheehan, Paddy Kelly, Declan O'Sullivan and Goulding, the home side maintained that three-point buffer.

Cooper provided some inspiration for Kerry as they sought to pull that deficit back. He sent over a free and did likewise after Jamie O'Sullivan had floored him with a hand trip.

Cork were suddenly struggling as Kerry, helped by the influence of Galvin and fellow substitute Micheal Quirke, tightened things up around the middle.

When Canty felled the onrushing Cooper in the 65th minute and referee Pat McEnaney reached for his red card, Cork were on the brink of imploding. Cooper mopped up with the levelling free.

A ball in from Colm O'Neill broke to Ciaran Sheehan who managed to squeeze the ball through the uprights for the lead score, but in the second minute of injury-time, a last-gasp raid down the left resulted in Donaghy cleverly putting Ó Sé through for the point that ensured extra-time.

With Cork restored to 15 players for extra-time – John Miskella was introduced for Canty – a high quality effort from substitute Fintan Goold edged the hosts back in front at 1-12 to 1-11.

Kevin McMahon, another new man in, struck a wide from the left as Cork's Jekyll-and-Hyde performance continued and they paid the price when Cooper converted a free and Donaghy put Barry John Keane through for a classy score.

McMahon kicked another wide after good work from Colm O'Neill, and Kerry finished the opening period of extra-time 1-14 to 1-12 ahead, with Donaghy again teeing up Keane.

Paddy Kelly hit a wide as Cork continued their struggle for scores in the second period. A Cooper point attempt bounced back off a post, before Noel O'Leary got forward to close the gap to a single point.

A dubious foul by substitute Eoin Cadogan on Donaghy allowed Cooper steady Kerry at 1-15 to 1-13, and although John Hayes' late free produced a helter-skelter conclusion, Kerry held on to secure their first replay win in Cork since 1976.

CORK: A Quirke; R Carey, G Canty, J O'Sullivan; N O'Leary (0-01), M Shields (0-01), P Kissane; A O'Connor, A Walsh; P O'Neill, D O'Connor (0-04), P Kelly (0-01); D Goulding (1-03), C Sheehan (0-02), P Kerrigan
SUBS: D Kavanagh for Walsh; E Cadogan for O'Leary; C O'Neill for Goulding; F Goold (0-01) for Kavanagh; K McMahon for Kerrigan; J Miskella for Canty; E Cotter for O'Sullivan; N O'Leary for Miskella; J Hayes (0-01) for O'Connor

KERRY: B Kealy; M Ó Sé (0-01), T Griffin, T O'Sullivan; T Ó Sé, M McCarthy, K Young; S Scanlon, A Maher; D Moran, Declan O'Sullivan (0-02), D Walsh; C Cooper (0-06), K Donaghy (1-01), B Sheehan (0-03)
SUBS: P Galvin for Moran; M Quirke for Maher; BJ Keane (0-02) for Sheehan; Darran O'Sullivan for Walsh; D Bohane for T Ó Sé; A O'Connell for Young; D Walsh for Scanlon

REFEREE: P McEnaney (Monaghan)

MEATH 2-13 1-16 **LAOIS**

13 June 2010

Meath and Laois will meet again after their Leinster Senior Football Championship quarter-final finished level at Croke Park.

Even extra-time could not separate them, after the O'Moore men refused to accept defeat when faced with dire situations at various stages of a thrilling encounter.

Their bench proved vital, with substitutes contributing seven valuable points, including Padraig Clancy's late equaliser in normal time, and the two late scores from John O'Loughlin that set up a second meeting.

Laois looked beaten when a fortuitous goal from Meath substitute Cormac McGuinness opened out a three-point lead 15 minutes into extra-time, but they displayed immense courage to get themselves back on level terms.

Darren Strong and Cian Ward had traded early points before Graham Reilly grabbed a fifth minute goal for Meath.

Ward's long ball was picked up by Joe Sheridan who offloaded to Reilly for a close-range finish to the roof of the net.

Laois, to their credit, quickly recovered, and responded with a couple of converted frees from Donie Kingston.

But by the end of the opening quarter, the Royals, with Mark Ward and in particular Brian Meade imposing themselves on the midfield battle, had edged ahead by 1-04 to 0-03, with Sheridan drilling over a superb point from wide on the right.

They could have been further ahead had Shane O'Rourke not landed a couple of timid efforts into the arms of goalkeeper Michael Nolan.

Cian Ward did stretch it out to four with his second converted free, but Ross Munnelly and Kingston, with a wonderful effort, kept the O'Moore men in touch.

O'Rourke finally found the range from Sheridan's searching delivery to send Meath in with a 1-06 to 0-05 interval lead

Padraig Clancy's introduction as a target man full-forward almost paid off for Laois in the 52nd minute when another replacement, MJ Tierney, sent in the high ball which the towering Timahoe man fielded. His shot was smothered out for a '45', which Tierney stroked between the posts to give his side a much-needed lift.

Meath quickly countered, with Sheridan yet again providing the assistance for Reilly to bring his tally to 1-04. Soon afterwards, however, the elegant wing-forward was forced out of the game by injury.

And Laois stunned their opponents with a brilliant goal from captain and corner back Padraig McMahon, smashed past Paddy O'Rourke from Ross Munnelly's pass.

Shane O'Rourke restored the Royals' three-point advantage, but Laois scored the last three of the game, through substitutes Clancy and Tierney to tie it up at 1-10 each and send the tie to added time.

Sheridan and substitute Conor Gillespie traded points with Kingston and Cahir Healy, and the sides remained deadlocked, 1-12 each, midway through extra-time.

Sub Cormac McGuinness hit a second Meath goal, his hopeful delivery fumbled into the net by goalkeeper Michael Nolan, but once again Laois dug deep, dominated the final five minutes and went level with scores from Tierney and O'Loughlin.

MEATH: P O'Rourke; C O'Connor, K Reilly, E Harrington; M Burke, A Moyles, C King; B Meade M Ward; S Kenny, J Sheridan (0-03), G Reilly (1-04); C Ward (0-02), S O'Rourke (0-02), S Bray (0-01) **Subs:** P Byrne for G Reilly; J Queeney for C Ward; G O'Brien for King; C Gillespie (0-01) for Kenny; B Farrell for Bray; C McGuinness (1-00) for Moyles; Bray for Farrell

LAOIS: M Nolan; P O'Leary, M Timmons, P McMahon (1-00); C Healy (0-01), C Ryan, C Begley; B Quigley, K Meaney; B Sheehan, C Rogers, D Strong (0-01); P Cahillane, D Kingston (0-06), R Munnelly (0-01) **Subs:** P Clancy (0-02) for Cahillane; J O'Loughlin (0-02) for Sheehan; MJ Tierney (0-03) for Strong; P Lawlor for Rogers; D Booth for Ryan; N Donoher for Munelly

REFEREE: M Duffy (Sligo)

DUBLIN: S Cluxton; M Fitzsimons, Rory O'Carroll, P McMahon; D Bastick, C O'Sullivan, B Cahill; E Fennell, R McConnell; N Corkery, D Henry, P Flynn (0-01); C Keaney (0-03), B Brogan (2-04), K McManamon

SUBS: G Brennan for O'Sullivan; A Brogan (0-02) for Fennell; E O'Gara for McManamon; MD MacAuley (0-01) for Henry; T Quinn (0-04); B Cullen (0-01); Fennell for Corkery; K Nolan (0-01) for Flynn; P Andrews for B Brogan

WEXFORD: A Masterson; J Wadding, G Molloy, B Malone; C Morris, D Murphy, A Doyle; D Waters, E Bradley (0-01); S Roche (0-02), R Barry (0-02), A Flynn (0-01); C Lyng (0-01), PJ Banville (0-01), M Forde (0-07)

SUBS: D Fogarty for Waters; A Morrissey for Doyle; B Doyle for Bradley; C Byrne for Morris; B Brosnan

REFEREE: M Higgins (Fermanagh)

Dublin's Ross McConnell and Brian Malone of Wexford

DUBLIN 2-16 | 0-15 WEXFORD

13 June 2010

Dublin recovered from a disastrous first half, coming from behind to defeat Wexford after extra-time to book their place in the Leinster Senior Football Championship semi-finals.

Pat Gilroy's side turned a seven-point deficit into a seven-point win, but the boss will be seriously concerned over the ineptitude displayed by his side in an opening 35 minutes that drew boos and jeers from their supporters among a crowd of 49,757 at Croke Park.

Totally outplayed in the opening half, Dublin looked to be on their way to a first Leinster Championship defeat since 2004, but they turned the game around, despite being reduced to 13 men late in normal time.

Wexford displayed all the hunger and desire in the opening half, running confidently at an inept Dublin side, often with little or no resistance.

The Dubs scored just two first half points, both from Bernard Brogan, and could find no way to break down a tenacious Wexford defence.

Matty Forde, returning from a two-year injury nightmare, swept over four frees, three of them

from 45 metres, while Redmond Barry drilled a '45' between the posts.

Eric Bradley and Ciaran Lyng also hit the target, while Pat Gilroy reacted to his side's problems at midfield by calling Eamonn Fennell ashore after just twenty-one minutes.

Still, they failed to spark, displaying an apparent lack of appetite and direction, their support play vastly superior to that of Jason Ryan's side.

As the Dublin players left the field with a 0-08 to 0-02 deficit at the interval, they were jeered by their own supporters.

Derision on the Hill grew louder when Forde stretched Wexford's lead, and the Dubs shot a succession of wides, some of them well off the mark.

Paul Flynn did manage to hit the target from a difficult angle, and Dublin spirits received a much-needed lift when substitute Alan Brogan landed a superb point.

Bernard Brogan reduced the deficit to four in the 53rd minute when he blazed over after Anthony Masterson had saved from Eoghan O'Gara, and finally, there was a sense that the tide was turning.

Substitutes O'Gara and Michael Dara MacAuley added a spark to Dublin's attacking dynamic, and despite the straight red card dismissal of wing-back Denis Bastick in the 57th minute, they continued to prosper.

The breakthrough came just a minute later when Bernard Brogan collected Conal Keaney's superb pass to crash home a goal, and they took the lead for the first time in the 64th minute through Keaney.

But Forde came to Wexford's rescue, his sixth converted free making it 1-09 to 0-12, and for the second time on a drama-packed afternoon, Croke Park went to extra-time.

The Dubs, who had finished with 13 men following a second booking to Ger Brennan in stoppage time, were restored to the full complement, with Tomás Quinn and Bryan Cullen joining the action.

Bernard Brogan grabbed his second goal, hitting the roof of the net after Quinn's shot for a point had come back off a post two minutes into extra-time, and midway through added time, Dublin led by 2-11 to 0-12.

Wexford had given their all, and had nothing left in the tank as Quinn reeled off four points and the Dubs stormed into the last four.

MEATH 2-14 0-10 LAOIS
19 June 2010 (replay)

Meath overcame the 54th minute dismissal of goalkeeper Paddy O'Rourke to claim a ten-point Leinster Senior Football Championship quarter-final replay win in Tullamore.

Joe Sheridan and Graham Reilly were Laois' tormentors-in-chief, as the Royals advanced to a mouth-watering Leinster semi-final against Dublin next weekend.

Meath led by 2-05 to 0-06 at half-time, thanks to Sheridan's goals, with MJ Tierney and Donal Kingston keeping Laois in touch.

However, Laois failed to score from play on the restart, allowing Meath to coast home.

O'Rourke's dismissal, following a straight red card, was referee Maurice Condon's only sending-off, but he issued nine yellow cards, including five for the Royals, in what was a hard-fought contest.

With the strong contributions of MJ Tierney, John O'Loughlin and Padraig Clancy as substitutes for Laois in their last drawn game, the trio were expected to make some impact in the replay.

But between them they could only muster four points this time around, with all of those scores arriving from the boot of Tierney – three from placed balls.

Laois replicated their opening move from the drawn encounter, with Darren Strong picking off the first score of the game inside the opening 30 seconds.

However, the O'Moore men suffered an early blow when Meath hit back with a sixth-minute goal. Cian Ward outpaced Laois centre-back Cathal Ryan to put Sheridan through and he clinically palmed the ball to the net.

Both sides had to cope with injuries as the first half wore on.

Although Laois pegged two points back through Padraig McMahon and Donal Kingston,

a second Sheridan goal, in the fourth minute of injury-time, edged his side into a 2-05 to 0-06 interval lead.

Meath looked solid as they pushed four points clear, helped by a brace of scores from Graham Reilly and Shane O'Rourke, and Sheridan swooped on a loose ball to rifle home and add some cushion to their advantage.

Meath showed great pace and vision on the restart as they used their dominance in the midfield sector to great effect.

Laois were punished on four occasions inside a five-minute spell, as Meath raced into a 2-09 to 0-06 lead. Half-back Caoimhín King was on the end of a move involving Cian Ward and Gary O'Brien, edging the Royals six points clear.

Graham Reilly followed up with two more points and a well-taken Sheridan score opened up a double scores lead by the 40th minute.

Laois were finding it tough going, and a number of poor wides did little for their confidence. A second Kingston free was the lone score for Laois in the third quarter as Meath continued to show the greater cutting edge in midfield and up front.

Paddy O'Rourke was then handed his marching orders by referee Condon, after lashing out at Laois captain Padraig McMahon, but despite the absence of their net minder, Meath had a relatively untroubled finish.

Failing to plunder a score from play, a frustrated Laois were curtailed to four points from placed balls in the closing 35 minutes, as Meath deservedly won through to Leinster's last four.

MEATH: P O'Rourke; C O'Connor, K Reilly, E Harrington; A Moyles, M Burke, C King (0-01); B Meade (0-01), M Ward; S Bray, G Reilly (0-04), S Kenny; J Sheridan (2-02), C Ward (0-03), S O'Rourke (0-03)
SUBS: C Gillespie for M Ward; O Lewis for Burke; G O'Brien for Moyles; B Murphy for Bray, C McGuinness for Kenny

LAOIS: M Nolan; P O'Leary (0-01), M Timmons, P McMahon (0-01); C Healy (0-01), C Ryan, C Begley; B Quigley, K Meaney; J O'Loughlin, D Strong (0-01), C Rogers; MJ Tierney (0-04), D Kingston (0-02), R Munnelly
SUBS: D Booth for Begley; B Sheehan for Ryan; P Clancy for Strong; P Lawlor for Rogers; D Rooney for Quigley

REFEREE: M Condon (Waterford)

Semi-Final

TYRONE	0-14	0-10	DOWN

19 June 2010

Ulster champions Tyrone qualified for another Ulster Senior Football Championship final with a four point win over Down at Casement Park.

The Red Hands recovered from a shaky start which saw James McCartan's men open out a four-point lead.

They also had to cope with the loss of ace attacker Stephen O'Neill, who limped out of the action with a heel injury after just 11 minutes.

O'Neill is expected to be fit for the Ulster final against either Monaghan or Fermanagh.

But his replacement, Brian McGuigan, rolled back the years with an imperious display as playmaker, making a massive contribution to his side's four-point success.

Had goalkeeper Pascal McConnell not pulled off two excellent saves, one in the first half from Benny Coulter, and another after the break from Dan Gordon, the outcome might have been different.

Down displayed all the early urgency, sweeping into a 0-06 to 0-02 lead, with Mark Poland, Martin Clarke and Dan Gordon hitting some eye-catching scores.

Following the loss of O'Neill, Sean Cavanagh moved inside and McGuigan adopted a playmaking role.

Brian Dooher swept over two points and Martin Penrose converted a free, but Tyrone trailed by 0-08 to 0-04 on 20 minutes.

Tyrone scored the final six points of the half, with Joe McMahon and Cavanagh both scoring magnificent efforts from distance, and corner-back Dermot Carlin also getting in on the act.

Cavanagh posed a massive threat in the inside line,

Down's Damian Rafferty tries to block a shot by Tyrone's Owen Mulligan.

particularly with McGuigan on form with his perception and ability to pick out a killer pass.

At the break, Tyrone led by 0-10 to 0-08 after Poland had missed an easy free, with Clarke also having difficulty in finding his range from placed balls.

Early in the second half, Gordon did break free of Joe McMahon, but with no support was forced to shoot from a tight angle and goalkeeper Pascal McConnell saved comfortably.

Coulter, meanwhile, could never get into the game, starved of quality possession and closely watched by Justin McMahon.

As the game became sloppy and untidy, almost 20 minutes elapsed without a score, before Sean Cavanagh created the opening for Penrose to hit his first from play.

Clarke did likewise at the other end and carved the opening for Danny Hughes to get in for a glorious goal chance.

His shot was superbly saved by Pascal McConnell, but Paul McComiskey had perhaps a better opportunity from the rebound, but skewed his shot badly wide.

And Penrose drove home the final nail with his fifth score to seal Tyrone's place in the decider.

Down and Tyrone players compete for a high ball

Tyrone's Sean Cavanagh with James Colgan of Down

TYRONE: P McConnell; M Swift, Justin McMahon, D Carlin (0-01); P Harte, C Gormley, P Jordan; C Cavanagh (0-01), K Hughes; B Dooher (0-02), S Cavanagh (0-03), Joe McMahon (0-01); M Penrose (0-05), S O'Neill, O Mulligan (0-01)
SUBS: B McGuigan for O'Neill; Sean O'Neill for Swift; T McGuigan for Harte; R Mellon for Dooher; C McCullagh for Mulligan

DOWN: B McVeigh; D Rooney, B McArdle, D Rafferty; K McKernan, J Colgan, C Garvey; A Rogers (0-02) K King; D Hughes (0-01), M Poland (0-02); B Coulter; C Maginn, D Gordon (0-01), M Clarke (0-03)
SUBS: P McComiskey (0-01) for Poland; D O'Hagan for Garvey; P Fitzpatrick for King

REFEREE: G Ó Conamha (Galway)

Semi-Final

ROSCOMMON | 1-13 | 0-11 | LEITRIM

20 June 2010

Roscommon got on top in the second half at Dr Hyde Park as they qualified for their first Connacht Senior Football Championship final since 2004.

Donie Shine's 39th-minute goal put the Rossies four points clear and Leitrim could not muster a comeback in sweltering conditions.

Free-takers Shine and Michael Foley shared out 11 points in a first half that ended 0-08 to 0-07 in Leitrim's favour.

But Leitrim, who had Tomás Beirne sent off in the closing stages, struggled after the restart as Fergal O'Donnell's men deservedly progressed to the 18 July decider.

O'Donnell made one change to the team that saw off London in the last round, with David Casey coming in for the injured Mark O'Carroll (knee) at wing-back and the Boyle clubman turned in a man-of-the-match performance which included a vital point early in the second half.

There was a minute's silence held before the start to acknowledge the tragic passing of Leitrim footballer Philly McGuinness, and his

Roscommon's David Casey and Ray Mulvey of Leitrim

team-mates, in their first championship outing since his death, broke into an early 0-04 to 0-02 lead.

The early exchanges were dominated by frees, with Foley notching a long-range opener by punishing Sean Purcell for over-carrying. Shine replied with a fourth-minute effort off the ground, and the tit-for-tat continued.

Shine and Foley exchanged frees again before Leitrim linked two points together in as many minutes, newcomer McKeon and David O'Connor doing well to set up full-forward James Glancy for a score, and influential wing-forward Foley followed up with an effort from play.

Both sides were opting for the long-ball tactic, lobbing deliveries in towards Shine and Glancy, and the former curled over two excellent frees to level the game by the midpoint of the first half.

Foley's fourth point – third from a free – nosed his side into a 0-05 to 0-04 lead by the 21st minute and Leitrim's terrific work-rate in defence and attack allowed them maintain that lead for the break.

O'Connor added his name to the scoresheet, but two more frees from Shine, who also top-scored against London last time out, had Roscommon back on terms at 0-06 apiece.

The Rossies' opening point from play followed, Ger Heneghan registering it, only for Foley to reply with another textbook free from a wide position and a quick counter out of defence led to wing-back James Glancy restoring Leitrim's one-point advantage.

Roscommon corner-forward John Rogers had a glorious chance of a goal in injury-time, but he left-footed into the side-netting having done most of the hard work.

Would the miss come back to haunt the home side? In the end, no. Although they hit four early wides, Roscommon picked off points through Cathal Cregg and Karol Mannion as the second half action got underway.

The decisive goal put Leitrim in even more trouble. As David Keenan knocked a long ball through, Leitrim captain John McKeon was beaten by Shine who rounded goalkeeper Enda Lyons and finished to the net.

Shine knocked over a free soon after to take his tally to 1-07, but his team-mates also stepped up to the mark as Casey raided forward for a point and Cregg collected his second.

Leitrim failed to respond from open play, relying on three frees from Foley to keep them in touch. The Kilcock clubman finished with eight points altogether.

Foley's eighth of the day put four between the sides in the closing stages, and really Leitrim needed a goal. But Roscommon's control of midfield helped them set up Rogers for the clinching point.

The hosts could afford to hit three late wides as Leitrim's gallant challenge collapsed, losing hard-working midfielder Beirne to a second yellow card.

ROSCOMMON: G Claffey; S McDermott, P Domican, S Ormsby; S Purcell, C Dineen, D Casey (0-01); M Finneran, K Mannion (0-01); D Keenan, P Garvey, C Cregg (0-02); J Rogers (0-01), D Shine (1-07), G Heneghan (0-01) **SUBS:** D O'Gara for Garvey; K Higgins for Rogers

LEITRIM: E Lyons; D Beck, J McKeon, D Reynolds; J Glancy (0-01), S Foley, W McKeon; T Beirne, S Canning; C Clarke, D O'Connor (0-01), M Foley (0-08); R Cox, J Glancy (0-01), R Mulvey **SUBS:** D Reynolds for Beck; K Conlon for Cox; G Reynolds for J Glancy; B Prior for Foley; D Maxwell for Conlon

REFEREE: J McQuillan (Cavan)

Benny Coulter

CLUB: Mayo Bridge

COUNTY: Mayo

AGE: 28

HEIGHT: 6'

WEIGHT: 13st 4lbs

OCCUPATION: GAA Coach

Benny made his senior championship debut in 2000. The previous year he had won Ulster and All-Ireland Minor titles with Down. The senior manager at the time, Pete McGrath, saw much potential in Benny and gave him his senior bow against Antrim. Since then he has developed into a talismanic figure on the Down team.

Benny plays corner-forward for both club and county and is seen as one of the best attackers in the game. This year he has been quite vocal in his criticism of the blanket defence system many football teams are adopting, and, in his role as GAA coach, much of his work is aimed at developing the finer skills of the game.

Although Down lost in the Ulster Championship this year they came back through the qualifiers and caused one of the season's biggest upsets when they beat Kerry in the All-Ireland Senior Football Championship quarter–finals.

Benny played a key role in Down's victory over Kildare in a dramatic All-Ireland semi-final. Sadly for Benny he missed out on an All-Ireland medal when his side lost to Cork by the narrowest of margins in a most dramatic All-Ireland Football final.

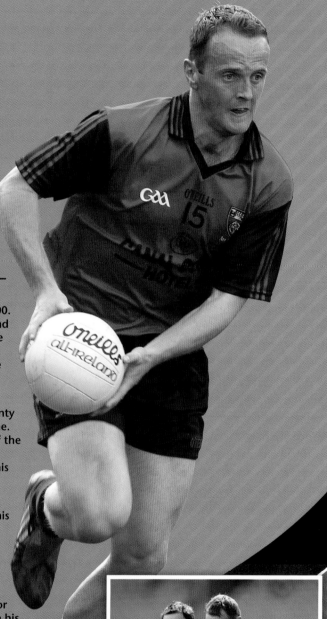

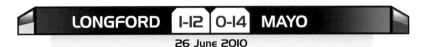

LONGFORD 1-12 0-14 MAYO

26 June 2010

John O'Mahony quit as manager of the Mayo football team after his side were dumped out of the All-Ireland Football Championship by Longford.

Longford caused the shock of the GAA Football Championship so far as they sent Mayo packing by 1-12 to 0-14 in their first-round qualifier at Pearse Park.

Alan Dillon had helped Mayo take a 0-07 to 0-04 interval lead but Paddy Dowd set up Longford substitute Paul Kelly for a galvanising goal and the dismissal of Keith Higgins left Mayo under all sorts of pressure.

After Alan Freeman had levelled twice for the visitors, Longford closed out a famous win with late points from Shane Mulligan and Sean McCormack.

Longford were hungrier for this win and clearly determined to bounce back from losing to Louth in the Leinster Championship.

Belief spread throughout the Glenn Ryan-managed outfit as they moved ahead in the second half, helped by a man-of-the-match performance from Dowd and key contributions from free-taker Francis McGee and goalscorer Kelly.

Looking to put their recent reversal to Sligo behind them, Mayo strode

Mayo's Alan Freeman and Alan Dillon tackle Barry Gilleran of Longford

confidently into an early 0-03 to 0-00 lead courtesy of points from Alan Freeman, Seamus O'Shea and Barry Moran.

McGee kicked two frees and Brian Kavanagh, who caused problems for marker Ger Cafferkey, added another as Longford opened their account.

Play was scrappy and neither side could take a stranglehold with Mayo frustrated by five early wides. The visitors did enough to warrant their three-point lead at the break though, with Andy Moran delivering two quick-fire points in the closing stages.

Longford lost the services of key forward Paul Barden who injured himself when scoring his side's first point from play in the 28th minute. Midfielder Bernard McElvaney secured possession and the ball was ferried on to Kavanagh who teed up the team captain. Nonetheless, his replacement Kelly went on to have a major role in the home win. Dillon and McGee traded points on the resumption before Longford picked up the pace and started to find holes in the Mayo defence.

O'Mahony introduced Peadar Gardiner and Mark Ronaldson but the pair had little influence on proceedings. The game swung in Longford's favour when Dowd took down a crossfield ball, picked out the advancing Kelly with a lovely centre and the substitute did the rest with a sidefooted finish past Mayo goalkeeper David Clarke.

Kavanagh tagged on a point for a sudden 1-09 to 0-09 lead. Mayo did not crack and took up the challenge with Freeman and Dillon getting them back level.

Tom Parsons was another Mayo substitute brought into the fray, as they sought to overhaul Ryan's strong-running side. Parsons' poor connection resulted in a poor point attempt but the attack was rescued by Barry Moran who gave Freeman a sight of goal. Unfortunately for the travelling support, the wing-forward's shot skimmed over the crossbar for a point.

Kavanagh moved Longford's total to 1-10, but Mayo were giving themselves every chance of rescuing the situation. Conor Mortimer made it a one-point game from a free.

Then, some ill-advised back chat from wing-back Higgins resulted in referee Gearóid Ó Conamha showing him a straight red card.

Mayo were on the brink of elimination from the championship and up popped Freeman with a terrific point to keep them somewhat on track.

In a dramatic finish, Shane Mulligan raced forward from his defensive position to fist Longford into a 1-11 to 0-13 lead with two minutes remaining.

Freeman levelled again with another top-drawer score, but it was not enough to save Mayo as McCormack kicked a match-winning point befitting such an outstanding night.

LONGFORD: D Sheridan; D Brady, B Gilleran, D Reilly; S Mulligan (0-01), E Williams, S Hannon; D Masterson, B McElvaney; P Dowd (0-01); P Barden (0-01); K Mulligan (0-01), F McGee (0-04), B Kavanagh (0-03), S McCormack (0-01)
SUBS: P Kelly (1-00) for Barden; P Foy for Hannon

MAYO: D Clarke; C Barrett, G Cafferkey, K Higgins; D Vaughan, T Howley, K McLoughlin; S O'Shea, P Harte; A Moran (0-02), A O'Shea (0-01), A Freeman (0-05); C Mortimer (0-02), B Moran (0-01), A Dillon (0-03)
SUBS: L O'Malley for McLoughlin; M Ronaldson for A O'Shea; T Parsons for Howley; BJ Padden for Harte

REFEREE: G Ó Conamha (Galway)

ARMAGH 2-14 0-11 DONEGAL
26 June 2010

Armagh coasted through this Ulster derby first-round football qualifier at Crossmaglen with a 2-14 to 0-11 win over a listless Donegal side.

Jamie Clarke's two early goals laid the foundations for an impressive win for the Orchard men, who are firmly back on track after suffering a heavy Ulster Senior Football Championship defeat at the hands of Monaghan.

However, manager Paddy O'Rourke will be keen to ensure that his players do not get carried away with what they achieved against a Donegal side which lacked spirit and direction as it made yet another early exit from championship football.

Clarke stunned Donegal with two goals in the opening six minutes, both finished soccer-style past a helpless Paul Durcan.

John Joe Doherty's men were able to muster little by way of response, struggling to create openings and scoring opportunities for front men Michael Murphy and Colm McFadden.

Clarke's initial shot was stopped by Durcan, but the Crossmaglen youngster followed up to slot the rebound to the corner of the net.

The men from the north-west had barely recovered when Clarke struck again, taking advantage of woeful defending to collect Steven McDonnell's cross and boot home his second from the breaking ball.

Murphy did pull back a couple of points, but Armagh, with Brendan Donaghy and Paul Duffy imperious at the back and Charlie Vernon lording midfield, continued to press forward.

They had points from Clarke, substitute Joe Feeney, Aaron Kernan and Gareth Swift, and went in at the break with a commanding eight-point lead, 2-06 to 0-04.

Amazingly, ace attacker Steven McDonnell didn't get his first score until the second half, and the gap had widened to 11 points within 10 minutes of the restart, with Gareth Swift drilling over a couple of classy points.

Murphy continued to represent Donegal's only scoring threat, steering another volley of scores between the posts.

Neil Gallagher and Adrian Hanlon also found the target during a brief revival, but they were reduced to 14 men after substitute Eamon McGee picked up a second yellow card six minutes from the end.

Mark McHugh brought Donegal's points tally into double figures, and as Armagh's resistance waned, Murphy brought his total to seven.

Paul Hearty had to make a brilliant save from Rory Kavanagh as Donegal continued their quest for redemption, but there was no way back for them.

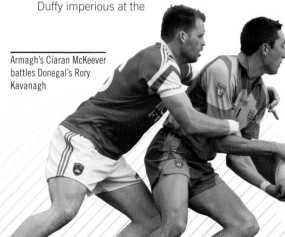

Armagh's Ciaran McKeever battles Donegal's Rory Kavanagh

ARMAGH: P Hearty; A Mallon, B Donaghy, V Martin; P Duffy, C McKeever, K Dyas; C Vernon (0-01), M Mackin; A Duffy, A Kernan (0-03), F Hanratty; G Swift (0-03), S McDonnell (0-03), J Clarke (2-02)
SUBS: J Feeney (0-02) for A Duffy; P McKeown for Mallon; T Kernan for Hanratty

DONEGAL: P Durcan; P McGrath, N McGee, K Lacey; M Maguire, B Dunnion, F McGlynn; N Gallagher (0-01), K Cassidy; M McHugh (0-01), R Kavanagh, D Walsh; C McFadden (0-01), M Murphy (0-07), C Dunne
SUBS: E Wade for McGrath; E McGee for Maguire; C Toye for Dunne; A Hanlon (0-01) for McFadden

REFEREE: M Duffy (Sligo)

KILDARE 0-15 0-15 ANTRIM
26 June 2010

Kildare and Antrim played out an entertaining 0-15 0-15 draw in their All-Ireland Football Championship first-round qualifier at Newbridge.

John Doyle and substitute Eoin O'Flaherty nudged Kildare ahead in extra-time, but free-taker Paddy Cunningham picked off a late brace to get the Saffrons back on terms for a final time.

It was an emotional night for Kildare midfielder Dermot Earley, whose father had been buried just hours earlier. The appreciative crowd honoured Dermot Earley Snr with a rapturous round of applause before the throw-in.

The Roscommon football legend would have been proud of his son's efforts, particularly in the second half as the hosts edged their way towards a likely win.

The Lilywhites, who kicked 12 first-half

Kildare's Thomas O'Connor hits his late goal chance off the post

wides, were 0-08 to 0-07 ahead at half-time, with Ronan Sweeney impressing.

Antrim played into a stiff wind in the opening period and Cunningham kicked them ahead, picking off a brace of frees, the second coming after a lengthy run from Tony Scullion.

Scullion and Thomas McCann ran hard out of defence all night, and Kildare struggled at times to take the right option, playing in towards a two-man full-forward line of John Doyle and Sweeney.

When they got it right, the scores duly arrived for Kieran McGeeney's men. But often their attacks resulted in wides and they could have proven particularly costly on another night.

Padraig O'Neill and Doyle got them back level at 0-02 apiece and O'Neill, with Doyle and Sweeney involved in the build-up, soon clipped over the lead point.

Kildare could have been further ahead, but John Doyle had his goal-bound effort smothered away after a short kickout from Antrim goalkeeper Sean McGreevy had been intercepted.

McCann thundered a shot off a crossbar for the visitors' best goal chance. Four well-taken scores from Cunningham had them well in the hunt at the break, and they had a 'zero' beside their wides column as the sides

headed for the dressing rooms.

Still, if Kildare had turned half of their disappointing wides tally over the opening 35 minutes into scores, the game would have had a completely different complexion to it.

In the second half, Sweeney continued to distribute well and set up chances for his colleagues. Doyle, adding to his four first half points, and James Kavanagh kept the hosts ahead, only for Cunningham and Kevin McGourty to make it 0-13 apiece and force extra-time.

The Ulstermen engineered two more scoring chances which could have left McGeeney's side floored. Cunningham had a free from distance which sailed wide and Scullion, raiding forward from defence once again, missed a final chance.

McGourty's point from long range still gave Antrim plenty of momentum for the two periods of extra-time. By half-time, Kildare were one ahead. Thomas O'Connor, on as a substitute for the home side, should have done better when presented with a goal-scoring opportunity but he missed the target.

Doyle took his tally to 0-07 but he was bettered by Cunningham who went into double figures as the sides played out a tense but thrilling stalemate.

KILDARE: S McCormack; P Kelly, H McGrillen, A Mac Lochlainn; M O'Flaherty, E Bolton (0-01), B Flanagan; D Flynn, D Earley; H Lynch, E Callaghan, J Kavanagh (0-01); P O'Neill (0-02), J Doyle (0-07), R Sweeney (0-02)
SUBS: G White (0-01) for Lynch; E O'Flaherty (0-01) for Flanagan; T O'Connor for O'Neill; K Donnelly for Earley; K Cribbin for M O'Flaherty; P O'Neill for Donnelly; M O'Flaherty for Callaghan; D Earley for E O'Flaherty

ANTRIM: S McGreevy; C Brady, A Healy, K O'Boyle (0-01); T Scullion, J Crozier, J Loughrey; B Herron, A Gallagher; K McGourty (0-03), K Niblock, T McCann (0-01); P Cunningham (0-10), M McCann, K Brady
SUBS: CJ McGourty for Brady; S Finch for T McCann; S Kelly for Healy; P Doherty for Niblock; T McCann for Herron

REFEREE: M Deegan (Laois)

Semi-Final

MEATH 5-09 0-13 DUBLIN

27 June 2010

Dublin's five-year reign as Leinster champions came to an end as Meath put on a goal-scoring blitz at Croke Park to win by 5-09 to 0-13 and book a Leinster final date with Louth.

Joe Sheridan and Anthony Moyles of Meath with Niall Corkery of Dublin

The Royals rattled Stephen Cluxton's net on five occasions as they reached their first provincial final since 2001, the year of their last title win.

The sides were level five times in the first half, ending it locked at 0-08 to 1-05.

Dublin's lack of scoring power hurt them after the break as Cian Ward, Joe Sheridan, Stephen Bray and Brian Farrell picked off the goals that made it Meath's day.

Bray was the man-of-the-match, finishing with 2-01 from play, while free-taker Ward kicked some excellent scores for a contribution of 1-04.

There was an expectant buzz amongst the 60,035 spectators as the game got underway, and Conal Keaney pointed a free from out under the Cusack Stand to get the defending champions off the mark.

Cian Ward missed his first two placed balls but Meath target man Shane O'Rourke got the better of his marker Rory O'Carroll to draw his side level in the fifth minute.

The Dubs opened up a two-point gap when Tomás Quinn converted a '45' and Brian Cullen and Alan Brogan combined for the former to score. Brogan, installed as team captain in the absence of David Henry, was leading by example and his distribution skills were central to a solid first 35 minutes from Gilroy's men.

However, they continued to have problems at the back. In the 11th minute, a slip by Barry Cahill was punished by Bray for Meath's first goal. He burst through on a pacey run in from the wing to leave Eamonn Fennell in his wake and beat Cluxton at his near post with a classy finish.

Bernard Brogan and O'Rourke traded points before Dublin, with their midfield pairing providing their fair share of ball, put on a spurt to lead by 0-07 to 1-02 by the midpoint of the half.

Quinn and Bernard Brogan were both on target, yet there was no sign of Meath panicking. Joe Sheridan teed up the elusive Bray for a point and a free from Ward brought the sides level for the fourth time. After a couple of wides, the same player scored from play to move O'Brien's outfit in front.

Dublin needed a score to end a barren spell and with the half coming to a close, Quinn delivered from a close-range free to make it 0-08 to 1-05 at the turnaround.

Meath's charge gathered serious pace between the 41st and 53rd minutes during which they scored three telling goals. Play resumed with O'Rourke and Quinn exchanging points, and then Ward, after linking with Bray, watched his deflected effort hit the back of the net for Meath's second goal.

The Dublin defence parted sufficiently, five minutes later, for the industrious Graham Reilly to raid through and pass for Bray who shook off Cullen and rounded goalkeeper Cluxton to complete his brace.

Just before that, luck was not on Dublin's side when Paul Flynn missed out on a much-needed goal, flicking a shot off the inside of the post.

You got a sense that it was not to be Dublin's day when play was called back for a free in Bernard Brogan's favour just as he managed to ripple the net. By that stage, Meath had scored their fourth goal. An error by Rory O'Carroll was punished by big centre-forward Sheridan who raced through to send a rocket of a shot past Cluxton's despairing dive.

In this match-winning spell, Meath had outscored their arch rivals by 3-02 to 0-01 and there was simply no way back for the boys in blue.

Bernard Brogan, from a free, and substitute

Dublin goalkeeper Stephen Cluxton leaps for a high ball

Kevin McManamon, from play, got the Dubs back on the scoring trail, with five minutes of normal time remaining.

However, Meath's rearguard was giving little away and there were certainly no goals to be plundered, Alan Brogan going closest as Murphy parried his shot.

Back up at the Hill 16 end, Meath mustered goal number five. Substitute Farrell, on for Anthony Moyles, found the right corner of the net with a measured finish and Dublin were out for the count.

MEATH: B Murphy; C O'Connor, K Reilly, E Harrington; A Moyles, G O'Brien, C King; B Meade, M Ward; S Kenny, J Sheridan (1-00), G Reilly (0-01); C Ward (1-04), S O'Rourke (0-03), S Bray (2-01)
SUBS: N Crawford for M Ward; C Gillespie for Meade; C McGuinness for G Reilly; J Queeney for King; B Farrell for Moyles

DUBLIN: S Cluxton; M Fitzsimons, R O'Carroll, P McMahon; B Cahill, B Cullen (0-01), G Brennan; E Fennell, R McConnell; N Corkery, A Brogan; P Flynn, C Keaney (0-01), B Brogan (0-03), T Quinn (0-07)
SUBS: E O'Gara for Keaney; K Bonner for McConnell; K Nolan for McMahon; K McManamon (0-01) for Quinn; D Henry for Corkery

REFEREE: P Hughes (Armagh)

Semi-Final

LOUTH	1-15	2-10	WESTMEATH

27 June 2010

Louth have reached their first Leinster football final in 50 years after a 1-15 to 2-10 win over Westmeath at Croke Park.

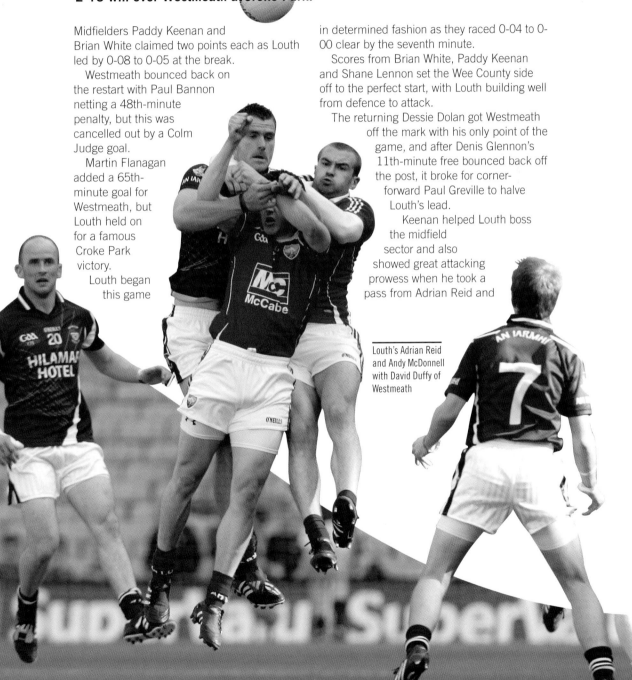

Midfielders Paddy Keenan and Brian White claimed two points each as Louth led by 0-08 to 0-05 at the break.

Westmeath bounced back on the restart with Paul Bannon netting a 48th-minute penalty, but this was cancelled out by a Colm Judge goal.

Martin Flanagan added a 65th-minute goal for Westmeath, but Louth held on for a famous Croke Park victory.

Louth began this game in determined fashion as they raced 0-04 to 0-00 clear by the seventh minute.

Scores from Brian White, Paddy Keenan and Shane Lennon set the Wee County side off to the perfect start, with Louth building well from defence to attack.

The returning Dessie Dolan got Westmeath off the mark with his only point of the game, and after Denis Glennon's 11th-minute free bounced back off the post, it broke for corner-forward Paul Greville to halve Louth's lead.

Keenan helped Louth boss the midfield sector and also showed great attacking prowess when he took a pass from Adrian Reid and

Louth's Adrian Reid and Andy McDonnell with David Duffy of Westmeath

claimed his side's fifth point.

Teenager Ger Egan, who was making his first championship start, landed a superb point for Westmeath in the 17th minute from an acute angle, before Reid quickly restored Louth's three-point advantage.

Westmeath knocked over some fine points in the opening half, including a 21st-minute effort from Paul Bannon, but a match-ending injury to Derek Heavin soon after was a setback.

Pat Flanagan's side got back on track as Glennon reduced the arrears in the 29th minute, but disappointing Dolan and Glennon both sent scoring chances into the welcoming arms of Louth goalkeeper Neil Gallagher.

At the opposite end, Lennon and Colm Judge tagged on scores as Louth broke into a 0-08 to 0-05 lead for half-time.

Westmeath made a lightning quick start to the second half. Greville grabbed his second point inside 20 seconds of the restart.

Indeed, the Lake County outfit looked hungrier in the third quarter, outscoring their opponents by 1-02 to 0-03 during a very good spell.

Westmeath's goal was a penalty knocked home by Paul Bannon. The strike cut the deficit to the minimum in the 48th minute after substitute Pádraic Smith and White had fired over for Louth.

A free-flowing move from Louth led to a 58th-minute goal as Westmeath's Glennon was dispossessed in an attacking situation and substitute Derek Maguire thundered through before unselfishly passing for Colm Judge to supply the killer finish.

Despite Mark Brennan cancelling out Greville's fifth point, Westmeath had more in the tank and mounted a late challenge.

They were handed a lifeline in the 65th minute when substitute Flanagan dummied and then knocked a well-placed shot straight into the net from a tight angle. Glennon raised a white flag in the next play to make it a one-point game and add to Louth's nerves.

But Judge popped up to land the match-winning score for the Wee men, sweeping onto his right to find the target from 30 metres out. Louth's defence stood tall in the dying minutes to see out the win, although John Smyth and Bannon will both have nightmares about failing to convert late chances.

LOUTH: N Gallagher; E McAuley, D Finnegan, R Greene; R Finnegan, M Fanning, J O'Brien; P Keenan (0-03), B White (0-04); A McDonnell, M Brennan (0-01), A Reid (0-01); C Judge (1-02), S Lennon (0-02), JP Rooney
SUBS: P Smith (0-01) for McDonnell; D Maguire (0-01) for Rooney

WESTMEATH: G Connaughton; F Boyle, D O'Donoghue, K Maguire; M Ennis, K Martin, D Harte; D Duffy, P Bannon (1-01); D Heavin, C Lynam, G Egan (0-01); P Greville (0-05), D Dolan (0-01), D Glennon (0-02)
SUBS: J Smyth for Heavin; J Keane for O'Donoghue; M Flanagan (1-00) for Lynam; T McDaniel for Egan; D Healy for Martin

REFEREE: S Doyle (Wexford)

Semi-Final

MONAGHAN	0-21	2-08	FERMANAGH

27 June 2010

Monaghan strolled into the Ulster Football Championship final with a 0-21 to 2-08 win over Fermanagh at Kingspan Breffni Park.

And even the concession of two late goals could not take the gloss off a handsome win for Seamus McEnaney's team.

Rory Gallagher and Daryl Keenan found the Farney net in the closing stages, but Monaghan had done enough to ease through to a 18 July decider against Tyrone.

Free-taker Paul Finlay pointed four times during a dominant first-half display from Monaghan – they led 0-14 to 0-03 at half-time.

Substitute Hugh McElroy got in on the scoring act in the second period and Fermanagh's late rally mattered little in the end.

Monaghan are now just one win away from lifting the Anglo-Celt Cup for the first time since 1988.

Monaghan manager Seamus McEnaney will have been frustrated by what Fermanagh offered in terms of opposition, however there were plenty of positives for the victors to take into the final.

Monaghan used the wind to their advantage in the first half, bossing play after an even enough opening. Points from Finlay,

Fermanagh's Niall Bogue with Ciaran Hanratty of Monaghan

Conor McManus and Damien Freeman had their side 0-03 to 0-01 ahead, before Paul Ward cut the gap for Fermanagh to the minimum.

The Ernesiders missed out on an early goal when Keenan opted to settle for a point when the goal loomed into view. It was an all-too-rare excursion into the danger area for O'Rourke's men, and leaking the next five points did little for their confidence.

Monaghan's defence and midfield had the beating of their opponents and their physicality and pace saw Fermanagh overwhelmed at times.

Points from Stephen Gollogly, Finlay and the two Freemans, Damien and Tommy, gave the Farney men some cushion at 0-08 to 0-02. Damien Freeman's deflected shot caught Fermanagh goalkeeper Ronan Gallagher napping and almost resulted in the game's opening goal.

Ward added his second point to give Fermanagh some hope but it was one-way traffic up to half-time as Monaghan strung together six more unanswered points, with Owen Lennon and Dick Clerkin adding their names to the scoresheet.

Seamus Quigley was introduced for the second period and although Rory Gallagher kicked Fermanagh's fourth point and Quigley and Ryan Carson also followed with scores,

Monaghan replied with four more from Finlay, the very effective McManus, Tommy Freeman and McElroy.

The remaining 25 minutes lacked the intensity of championship football and Monaghan were content to pick off their scores and conserve their energy on a hot summer's day.

Fermanagh kept battling for every ball and, adopting a more direct style, they found a way past net minder Hughes. A shot from Gallagher went in off the woodwork for the first goal and a pointed free from the same player cut the gap to ten points – 0-20 to 1-07 – with six minutes to go.

Monaghan boss McEnaney had emptied his bench at that stage and the sight of full-back JP Mone limping off with a leg injury caused some concern.

With Monaghan taking their foot off the pedal, Keenan grabbed a second goal for more consolation for Fermanagh who will need to regroup quickly for the All-Ireland qualifiers.

For McEnaney's side, another encouraging performance has earned them a deserved shot at provincial silverware and their first Ulster final appearance since 2007 when they lost to upcoming opponents Tyrone (1-15 to 1-13).

MONAGHAN: D Hughes; D McArdle, JP Mone, C Walshe; D Freeman (0-02), V Corey, G McQuaid; D Clerkin (0-02), O Lennon (0-01); S Gollogly (0-01), P Finlay (0-06), K Hughes; C Hanratty, C McManus (0-03), T Freeman (0-03)
SUBS: R Woods for Hanratty; H McElroy (0-01) for Gollogly; D Mone for McArdle; M McElroy (0-02) for Hughes; N McAdam for D Freeman

FERMANAGH: Ronan Gallagher; N Bogue, S Lyons, B Mulrone; D Ward (0-01), R McCluskey, T McElroy; J Sherry, M McGrath; D Keenan (1-01), R Carson (0-01), M Little; P Ward (0-01), Rory Gallagher (1-02), C O'Brien
SUBS: M O'Brien for Lyons; C Flaherty for Little; S Quigley (0-01) for Ward; K Cosgrove for McGrath; R Keenan (0-01) for O'Brien

REFEREE: M Duffy (Sligo)

Semi-Final

GALWAY 1-10 | 1-10 **SLIGO**

27 June 2010

Garreth Bradshaw kicked an injury-time free to earn a gutsy 1-10 to 1-10 draw for 14-man Galway in the Connacht Senior Football Championship semi-final.

Galway's Joe Bergin and Brendan Philips of Sligo

Sligo had the winning of this Salthill encounter, having built a 1-08 to 0-02 half-time lead with a blustery wind behind them in front of a 12,829 attendance.

Galway lost Sean Armstrong to a second yellow card, just four minutes into the second half, and Joe Kernan's men had it all to do.

But championship veteran Pádraic Joyce stepped up to the plate, inspiring his side with a six-point tally and hand-passing through for Eoin Concannon to collect a crucial late goal.

That left a single point between the sides and substitute Michael Meehan drew a foul in the third minute of injury-time that resulted in Bradshaw's levelling score.

The early exchanges were typically fast-paced and Galway opened the scoring in the fourth minute as Joe Bergin swooped on a ball in from Gary Sice and fisted over from the edge of the square.

Sligo's response was swift, Colm McGee bending a free over from the left wing and David Kelly turning smartly to point from close range.

Keelan Cawley clipped a lovely low ball in to Kelly who gathered and turned onto his right for a tidy finish.

The Galway markers were not as tight as their Sligo counterparts, as evidenced by comfortable scores for Alan Costello and Mark Breheny.

Replying to a free from Pádraic Joyce, Costello sent over a towering point off his left and Breheny made it 0-04 to 0-02 to Sligo. The Galway forwards were coming deeper and deeper in pursuit of possession and their frustration grew as Sean Armstrong dropped a point attempt short of the uprights and Bergin was foiled by a well-timed challenge from Charlie Harrison.

Sligo's industry and hard running helped set up a well-taken point from Tony Taylor on the left, after Breheny and Costello had secured a quick turnover of possession.

Taylor and Stephen Gilmartin, Sligo's midfield pairing, were beginning to set the tone in centrefield and when Cawley polished off a point, following a quick one-two with Johnny Davey, Galway were 0-06 to 0-02 in arrears.

Corner-forward Kelly dummied a pass and raced past Alan Burke before stabbing a right-footed shot to the bottom right corner of the net and McGee followed up with two more frees.

Kernan's charges opened the second half with a point from Concannon, but a mistimed challenge by Armstrong on Davey saw referee David Coldrick reach for his yellow and red cards.

That was the signal for the introduction of Michael Meehan, who with his right knee heavily bandaged was clearly not match fit, but his presence gave Sligo some extra headaches.

Joyce kicked the next four points for the home side, two of which were from play. Joyce and Kelly traded points before the former landed a free for a 1-09 to 0-05 scoreline.

The Killererin ace then wormed his way past three Sligo defenders to claim the point of the match and although Galway kicked three subsequent wides, Joyce delivered again with a slick point off his left.

Meehan was wayward with two point attempts and Sligo were also looking jittery in attack. They broke forward and should have punished some lacklustre Galway defending, only for Costello to drop his shot short of the posts and an unmarked Cawley was too casual when drifting his effort to the left and wide.

With two minutes of normal time remaining, Meehan was involved in a move that ended with Sice splitting the posts for 1-09 to 0-08.

Kelly wrong-footed two Galway players before stroking over a much-needed score for Sligo and with O'Hara stationed in defence, they had three minutes of injury-time to survive whatever the Tribesmen could throw at them.

Joyce crept his side closer with another solid strike off his left and Bergin and Joyce did the donkey work in setting up the onrushing Concannon for a lovely left-footed dink to the net.

In the dying seconds, Galway forced a late attack and when Meehan was grounded by O'Hara's outstretched leg, Bradshaw stepped up to slot over from close range and complete his side's comeback.

GALWAY: A Faherty; K Fitzgerald, F Hanley, A Burke; G Bradshaw (0-01), D Blake, G O'Donnell; P Conroy, N Coleman; G Sice (0-01), S Armstrong, J Bergin (0-01); E Concannon (1-01), P Joyce (0-06), M Clancy
SUBS: M Meehan for Clancy; D Cummins for Conroy

SLIGO: P Greene; C Harrison, N McGuire, R Donovan; K Cawley (0-01), B Philips, J Davey; T Taylor (0-01), S Gilmartin; M Breheny (0-01), A Costello (0-01), E O'Hara; C McGee (0-03), K Sweeney, D Kelly (1-03)
SUBS: E Mullen for Sweeney; S Coen for McGee

REFEREE: D Coldrick (Meath)

JOANNE CANTWELL

'Just don't ask me about Semplegate!' cries Donie Bergin throwing his head back with laughter.

When the dust settled on that 2007 summer's day, after the hurling teams of Cork and Clare had made their entrance through the tunnel of Semple Stadium at the exact same time, their fiery actions raised plenty of questions – for the players, their managers, the team-officials, the GAA... and one man in an orange vest.

Donie Bergin, the Assistant Head Steward of Semple Stadium, had been the man to give the teams their three-minute warning, the man who told them it was time to come out, each at the correct time, each at separate times. Donie Bergin was the man who had to have a full report in to Croke Park by nine o'clock the next morning. All in a day's work.

Donie Bergin isn't looking for any sympathy. It's a Wednesday morning, and he's in the place he loves, chuckling away at favourite memories with Robert Ryan, the Deputy Chief Steward of Semple Stadium and Donal Fitzgibbon, Chairman of the Munster Stewarding and Safety Committee for Major Grounds. This is their land: Semple Stadium, or any Munster stadium, big or small, where they spend almost every Saturday and Sunday of their lives. As much as Brian Cody or Liam Sheedy, Jack O'Connor or Conor Counihan, the championship is their life, and they play a massive role in ours.

The truth is that 'Semplegate' doesn't rank very highly among the great things they've seen, such as Maurice Fitzgerald's pointed sideline ('probably the greatest score I ever saw in any sport'); or the Toomevara father who insisted he be let on to the sideline during a Munster Club Championship meeting against Mount Sion so he could deliver some suggested changes to the manager, which ultimately turned certain defeat into victory for the Tipperary side; or the request from a hurling management team for 'a hammer and a vice-grips'.

Approximately 300 stewards work on Munster Championship games, whatever the venue – 100 official Munster stewards plus 200 'voluntary stewards', (a strange name, given they're all voluntary). The majority don't even get to see the games they're stewarding, although some are as close to the action as you can get. All sorts of action.

Hurling fans will remember this year's National League meeting between last year's All-Ireland finalists, and the heated exchange between Kilkenny manager Brian Cody and Tipperary boss Liam Sheedy on the sideline. Robert Ryan was closer than anyone.

'The only thing you'd ever worry about is someone else coming in to get involved. There's plenty of room for the managers to argue away, like. Cop on does take over in a few seconds. If you took that out of it, it would be a very dull and boring game. That day I just walked over, there was another person walked over, and I just said "no", and he went back.'

'The thing is to be discreet. It was gas now, the following day a fella' said to me, "oh I heard exactly what Sheedy said to him". Now there was Liam Sheedy, Brian Cody, the referee and myself, and I know the three of them didn't say anything and I didn't say anything, so how did he know what was said?'

Even problems in the game itself can require involvement from the stewards. It's not uncommon for the referee to find himself unpopular with those watching the game, and Garda escorts for the men in the middle have become an occasional feature of the game.

'It's no secret, if there's a tricky point in the game, we always advise the referees to be as close to the dressing room as is possible,' says Donal Fitzgibbon. 'Still the odd clown decides to be at the far end when the final whistle goes... it's not an official thing, but it's common sense.'

It's Robert's job to make sure the referee gets off the pitch safely. 'My role, more or less, would be to call in the Gardaí or extra stewards if I think we need them. You'd know how hostile the game is getting. Most of the time there'd never ever be any problem. It's usually not a genuine supporter who has anything to say. It's very rarely a player – he might pass comment or something, but he'd never be a threat to a referee. There'd never be a threat from any officials or anything like that. Some fella tanked up with beer and has obviously money or something on it; usually he's the only threat.'

Much like the way the games of hurling and football are played at a standard and intensity that seem so far from 'amateur', the level of training for stewards has also hit new heights. Almost every one of the official Munster stewards has a FETAC qualification, level four – an internationally-recognised training that can only be acquired after a two-day intensive course and an exam. The hope is that by the end of the year, 250 stewards in the Munster area will have this qualification.

'It's become a very structured set-up. Every steward knows on the Tuesday before the game where they're going to be,' says Donal Fitzgibbon. 'All the stewards will have left home seven, half-seven in the morning, and it could be nine or ten at night before you get home. And they've to go to work the next morning.'

But you won't hear any of these stewards complaining. For three or four hours each Sunday, the stewards in the stands in Thurles, Killarney, Cork, have a link with each fan in their section, and of course, they get to meet some of the greatest characters in the games of football and hurling.

'I found Nicky English an out and out gentleman, and John Allen, I'd have to put Davy in too, 'cos I think I'm the only one who can handle him!' laughs Donie.

In fact, the 'Davy' in question – current Waterford boss Davy Fitzgerald – brings a smile to all three faces.

'Davy is very entertaining,' Robert agrees. 'He's a kind of a love-hate character. When he was playing he attracted so much attention from the terraces from the opposition and he was part of the game. Now I suppose it's carried on to his management. He's so easy to work with, I have to say, he's no problem whatsoever.'

'Once he goes back in there, he's a completely different man,' Donie adds, before Robert continues.

'Coming up to the game or anything like that, he always has a word for everyone coming in, and he acknowledges stewards and everyone so there's no airs and graces about any of them... Brian Cody, you'd often meet him coming in here to "spy on the opposition", as I always say to him. He's the most low-key person you will ever meet. He comes up along through the crowd there, himself and the wife. He's not looking for any attention, doesn't look for any special treatment or anything like that – goes in, quiet. They are great now, always acknowledge you.'

And when Brian Cody, Davy Fitzgerald and co. pack up for the day, the same people who opened up the stadium – who prepped it, guided players and managers to the correct dressing rooms, gave that famous three-minute knock, directed supporters to their seats, told them where the nearest toilet was, told them when car parks would be re-opening, helped them find a lost child, directed them to first-aid – they're still there, just like they will be every Saturday and Sunday. Because the championship is part of who they are, and they are part of the championship.

Graham Canty

CLUB: Bantry Blues

COUNTY: Cork

AGE: 30

HEIGHT: 6'2"

WEIGHT: 13 stone 10lbs

OCCUPATION: Engineer

Graham Canty, the current Cork captain, has been one of the counties finest servants and a talismanic figure in the centre of the Cork defence for nearly 10 years. He made his championship debut in 2001 as a full-back after earning Munster Under-21 honours as team captain.

Since then he has won four Munster Senior Football titles and has also represented Ireland in the International Rules Series. He was vice captain when Ireland beat Australia down under in 2008.

At senior level he suffered defeat in the All-Ireland Football finals of 2007 & 2009 but his heroic efforts finally paid dividends in 2010 when he helped put an end to Cork's unenviable record of losing finals and bring the Sam Maguire back to Cork for the first time in 20 years.

Although injury prevented him from starting the game he came off the bench in the second half and played a hugely influential role in turning the game around for Cork. Afterwards, in an interview on *The Sunday Game*, the modest captain said, 'It was good to run on in the second half but I was only part of a jigsaw. We all pull together, we all do our bit and my bit today was coming off the bench and doing my bit for the team.'

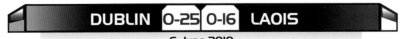

DUBLIN 0-25 0-16 LAOIS

6 June 2010

Dublin are through to the Leinster Hurling Championship semi-finals after a win over Laois at Nowlan Park.

All bar three of Dublin's points came from open play as they advanced to a Leinster semi-final against Kilkenny.

Shane Durkin, Liam Rushe and All-Star Alan McCrabbe impressed for Anthony Daly's men, scoring 0-14 between them, while Willie Hyland and John Brophy kept Laois in touch.

However, Dublin were strongest on the restart, with Laois reduced to 13 men following second yellow cards for Brian Campion and Colin Delaney.

Last year's beaten Leinster finalists certainly looked the more composed side in the opening half, and quickly claimed the first score of the game from full-forward Simon Lambert in the second minute.

Laois had a good grip on the midfield sector, where Conor Dunne and James Walsh performed strongly early on, but were let down by a wasteful attack.

The O'Moore men registered eight first-half wides, but were level on six occasions with the Metropolitans during that spell.

Indeed, Laois led Dublin twice in the opening 12 minutes, with scores from Hyland and Zane Keenan giving them a 0-02 to 0-01 lead in the sixth minute.

A long-range clearance by Joey Boland was gathered by Rushe to tie the game at 0-02 apiece in the ninth minute, but Laois regained the lead thanks to a brace of Hyland points.

Durkin, Rushe and Paul Ryan claimed scores in quick succession as the Dubs went 0-05 to 0-04 in front by the end of the opening quarter.

Team captain Brian Campion and fellow half-back Matthew Whelan marshalled well in the Laois defence, but the underdogs'

forwards amassed six wides between the 18th and 25th minutes.

The sides were level for the sixth time when a second John Brophy point tied the game at 0-07 apiece in the 32nd minute, but Dublin found an extra gear before the break.

Daly's charges were now hitting top form and outscored Laois by three points to one in the closing stages of the opening half, with Durkin, McCrabbe and John McCaffrey ensuring a 0-10 to 0-08 buffer.

Laois' strike rate failed to improve as the second half started as Tommy Fitzgerald and Joe Fitzpatrick registered wides inside 45 seconds.

Lambert, Paul Ryan and Rushe fired quick points to push the Dubs 0-13 to 0-08 ahead by the 39th minute, before Hyland and Whelan replied for Laois.

However, a three-point deficit was as close as the O'Moore men would get to Dublin in the closing 35 minutes. Campion's dismissal, ten minutes into the second period, was a major blow to his side's chances.

The 14 men of Laois tried to show more urgency but their wides tally increased and Dublin added some cushion to their lead thanks to scores from McCrabbe, Rushe, McCaffrey and Peter Kelly.

Points from Laois substitutes Colin Delaney and John Purcell left four points between the sides with 12 minutes remaining, but Dublin were doing just enough to look comfortable and closing points from McCaffrey and Liam Ryan completed the job.

Laois' woes were compounded when Colin Delaney walked late on for a second bookable offence.

DUBLIN: G Maguire; N Corcoran, T Brady, O Gough; S Hiney, J Boland, M O'Brien; J McCaffrey (0-03), S Durkin (0-05); P Kelly (0-03), L Rushe (0-04), P Ryan (0-02); D O'Callaghan, S Lambert (0-02), A McCrabbe (0-05)
SUBS: K Flynn for O'Callaghan; L Ryan (0-01) for Flynn; P Carton for P Ryan; S Ryan for Brady; R Trainor for Gough

LAOIS: E Reilly; J A Delaney, D Maher, C Healy; B Campion, M Whelan (0-01), M McEvoy; C Dunne, James Walsh (0-01); J Fitzpatrick, Z Keenan (0-02), W Hyland (0-06); T Fitzgerald (0-01), N Foyle, J Brophy (0-03)
SUBS: C Delaney (0-01) for Foyle; J Purcell (0-01) for Fitzpatrick

REFEREE: C McAllister (Cork)

Semi-Final

| WATERFORD | 0-22 | 1-15 | CLARE |

7 June 2010

Waterford overcame Clare's battling youngsters to reach the Munster Senior Hurling Championship final at Semple Stadium.

A cracking Bank Holiday encounter was level seven times and hung in the balance right until the final stages, before the experienced Waterford men pushed for home with a powerful surge.

Clare boss Ger O'Loughlin handed out six debuts and by the end of the game ten members of last year's All-Ireland U21 winning team had joined the action.

But it was the Waterford bench that turned the tide after the Banner had gone in at the break with a four-point lead.

Declan Prendergast fired over three superb points, with Seamus Prendergast and Ken McGrath also coming on to shoot inspirational scores.

Despite their inexperience, Clare embraced the challenge with confidence and conviction, and looked intent on causing an upset with their high energy approach in the first half.

It seemed as if the script was to be followed to the letter when Stephen Molumphy and John Mullane flighted over early Déise points.

But Clare, with Pat Donnellan and Cian Dillon performing heroics at the back, tackled like demons, and forced a series of turnovers which created the scoring opportunities for Sean Clancy, Jonathan Clancy and John Conlon to put away.

By the 21st minute, they had opened out a 0-08 to 0-03 lead, with rookie midfielder Nicky O'Connell helping himself to three excellent scores.

Eoin Kelly kept a flagging Waterford side in touch with long-range frees, and Mullane executed an overhead gem for the second time.

Waterford's Eoin Kelly celebrates

Waterford had narrowed the gap to two points when Banner full-forward Darach Honan picked up a loose ball to blast home a brilliant 33rd-minute goal.

Kelly and Kevin Moran responded with points, but at the break, it was the Clare men who led by 1-10 to 0-9.

Once Waterford got the wind in their backs in the second half, they carried a much greater threat.

With 37-year-old veteran Tony Browne driving his younger colleagues on from the half-back line, they set about dismantling Clare's lead.

Kevin Moran, Molumphy, Maurice Shanahan and Mullane were all on target, with Declan Prendergast firing over three gems.

Clare were far from finished, though, and went back in front through substitute Cormac O'Donovan and Honan.

But Waterford had the will to produce a response each time their opponents registered, and late scores from Kelly, McGrath and Seamus Prendergast sealed the win and a place in the decider.

Waterford's Shane O'Sullivan and Brian O'Connell of Clare

WATERFORD: C Hennessy; E Murphy, L Lawlor, N Connors; T Browne, M Walsh, J Nagle; S O'Sullivan, R Foley; D Shanahan, K Moran (0-02), S Molumphy (0-03); J Mullane (0-03), E Kelly (0-06), M Shanahan (0-02).
SUBS: D Prendergast (0-03) for Nagle; S Prendergast (0-02) for M Shanahan; S Walsh for D Shanahan; K McGrath (0-01) for Moran; E McGrath for Molumphy

CLARE: D Touhy; P Vaughan, C Dillon, C Cooney; B Bugler, D McMahon, P Donnellan; B O'Connell, N O'Connell (0-03); S Collins (0-02), J Conlon (0-01), J Clancy (0-03); F Lynch, D Honan (1-03), C Ryan (0-01).
SUBS: C O'Donovan (0-01) for Ryan; D O'Donovan for B O'Connell; D Barrett (0-01) for Lynch; A Markham for Clancy

REFEREE: B Galvin (Offaly)

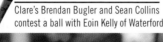

Clare's Brendan Bugler and Sean Collins contest a ball with Eoin Kelly of Waterford

Semi-Final

CORK 2-19 0-12 LIMERICK
20 June 2010

Substitute Paudie O'Sullivan's late goal put the seal on a comfortable Munster Senior Hurling Championship semi-final win for Cork, as 14-man Limerick's resistance eventually petered out at Páirc Uí Chaoimh.

This inexperienced and youthful Limerick side started well under a strength-sapping sun, but Sean Herlihy's first half dismissal for striking was a serious setback.

Cork were 1-10 to 0-06 ahead by half-time, with Pat Horgan netting from a penalty and Graeme Mulcahy impressing for the underdogs with three points.

The second half was a one-sided affair, however, and although midfielder Tommy O'Brien finished with six points for the Shannonsiders, Cork's man-of-the-match Niall McCarthy (0-05) was just as influential.

With the dispute between last year's panel and manager Justin McCarthy still not resolved, the Limerick starting line-up included nine championship debutants.

David Breen, Paul Browne, Paudie McNamara, new captain Bryan O'Sullivan and James O'Brien were the only survivors from last August's All-Ireland semi-final loss to Tipperary.

It was a cagey opening from both sides with little final product. James O'Brien, Pat Horgan, Niall McCarthy and Tommy O'Brien all hit wides before Paudie McNamara converted a sixth-minute free for the lead score.

Andrew Brennan darted forward for Limerick's second point, sandwiched between Cork's opening efforts from Jerry O'Connor and Horgan.

But the Rebels took a lead they would not relinquish, courtesy of an 11th-minute penalty which was won and sent to the net by corner-forward Horgan. Amid a spell of fluent, fleet-footed attacking from Cork, Horgan then took his tally to 1-02 with a well-taken point.

Cork's Sean Óg Ó hAilpín clears the danger

Limerick stuck stubbornly to their task, albeit with McNamara struggling from placed balls. A brace of points from Mulcahy moved Limerick onto 0-04, but with ten minutes remaining in the half, Cork had cantered on to 1-07.

Cork's Patrick Horgan

McCarthy, McLoughlin and Ben O'Connor all pointed during that period and Horgan missed a second penalty – Shane O'Neill, the defender who fouled him, doing well to block the shot and clear.

An Anthony Owens point was followed by two from the O'Connor twins, Jerry and Ben, with the latter's being probably the point of the half – a sublime strike from a tight angle near the right sideline.

Cork seemingly had the quality to pull clear, but with target man Aisake Ó hAilpín kept quiet by David Breen, Limerick were growing in confidence by the minute.

They earned a penalty of their own when John Gardiner floored the onrushing James O'Brien. Yet Cork goalkeeper Donal Óg Cusack rescued his wing-back when he saved McNamara's penalty effort and the danger was averted.

A knee injury to corner-back Brian Murphy left Cork having to readjust and Limerick suffered a huge blow in injury-time when referee James Owens gave a straight red card to Limerick wing-forward Sean Herlihy as he was seen swinging out at Cork substitute Shane Murphy in retaliation.

The sides split two points as the half came to a close, Mulcahy and Cork captain Kieran Murphy on target, and Walsh's side were able to build a match-winning lead in the opening minutes of the second period.

Tommy O'Brien nipped it back to 1-10 to 0-07 for Limerick, before scores from Ben O'Connor, McCarthy and Jerry O'Connor launched Cork towards a double-figures lead.

McCarthy's youngsters were fading, despite the best efforts of top-scorer O'Brien, and they had goalkeeper Tadhg Flynn to thank for a smart save as he denied Paudie O'Sullivan a goal after a clever attack involving Sean Óg Ó hAilpín.

O'Brien had closed the gap back to 1-15 to 0-09 prior to that. Cork replied through wing-forward McCarthy who hit another gear in the second half. He tagged on two excellent scores.

Cusack did well again to prevent Mulcahy from rippling the net. It was a goal that Limerick's dogged efforts had deserved, but it never came and O'Sullivan, taking a pass from fellow substitute Michael Cussen, thundered through to bat home Cork's second in the 69th minute.

Cork skipper Murphy struck the final point to make the winning margin 13 points. A satisfactory scoreline for the Rebels who march into their first Munster final since 2006, while Limerick can, at least, take some positives from today into the All-Ireland qualifiers.

CORK: D Óg Cusack; S O'Neill, E Cadogan, B Murphy; J Gardiner (0-01), R Curran, S Óg Ó hAilpín; L McLoughlin (0-01), C Naughton (0-01); B O'Connor (0-03), J O'Connor (0-03), N McCarthy (0-05); K Murphy (0-02), A Ó hAilpín, P Horgan (1-02)
SUBS: S Murphy for B Murphy; M Cussen for A Ó hAilpín; P O'Sullivan (1-01) for Horgan; G Callanan for Naughton; R Ryan for S Óg Ó hAilpín

LIMERICK: T Flynn; S O'Neill, D Breen, K O'Rourke; S O'Riordan, B O'Sullivan, P Browne; T O'Brien (0-06), A Brennan (0-01); P McNamara (0-01), J O'Brien, S Herlihy; G Mulcahy (0-03), A Owens (0-01), R McKeogh.
SUBS: L O'Dwyer for O'Riordan; C Mullane for McNamara; P Russell for McKeogh; N Quaid for Brennan; A O'Connor for Owens

REFEREE: J Owens (Wexford)

Semi-Final

GALWAY 2-19 3-16 OFFALY
20 June 2010

Galway and Offaly will meet again next Sunday after their thrilling Leinster Senior Hurling Championship semi-final finished level at Croke Park.

Shane Dooley earned a replay for the Faithful County with a long-range free in stoppage time.

Offaly stunned the pre-match favourites with three first-half goals to open up a seven-point lead, but Galway hit back with strikes in the second half from Joe Canning and Ger Farragher.

John McIntyre thought he had secured the win over his former county when Canning and Iarla Tannian drilled over late points, but Dooley scored twice at the death to rescue Offaly in front of a crowd of 25,260.

Galway reeled off the first four points of the game, but Offaly were ahead by the 15th minute.

Damien Hayes, Ger Farragher and Iarla Tannian all swept over points to delight the Tribal following.

But it soon became evident that the Connacht side's defence could be exploited, and a fired up Offaly side did just that.

It was in the 12th minute that Shane Dooley cut in front from the right, and when his shot was blocked, Joe Brady gathered to crash to the net from close range.

Offaly had the lead for the first time, but they weren't content to sit on it. They continued to press forward, and added points through Brian Carroll and Joe Bergin, before Shane Dooley cracked home a second goal on 20 minutes.

He turned his marker in alarmingly comfortable fashion before slotting low to the net from a difficult angle.

And when he added a free soon afterwards, the Faithful had turned a four-point deficit into a four-point lead.

Joe Canning finally escaped the shackles of David Kelly to slot his first point from play, but with Stephen Egan and Derek Moran solid at the back, there was little room to manoeuvre for the other Galway attackers.

Paul Cleary's booming clearance set up the third goal in the 26th minute for full-forward Bergin, who rounded Shane Kavanagh to slot past Colm Callanan for a 3-04 to 0-07 lead.

Dylan Hayden and Brady swapped points with Farragher and Aonghus Callanan late in the half, and Offaly turned around with a 3-07 to 0-11 lead.

But Galway made a devastating start to the second half. Farragher and substitute Niall Healy cut the deficit to three within two minutes of the restart.

Then came a 2-02 salvo in the space of four minutes. Cyril Donnellan knocked the ball back to Canning to smash to the net, and it was Farragher who finished to the net after Aonghus Callanan's shot had been kept out by James Dempsey.

Offaly were reduced to 14 men when substitute Daniel Currams received a straight red card for a challenge on David Burke in the 46th minute, but they scored the next three points, through Dooley, Dylan Hayden and Bergin, to narrow the gap to a point.

There was nothing to separate the sides as they headed for a gripping final quarter, with Canning, for the second time, scoring exquisitely from a sideline cut, only to see Rory Hannify and Dooley bring the sides level.

Canning's long-range effort, and a second for Tannian, eased the Connacht side two clear in the dying moments, but Dooley emerged as the saviour, bringing his tally to 1-07.

GALWAY: J Dempsey; D Franks, P Cleary, J Rigney; S Egan, D Kenny, D Morkan; R Hanniffy (0-01), D Hayden (0-02); B Carroll (0-02), J Brady (1-01), D Molloy (0-01); B Murphy, J Bergin (1-02), S Dooley (1-07)
SUBS: J Lee for Barry; N Healy (0-01) for Harte; K Hynes for Donnellan; J Gantley for Hynes

OFFALY: J Dempsey; D Franks, P Cleary, J Rigney; S Egan, D Kenny, D Moran; D Hayden (0-02), K Brady; B Carroll (0-02), J Brady (1-01), R Hanniffy (0-01); D Molloy (0-01), J Bergin (1-02), S Dooley (1-07)
SUBS: D Currams for Molloy; B Murphy for Brady; G Healion for J Brady; O'Kealey for Carroll

REFEREE: J Ryan (Tipperary)

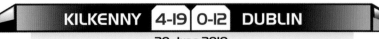

Semi-Final

KILKENNY `4-19` `0-12` **DUBLIN**

20 June 2010

Henry Shefflin smashed Eddie Keher's all-time scoring record as Kilkenny completed a 19-point drubbing of Dublin in the Leinster Senior Hurling Championship semi-final.

Dublin were never far away in a first half that saw them compete point-for-point with the All-Ireland champions, but after the break Kilkenny stepped up a gear and put the game out of sight with ease.

Two late goals from substitute Aidan Fogarty made it a rout in the end, after Richie Power had netted to add to Eddie Brennan's first-half strike.

Kilkenny had the ball in the net after just 45 seconds, Eddie Brennan giving them a dream start as he crashed the ball to the net from TJ Reid's lay-off.

They eased into a 1-02 to 0-01 lead with Shefflin hitting a couple of points, but Dublin displayed grit and courage to play themselves back into the game.

Tomás Brady and Joey Boland led by example at the back and Alan McCrabbe provided the finishing power with a succession of converted frees.

Two of them came as a result of illegal hand-passes by Kilkenny defenders who got to grips with the new directive as the contest progressed.

When Boland drove over a long-range score in the 16th minute just a point separated the sides, but as Jackie Tyrell and Tommy Walsh stamped their authority on proceedings at the back for the Cats, they opened out a four-point lead.

Shefflin drilled through two points from '65's, one of them a result of a superb double save by Dublin goalkeeper Gary Maguire who denied Richie Power and Reid.

Another uplifting score from a Dublin defender – this time Maurice O'Brien splitting the posts from distance – raised Metropolitan hopes, but Shefflin and Reid responded to send the All-Ireland champions in with a 1-10 to 0-8 interval lead.

Peter Kelly steered over two Dublin points early in the second half to keep hope alive, but in the 49th minute Richie Power raced through to flick home the goal that effectively ended Dublin's challenge.

Shefflin continued to hit the target, and Dublin's attempts to drag themselves back into contention suffered a setback when Paul Ryan's penalty was kept out by Noel Hickey.

As desperation grew, McCrabbe went for goal from a couple of 20 metre frees, but one was stopped by goalkeeper PJ Ryan and the other deflected out for a '65' which John McCaffrey converted.

There was a certain inevitability about the manner in which Brian Cody's side closed out the game.

Fogarty slotted an opportunist 63rd-minute goal after Gary Maguire had saved from Shefflin and it was substitute Fogarty who sealed a big win with a brilliant solo goal three minutes from the end.

KILKENNY: PJ Ryan; J Dalton, N Hickey, J Tyrrell; T Walsh, B Hogan, JJ Delaney; M Rice (0-02), M Fennelly; M Comerford (0-01), R Hogan (0-01), H Shefflin (0-12); E Brennan (1-01), TJ Reid (0-02), R Power (1-00)
SUBS: E Larkin for Hogan; J Mulhall for Reid; A Fogarty (2-00) for Brennan; D Lyng for Power

DUBLIN: G Maguire; N Corcoran, T Brady, O Gough; S Hiney, J Boland (0-01), M O'Brien (0-01); J McCaffrey (0-01), S Durkin; S Lambert, P Kelly (0-02), L Ryan; D O'Callaghan (0-01), L Rushe, A McCrabbe (0-06)
SUBS: P Ryan for Lambert; M Carton for O'Brien; D O'Dwyer for Durkin; D Treacy for O'Callaghan; K Flynn for L Ryan

REFEREE: D Kirwan (Cork)

Semi-Final

GALWAY 3-17 | 2-18 OFFALY

26 June 2010 (replay)

Joe Canning and Ger Farragher hit injury-time points as Galway won an epic Leinster Hurling Championship semi-final replay over Offaly by 3-17 to 2-18.

Level in stoppage time, John McIntyre's side finished with a flourish as Joe Canning landed the decisive score amid another brilliant comeback from Offaly.

Meeting for the second time in the space of six days, Galway's explosive start was rewarded with a burst of scores as Offaly failed to match the Tribesmen's passion early on.

Leading by 0-04 to 0-01 after 10 minutes courtesy of scores from Andy Smith, Damien Hayes, Iarla Tannian and Ger Farragher, Galway were in the ascendancy and they then bagged their first goal with a smashing move.

The game had just ticked into its 11th minute when Farragher found the excellent Hayes, who burst clear to rattle home an opportunistic goal.

Offaly were in deep distress, and the westerners grabbed a second goal in the 24th minute with Farragher again heavily involved. Ollie Canning started the move, Farragher kept the sliotar moving, and Joe Canning supplied a typically crisp finish to edge Galway nine points ahead.

Brian Carroll was effective for Offaly and struck over a couple of smartly taken points, but Galway still went in at the break armed with a commanding 2-09 to 0-07 advantage.

They added two more points after the restart courtesy of Farragher and Hayes, but Offaly, rediscovering the sort of form they showed at Croke Park last Sunday, came thundering back.

Substitute Ger Healion announced his arrival into the game with a well-taken point and a goal shortly after in the 42nd minute.

It was a smashing encounter, but Galway remained composed, and Hayes swept home a 51st-minute goal that put them six clear again.

Referee Cathal McAllister then took centre stage in the 54th minute when controversially red-carding Galway midfielder David Burke for retaliation.

Offaly then hit an equalising goal in the 59th minute when Joe Bergin buried a shot from an acute angle as the match continued to excite.

It was tight and tense in the closing stages as the lead swapped hands, but Galway took the verdict to advance to their first ever Leinster decider.

Galway's Joe Canning and James Rigney of Offaly

GALWAY: C Callanan; D Joyce, S Kavanagh, O Canning; D Barry (0-01), T Óg Regan, J Lee; G Farragher (0-06), D Burke; E Ryan, A Callanan (0-01), A Smith (0-01); J Canning (1-03), D Hayes (2-03), I Tannian (0-02)
SUBS: N Healy for Ryan; J Gantley for Healy; A Cullinane for Smith

OFFALY: J Dempsey; D Franks, D Kenny (0-01), S Egan; J Rigney, P Cleary, D Morkan; K Brady, D Hayden; B Carroll (0-03), J Brady, R Hanniffy; S Dooley (0-10), J Bergin (1-01), B Murphy (0-02)
SUBS: G Healion (1-01) for Franks; M Verney for Egan; C Parlon for Kenny; O Kealy for K Brady

REFEREE: C McAllister (Cork)

Bernard Brogan

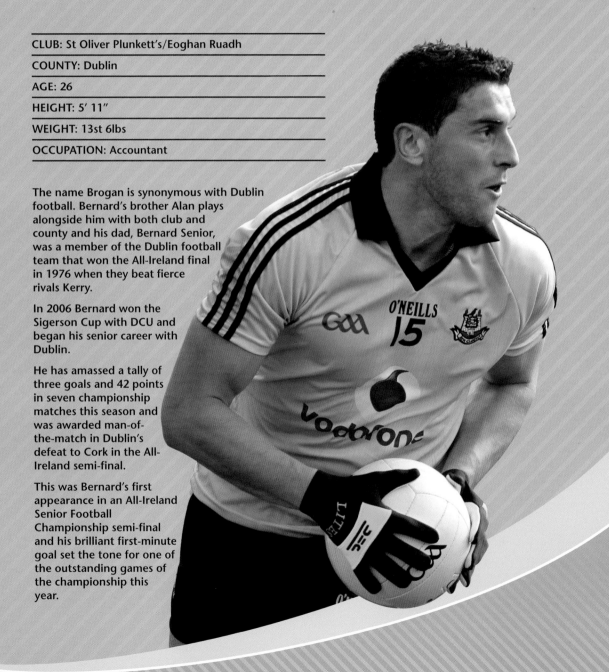

CLUB: St Oliver Plunkett's/Eoghan Ruadh

COUNTY: Dublin

AGE: 26

HEIGHT: 5' 11"

WEIGHT: 13st 6lbs

OCCUPATION: Accountant

The name Brogan is synonymous with Dublin football. Bernard's brother Alan plays alongside him with both club and county and his dad, Bernard Senior, was a member of the Dublin football team that won the All-Ireland final in 1976 when they beat fierce rivals Kerry.

In 2006 Bernard won the Sigerson Cup with DCU and began his senior career with Dublin.

He has amassed a tally of three goals and 42 points in seven championship matches this season and was awarded man-of-the-match in Dublin's defeat to Cork in the All-Ireland semi-final.

This was Bernard's first appearance in an All-Ireland Senior Football Championship semi-final and his brilliant first-minute goal set the tone for one of the outstanding games of the championship this year.

DARRAGH MALONEY

The Sunday Game was first broadcast on 8 July 1979 and it has become one of the longest running shows on Irish television.

Presenter Michael Lyster followed Jim Carney in 1984 while Des Cahill is in his second year presenting the highlights programme following Pat Spillane.

The *2010 Sunday Game* divides into two parts: *The Sunday Game Live* which is presented by Michael and *The Sunday Game* which is fronted by Des. Each show has two separate teams of people working behind the scenes at RTÉ in Dublin and at the match venue. Editors, producers, video operators, cameramen and women, sound technicians, graphics operators, statisticians, floor managers, broadcast co-ordinators, set designers and autocue operators join the commentators, presenters and reporters to bring you what you see every Sunday of the summer.

Just as Croke Park has changed dramatically over the last 15 years, so too has the coverage RTÉ provides. When I first started to go to matches in the 1980s with my dad, I used to try and sneak a look at the RTÉ presentation position which was used by Michael Lyster for the live coverage of the All-Ireland semi-finals and finals. It was located in the old Nally Stand and was a platform suspended from the roof of the stand! Michael and his panel along with the camera people, the floor manager and others had to climb up a big ladder to get to their seats. Once the games were finished, the ladder was taken away so I never did get to see the 'studio' they used all those years ago.

The commentary position has also changed in the last few years with the construction of the new Hogan Stand. I did manage to get into the old commentary box after big matches in the 80s to see where Mícheál O'Hehir and Mícheál Ó Muircheartaigh and later Ger Canning and Marty Morrissey were

The coverage back then was basic by 2010 standards but it was cutting-edge 31 years ago. Jim Carney presented highlights of the Munster Senior Hurling Championship final between Cork and Limerick and that night set in motion a show that has become an important part of Irish culture.

The first time Gaelic Games were seen on television in Ireland was on Saint Patrick's Day in 1962 when RTÉ showed the Railway Cup finals, just three months after Telefís Éireann was established. During the 60s, 70s and most of the 80s, RTÉ broadcast the All-Ireland semi-finals and finals live along with the Railway Cup finals, but in 1989, the Munster Hurling final was shown live for the first time and the debate began about showing more and more live matches.

There were concerns about the effect on attendances but the GAA awarded the broadcasting rights to RTÉ and the coverage grew year after year. In 2010 RTÉ showed 40 championship matches live.

broadcasting from. It was not as glamorous as you might think as it was a very tight, cramped space, but I did find the odd script and programme running order lying around which I still have at home today.

The commentary positions now are the best seats in the house, giving a perfect view of the pitch and everything happening down on the sideline.

I have been fortunate enough to work on *The Sunday Game* since 2000 as a reporter, presenter and commentator. As in any team environment you are one part of a vast machine which grows and changes year after year. When you are at home watching the match, you see the presenter and the panel and you hear the commentator and co-commentator but you do not see the army of people working in the background.

The RTÉ coverage of the All-Ireland finals is planned months in advance with a staff of over 100 people working on each game and a worldwide television audience of millions. Since 2002, RTÉ has used the services of an outside broadcast company called Observe for the All-Ireland finals. They provide the cameras and camera people, the vision mixers, video and graphics operators and many others on the big day.

On the Friday ahead of All-Ireland final Sunday, Alan Burns and his team arrive in Croke Park in a giant outside broadcast Unit called HD1 which is worth around €4 million. It takes the crew two days to prepare the venue, using 10 miles of cable to connect 18 cameras to HD1. By Sunday, Observe will have 45 staff working with RTÉ personnel as the broadcast begins.

Inside HD1, the Observe staff is joined by the RTÉ match director, programme editor and broadcast co-ordinator while the commentators take their places in the Hogan Stand. Michael Lyster and his panel are in their studio along with their floor manager, lighting and sound technicians, camera and autocue operators and stage hands who have built the set for the big match.

The reporters wait down on the sideline with the floor manager. Outside Croke Park, reporters and cameramen are busy talking to and filming supporters as they arrive at the ground, giving viewers all over the world a flavour of the biggest day in Irish sport.

Once the commentator puts on the headphones, a lot of the activity in HD1 can be heard. The match director calls the shots you see on television as he or she goes from camera to camera to give you the best view of the action. The director calls in the replays of the key incidents at the appropriate times and calls in the state-of-the-art graphics that feature player information or the live statistics that contain information about possession or scoring chances.

While the match is on-going, Michael and the panel are busy calling for various incidents to be included in the half and full-time analysis. The video editors cut the pieces together and Ger, Cyril, Tomás, Pat, Joe and Colm offer their opinions when the clips are shown on air.

Des and his night-time show team watch the match back at base and prepare for their broadcast which features highlights of the match and reaction from the panel and from the key players involved. Once the full-time whistle is blown, the interviews are done and the panel give their verdicts, while the night-time team get ready for the latest edition of the show.

Editors race around cutting the shorter version of the match to be shown that evening while Des and the panel agree the content of their discussions with the programme editor. On All-Ireland final night, another Observe OB is used at the hotel where the winners are staying. As soon as the final whistle blows there is a race to the winners' hotel to get the cameras in position for the latest reaction from the All-Ireland champions.

Des presents the show from RTÉ so another group of camera, sound, lighting and stage professionals are involved on the night along with directors, producers, and editors from *The Sunday Game*.

By 11pm on the night of the All-Ireland final, well over 100 people will have been involved in the production and the broadcast of the biggest event in the Irish sporting calendar.

All in a day's work!

Semi-Final

SLIGO 1-14 0-16 GALWAY

3 July 2010

Sligo held their nerve to overcome Galway at Markievicz Park and claim a place in the final.

Alan Costello bent a point over into the stiff wind, after just 36 seconds, to get Sligo off to a swift start. Pádraic Joyce levelled with a third minute free.

But Sligo looked the more threatening and Stephen Coen's rising shot, which cannoned back off the crossbar, could easily have resulted in the game's first goal. As it was, the ball broke for Adrian Marren to clip over a point and Keelan Cawley was able to fist over for the hosts' third, latching onto a low-slung free from Marren.

Joe Kernan's side had the game squared up by the seventh minute, the elusive Matthew Clancy and Eoin Concannon adding points from play. They tightened their grip on centre-field, giving their forwards the time and space to kick a succession of scores – five in all.

With the elements favouring them, the Tribesmen really went at it and Joyce, Clancy, Sean Armstrong and Michael Meehan all found the target during a productive spell. Sligo's only response was from Marren as, by the half-hour mark, they were left trailing by 0-08 to 0-04.

Ending the home side's 17-minute scoreless run, Mark Breheny slotted over following a

Galway's Matthew Clancy and Alan Costello of Sligo

Galway's Pádraic Joyce

free-flowing move involving Coen and David Kelly, and the latter opened his scoring account just before the interval to whittle Galway's lead down to two points.

On general play, Galway had done enough to be further ahead and they immediately got back on the attack as the second half resumed, Joyce setting up Joe Bergin for a fisted effort.

But, three minutes in, Sligo were gifted a priceless goal. Gareth Bradshaw had a nightmare moment when he tried to kick a sideline ball back to goalkeeper Adrian Faherty. Kelly was well placed to intercept and fire home his second goal in as many championship games.

Galway showed great resolve to respond with three successive points, Bradshaw setting up a free for Armstrong who pointed again shortly afterwards and wing-back Garry O'Donnell also swept a shot over from the right.

This was now a huge test for Sligo and they

71

showed their class as Breheny drilled a free over and Kelly, darting onto a Marren delivery, outfoxed the Galway defence for an inspirational point from play.

The second period continued to ebb and flow, Joyce boosting Galway with a quality score from 35 metres out. The Killererin clubman was taking on more responsibility, after a leg injury forced Meehan out of the game.

By the midpoint of the half a Marren free had cut the gap to a single point – 0-13 to 1-09 – and the same player then won a free which Breheny converted to produce huge roars from the Sligo faithful.

With five minutes left on the clock, Joyce popped over a rousing score, and then turned provider as he laid off for Armstrong to land his fourth point from an acute angle.

It was real end-to-end, helter skelter

championship action as Sligo raided forward and Colm McGee, on as a substitute, split the posts under all sorts of pressure.

Scores were at a premium and when another new man in, Paul Conroy, threaded the ball through the posts in outstanding fashion; the difference was back to two.

However, Kevin Walsh's charges dug deep to engineer the sort of finish that would have got them over the finish line six days ago.

Ken Sweeney and the excellent Breheny brought the home side level as the game ticked into injury-time, and it was left to McGee to plunder the winner, which had a good deal of controversy attached to it as the Galway players felt the wind had taken the ball to the right and wide.

The score stood and there was no stopping Sligo this time.

SLIGO: P Greene; C Harrison, N McGuire, R Donavan; K Cawley (0-01), B Philips, J Davey; E Mullen, S Gilmartin; A Costello (0-01) M Breheny (0-04), E O'Hara; S Coen, A Marren (0-03), D Kelly (1-02)
Subs: C McGee (0-02) for Coen; S Davey for Costello; K Sweeney (0-01) for O'Hara; F Quinn for Marren

GALWAY: A Faherty; K Fitzgerald, F Hanley, A Burke; G Bradshaw, D Blake, G O'Donnell (0-01); J Bergin (0-01), N Coleman; G Sice, S Armstrong (0-04), M Clancy (0-02); M Meehan (0-01), P Joyce (0-05), E Concannon (0-01)
Subs: P Conroy (0-01) for Meehan; D Reilly for Hanley

REFEREE: M Deegan (Laois)

Sligo's Eugene Mullen and Stephen Gilmartin with Niall Coleman of Galway

Final

KERRY 1-17 1-14 **LIMERICK**

4 July 2010

Limerick suffered Munster final heartbreak once again as Kerry won a closely fought Killarney duel for their first provincial success since 2007.

Kerry players block a free on the goal mouth line as Limerick attempt a last-minute goal

Despite Kerry playing in fits and starts, they showed enough of a killer instinct to win out in front of a 23,864-strong crowd.

The Shannonsiders were 0-03 to 0-00 up within two minutes of the start. Midfielder John Galvin powered forward straight from the throw-in to fist over after just 14 seconds, and Ger Collins followed up with a towering free and a point from play, the latter set up by Stephen Kelly.

Limerick moved 0-04 to 0-00 ahead when Ian Ryan forced Tommy Griffin away from the Kerry square and Collins darted into the space to knock over his third point. Tomás Ó Sé punched over Kerry's opening score in response, and Colm Cooper converted a free after a foul by Stephen Lucey.

Some terrific movement in the Limerick attack set up a right-footed score from Jim O'Donovan, before the open, expansive football continued at the other end – Mike McCarthy setting up a drilled effort from Darran O'Sullivan.

The pace of the Kerry half-forwards was beginning to put Limerick on the back foot, and Bryan Sheehan fired over a free to close the gap to 0-05 to 0-04. Limerick responded with three points in quick succession.

Net minder Brian Scanlon strode forward to knock over a long-range free, and Kelly held his composure to score off his left, in spite of a late challenge from Tomás Ó Sé. Then Scanlon doubled his tally with another free from distance, making it 0-08 to 0-04.

Sheehan tapped over his second free before James Ryan, latching on to a superb diagonal ball from Seanie Buckley, claimed Limerick's ninth point. Their tenth followed when captain Buckley outfoxed Tomás Ó Sé close to the sideline and split the posts from a tight angle.

However, Kerry took some much-needed momentum into the second half courtesy of late points from McCarthy, who was playing in an advanced role, and Cooper.

The first 15 minutes of the second half were all Kerry as they clinically picked off a succession of scores and seemingly suffocated the life out of Limerick.

By the 41st minute, the sides were level at 0-10 apiece, following a fisted point from Micheal Quirke and another Cooper free off his left.

McCarthy increased his influence by breaking on to a loose ball and setting up Declan O'Sullivan for the lead score, and O'Sullivan then played a one-two with Kieran Donaghy before rifling over Kerry's seventh point on the trot.

Kerry were ominously hitting their stride, with Cooper sending a well-weighted ball over the top for the overlapping McCarthy to fist over for 0-13 to 0-10. The divisional divide was becoming more and more obvious as Declan O'Sullivan smacked over a skyscraper point off his left.

Limerick's defence was cut wide open in the 50th minute, Donnacha Walsh side-footing a breaking ball through for the unmarked Cooper to smash high past Scanlon for what looked to be a decisive goal.

Trailing now by 1-14 to 0-10, Limerick needed a huge response and they got it, inspired by the talismanic Galvin.

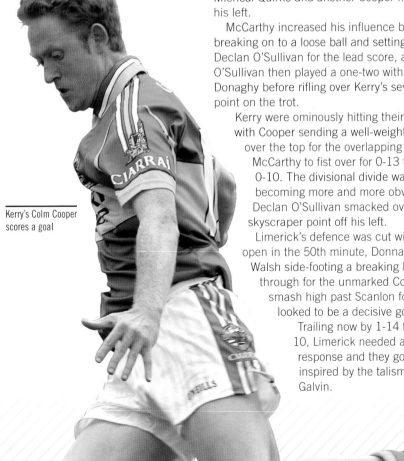

Kerry's Colm Cooper scores a goal

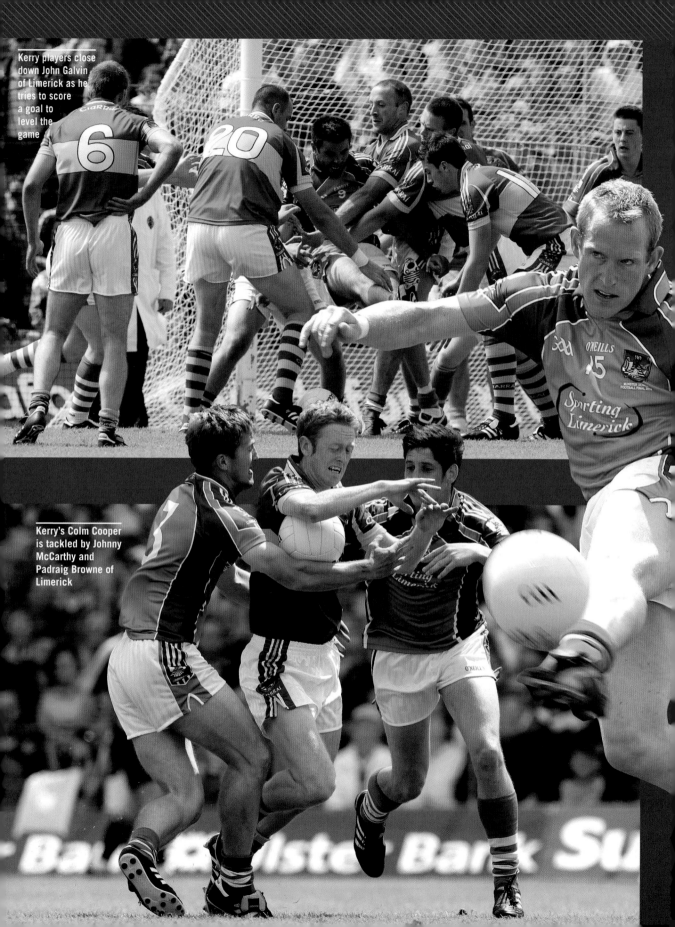

Kerry players close down John Galvin of Limerick as he tries to score a goal to level the game

Kerry's Colm Cooper is tackled by Johnny McCarthy and Padraig Browne of Limerick

Collins cut on to his left to notch Limerick's first point in 22 minutes and a quick dispossession from the resulting kickout led to the unchallenged Galvin blasting to the middle of the net, over Brendan Kealy, for a priceless 54th-minute goal.

Limerick, with the bit between their teeth, tagged on three more points. James Ryan fisted over from a tight angle; Collins, who dominated his marker Tom O'Sullivan, converted a free, and Galvin then broke through the middle, evading Walsh's challenge to kick his side level at 1-14 apiece.

The tension was palpable as Sheehan, Seamus Scanlon twice and substitute David Moran missed point-scoring chances.

Kerry boss Jack O'Connor emptied his bench, trying to give his side some fresh impetus up front. Cooper found the woodwork as he tried to fist over from a tight angle, and substitute Barry John Keane failed to find the target from further out.

The match-winning run was kick-started by a Cooper effort, Kerry's first score in 18 minutes, and Keane set up an unmarked Moran for a quickfire second. Stretching Limerick's rearguard to the maximum, Tomás Ó Sé thundered through for a trademark point off his left, and suddenly the scoreboard read 1-17 to 1-14.

After substitute Eoghan O'Connor put his name to Limerick's twelfth wide, missing the target on the run, Limerick boss Mickey Ned O'Sullivan tried valiantly to create a goal that would square up this memorable contest.

Galvin was sent in towards the Kerry square and created enough havoc to force a close-range free in injury-time, and a dramatic conclusion. Goalkeeper Kealy brought seven team-mates back onto the line to assist him and Stephen Lavin's powerful shot was blocked out, confirming a frustrating fourth Munster final defeat for Limerick in eight years.

Late points from top scorer Colm Cooper, substitute David Moran and Tomás Ó Sé put the seal on a hard-fought win for Jack O'Connor's side who allowed Limerick back into the contest after moving 1-14 to 0-10 ahead.

KERRY: B Kealy; M Ó Sé, T Griffin, T O'Sullivan; T Ó Sé (0-02), M McCarthy (0-02), K Young; S Scanlon, A Maher; Darran O'Sullivan (0-01), Declan O'Sullivan (0-03), D Walsh; C Cooper (1-05), K Donaghy, B Sheehan (0-02)
Subs: M Quirke (0-01) for Maher; BJ Keane for Darran O'Sullivan; Padraig Reidy for T O'Sullivan; D Moran (0-01) for Scanlon; K O'Leary for Sheehan

LIMERICK: B Scanlon (0-02); M O'Riordan, J McCarthy, A Lane; S Lavin, S Lucey, P Ranahan; J O'Donovan (0-01), J Galvin (1-02); P Browne, J Ryan (0-02), S Buckley (0-01); G Collins (0-05), I Ryan, S Kelly (0-01)
Subs: J Mullane for Browne; S Gallagher for Lane; E Joy for Buckley; E O'Connor for Kelly; S O'Carroll for J Ryan

REFEREE: P Fox (Westmeath)

KILDARE 1-15 0-09 ANTRIM

3 July 2010

Kildare set up a second round qualifier clash with Leitrim as they ended Antrim's All-Ireland Championship hopes at Casement Park.

The Lilywhites scored seven unanswered points in a key second half spell, racing clear of a Saffrons side that relied heavily on free-taker Paddy Cunningham.

Team captain John Doyle helped himself to 1-06, with his 21st-minute goal nudging Kildare towards a 1-04 to 0-05 half-time lead. Doyle and company showed greater accuracy after that to run out impressive nine-point winners.

Kieran McGeeney's men kicked 21 wides in the drawn game in Newbridge last weekend, so they were keenly aware of the improvements they would have to make to prevail in the replay.

Both McGeeney and his Antrim counterpart, Liam Bradley, opted for unchanged starting line-ups, the latter also having the recalled Michael Magill to call on as a substitute.

Comfortable at their home venue, the Saffrons settled quickly and dominated possession for long stretches of the opening half – without too much end product. Cunningham pointed them ahead, but it came after wing-back James Loughrey missed out on an early goal.

Kildare seized control of the scoreboard courtesy of points from Ronan Sweeney, Eoin O'Flaherty and Doyle, and they were important scores in a first half that saw defences very much on top.

There was precious little room for forwards to operate in, with both sides tackling and harrying well. Kevin Brady and Cunningham got the home side back on terms at 0-03 apiece, before Doyle broke through for his goal.

Emmett Bolton created the opening for the Allenwood ace, who had missed a couple of kickable frees, to slot past Sean McGreevy. Morgan O'Flaherty tagged on a point, but Cunningham took his tally to four as he cut the gap to two at the turnaround.

Kildare had the wind behind them for the second half and they were increasingly comfortable on the ball, albeit with Cunningham making it a one-point game as play got back underway.

McGeeney's charges raised their game significantly to score the next seven points, Doyle, Eamon Callaghan, Dermot Earley and Padraig O'Neill doing the damage as the Antrim players let their efforts slip.

Sweeney also failed to convert a goal-scoring chance as Kildare began to stretch clear. The Ulstermen reeled them in slightly, thanks to points from Cunningham and Brendan Herron, but closing scores from Doyle, substitute Keith Cribben and Darryl Flynn ended the Saffrons' summer run.

ANTRIM: S McGreevy; A Healy, C Brady, J Crozier; T Scullion, K O'Boyle, J Loughrey; B Herron (0-01), A Gallagher; K McGourty, K Niblock, T McCann; P Cunningham (0-07), M McCann, K Brady (0-01)
Subs: M Magill for Healy

KILDARE: S McCormack; P Kelly, H McGrillen, A Mac Lochlainn; M O'Flaherty (0-01), E Bolton, B Flanagan; D Flynn (0-01), D Earley (0-01); J Kavanagh, P O'Neill (0-01), H Lynch; J Doyle (1-06), R Sweeney (0-01), E Callaghan (0-02)
Subs: D White for Mac Lochlainn; K Cribben (0-01) for E O'Flaherty (0-01); G White for Sweeney; M Foley for Flanagan; K Donnelly for Earley

REFEREE: J McQuillan (Cavan)

Antrim's Justin Crozier and Kildare's Dermot Earley

79

KILDARE 1-12 0-06 LEITRIM

10 July 2010

Leitrim's brave challenge petered out in Newbridge as Kildare maintained their All-Ireland Senior Football Championship bid with a nine-point qualifier victory.

James Kavanagh found the visitors' net in the 61st minute, confirming Kildare's progress into the third round.

Ray Mulvey and Michael Foley had Leitrim ahead early on, but the Lilywhites fought back to lead by 0-06 to 0-03 at half-time, helped by three late points.

John Doyle's scoring influence from play and placed balls increased in the second half, during which free-taker Foley and substitute Darren Sweeney were Leitrim's only scorers.

Leitrim set a flurry of nerves about St Conleth's Park as they made a business-like start, nudging ahead in the fifth minute through wing-forward Mulvey.

Foley also converted a free as they used the wind to good advantage and controlled possession around the middle of the pitch.

Mickey Moran's men should have been further ahead by the midpoint of the half, with five wides struck and two decent goal-scoring chances gone a-begging.

Defender Daniel Beck watched his shot hit the crossbar on a break forward, while a punt towards the Kildare square from James Glancy was spilled by goalkeeper Shane McCormack and Declan Maxwell really should have hit the target when the ball broke to him.

Kildare captain John Doyle missed two kickable frees before he opened his side's account in the 20th minute, bending over a terrific shot on the turn after a ball in from Brian Flanagan.

Padraig O'Neill added a second, four minutes later, and as Shane Canning and James Kavanagh traded scores, the rain stopped and the pace of the game quickened.

Kildare were tightening things up at midfield, and they used possession wisely in the closing minutes of the half, setting up points for Eamon Callaghan, Ronan Sweeney and Kavanagh.

Leitrim's hard work seemed to have been undone in a cruel five-minute spell, but they opened the second period with another free from Foley to cut the gap to 0-06 to 0-04.

As the rain began to fall once again and a degree of niggle crept into the game, Kavanagh's third point of the evening gave Kieran McGeeney's charges a three-point buffer with little over 20 minutes remaining.

The killer blow came with just under ten minutes to go. Callaghan pumped a long ball in, substitute Tomás O'Connor did brilliantly to field it and pass across the Leitrim rearguard for Kavanagh to knock it home.

Two excellent frees from Doyle and points from trying from Morgan O'Flaherty and substitute Hugh Lynch took Kildare out of sight, but Leitrim, to their credit, never stopped trying and late placed balls from substitute Darren Sweeney and Foley gave a more respectable look to the final scoreboard.

KILDARE: S McCormack; P Kelly, H McGrillen, A Mac Lochlainn; B Flanagan, E Callaghan (0-01), E Bolton; D Flynn, D Earley; M O'Flaherty (0-01), P O'Neill (0-01), E O'Flaherty; J Doyle (0-03), R Sweeney (0-01), J Kavanagh (1-04)
Subs: T O'Connor for E O'Flaherty; D Whyte for Earley; D Lyons for Mac Lochlainn; H Lynch (0-01) for Sweeney

LEITRIM: G Phelan; D Reynolds, C Egan, D Beck; W McKeon, J McKeon, G Reynolds; T Beirne, S Canning (0-01); R Mulvey (0-01), J Glancy, M Foley (0-03); P Howard, D Maxwell, B Gallagher
Subs: D O'Connor for Howard; C Clarke for Mulvey; D Sweeney (0-01) for Canning; B Prior for Beck

REFEREE: C Reilly (Meath)

DUBLIN 1-21 1-13 TIPPERARY

10 July 2010

The Brogan brothers, Alan and Bernard, exploited a tiring Tipperary defence as Dublin advanced in the All-Ireland qualifiers at Croke Park.

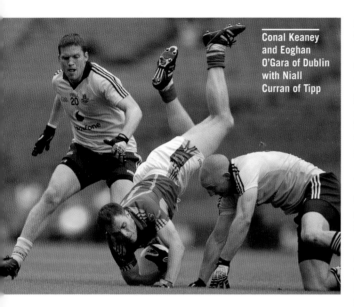

Conal Keaney and Eoghan O'Gara of Dublin with Niall Curran of Tipp

The Brogans shot 0-11 between them to drive Pat Gilroy's men to victory in a dour contest which gave little indication as to Dublin's All-Ireland credentials.

After an edgy first half, Gilroy's charges got their championship challenge back on the rails with an improved second-half showing.

Michael Dara MacAuley and Barry Grogan traded goals as Dublin led by 1-09 to 1-07 at half-time.

Grogan led Tipp's scoring with 1-05, but Dublin, with their bench proving influential, pulled through in front of just 22,107 spectators.

In rain-soaked conditions, Kevin McManamon got a glimpse of the Tipperary goal in the opening seconds but failed to find the target. It was left to Alan Brogan to open the scoring for Dublin, with Ross McConnell and Bernard Brogan making it 0-03 to 0-00 by the six-minute mark.

The Dublin team showed five changes to the one that succumbed to Meath last time out, with experienced campaigners like Bryan Cullen, Conal Keaney and Barry Cahill among the players to miss out.

Tipperary opened their account through wing-forward Stephen Hahessy, but Dublin pressed on for a 0-06 to 0-01 lead as goalkeeper Stephen Cluxton and Bernard Brogan converted three placed balls between them. Cluxton stepped up to knock over a '45', taking over from the benched Tomás Quinn.

While Dublin's wides tally mounted to five, Tipp's talismanic forward Grogan struck a free over off a post and Conor Sweeney, in the left corner, scored from play to reduce the arrears to three.

Then, in the 19th minute, Dublin engineered their only goal when Eoghan O'Gara turned and raced in from the right to pass for the advancing MacAuley to fist home and crown his first championship start with a goal.

Alan Brogan had time and space to follow up with a point, making it 1-07 to 0-03, but a slip by Dublin full-back Rory O'Carroll in the 21st minute allowed Grogan slide home a well-taken goal in response. George Hannigan's pinpoint through-ball was latched on to by Grogan who cut past Cluxton and fired home in front of a sparsely populated Hill 16. Grogan added a free to make it a three-point game.

The remainder of the first half was evenly contested with Dublin clearly rattled by the concession of that goal. Philip Austin nailed a point and Grogan and Sweeney tagged on two more frees, in between scores from Bernard Brogan and McManamon at the Davin End. Indeed, Dublin would have been celebrating a second goal by the break if O'Gara had not clipped a late shot wide.

Tipp kept in the hunt as the second half started, with scores from Grogan and Sweeney sandwiching a single effort from Bernard Brogan.

There were a lot of wides and frees conceded, but Dublin managed to add some much-needed cushion to their advantage, helped by a run of points from substitute Eamonn Fennell, Alan Brogan and O'Gara.

The life was sucked out of the game as, by the hour mark, Dublin were armed with a 1-17 to 1-10 buffer and had one foot in the next round. Substitute Conal Keaney came on and kicked two points; Ross McConnell raided forward to score and Bernard Brogan continued to cause problems for the Tipp defence, taking his haul for the afternoon to 0-07.

Their overall effort could not be questioned, but the Premier County side, hit by recent squad withdrawals, had no answer. Their closing points from Grogan, substitute Brian Coen and Brian Mulvihill were cancelled out by MacAuley, man-of-the-match Alan Brogan, and Keaney.

So, at the final whistle, it was a case of mission accomplished for Dublin who will be pleased with this return to winning ways. Nonetheless they had enough shaky moments to still leave a question mark over their ability to mount a serious challenge for All-Ireland honours.

DUBLIN: S Cluxton (0-01); M Fitzsimons, Rory O'Carroll, P McMahon; K Nolan, G Brennan, D Henry; MD MacAuley (1-01), R McConnell (0-02); P Flynn, A Brogan (0-04), N Corkery; B Brogan (0-07), E O'Gara (0-01), K McManamon (0-01)
Subs: E Fennell (0-01) for Flynn; C Keaney (0-03) for McManamon; B Cullen for Corkery; P Casey for Nolan

TIPPERARY: P Fitzgerald; P Codd, R Costigan, A Morrissey; C McGrath, B Jones, B Fox; G Hannigan, N Curran; S Hahessy (0-01), H Coghlan, P Acheson; P Austin (0-03), B Grogan (1-05), C Sweeney (0-03)
Subs: B Coen (0-01) for Hahessy; B Mulvihill for Jones; K Mulryan for Acheson; A Rockett for Coghlan; E Kearney for Codd

REFEREE: P McEnaney (Monaghan)

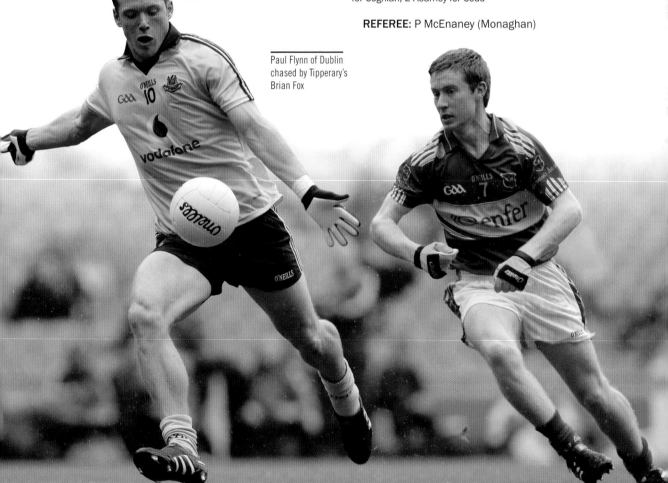

Paul Flynn of Dublin chased by Tipperary's Brian Fox

Cork's Paudie Kissane and Cavan's Ciaran Galligan.

CORK 1-19 | 0-04 **CAVAN**

10 July 2010

Cork were in cruise control as they cantered through to the third round of the All-Ireland Senior Football qualifiers at a very wet Páirc Uí Chaoimh.

Pearse O'Neill's 51st-minute goal effectively put the result beyond doubt, with Cork leading at that stage by 1-15 to 0-02.

Cavan looked a shell of the side that produced a tremendous comeback win over Wicklow, and substitute Cian Mackey was their only scorer as they trailed by 0-09 to 0-01 at half-time.

Ronan Flanagan and Seanie Johnston added points, but Cork were never troubled as they cleared the first hurdle towards an All-Ireland quarter-final berth.

Smarting from the loss of their Munster title, the Rebels' championship campaign was on the line against a Tommy Carr-managed Cavan outfit.

The Breffni men were keen to produce a big performance against one of the country's top sides, as Cork and Cavan clashed in the championship for the first time since 1967.

Watched by 3,172 spectators, Cork started against the wind in what was their first-ever home draw since the qualifiers were introduced in 2001.

Gradually, the hosts' greater physicality and finishing power shunted them into a comfortable lead and Cavan never really tested them.

Johnston, such a threat during a sparkling individual display against Wicklow, was kept quiet after two early misses.

Cork took the lead after just 19 seconds, with good work from Aidan Walsh and the returning John Miskella teeing up a point for young full-forward Ciaran Sheehan.

Both sides turned over possession with the conditions playing their part, and Paddy Kelly and Colm O'Neill nudged Cork further in front.

Two frees from Daniel Goulding made it 0-05 to 0-00 as Cavan continued to struggle, another Johnston wide and a Michael Brennan shot, which skimmed away from goal, doing little for their confidence.

Goulding, Sheehan, O'Neill and Kelly added four more points as Conor Counihan's men began to dictate. Mackey, who replaced full-forward Brennan, tapped over just before the break to spare his side's blushes.

Goulding took his free-taking tally to eight points and O'Neill mustered his third from play as Cork took a 0-15 to 0-01 advantage early in the second period.

The sending-off of centre-forward Gareth Smith, for his second bookable offence, sucked more life out of Cavan's challenge, although Johnston did manage to point a free.

As the rain continued to pelt down, Cork showed no mercy as they worked their centre-forward O'Neill through on goal and he smashed a powerful shot to the roof of the net for a 1-15 to 0-02 scoreline.

Cavan wing-forward Flanagan replied with a brace of points in the space of a minute, but Carr's charges had nothing left to give and the remaining action was mostly forgettable.

Importantly though for Cork's All-Ireland challenge, they managed to get some game-time for Nicholas Murphy as a second-half substitute. The Carrigaline midfielder has been troubled by a back injury all year.

CORK: A Quirke; R Carey, M Shields, J O'Sullivan; G Canty, J Miskella, P Kissane; A Walsh (0-01) A O'Connor; F Goold (0-01), P O'Neill (1-00), P Kelly (0-03); D Goulding (0-08), C Sheehan (0-02), C O'Neill (0-04)
Subs: N O'Leary for O'Sullivan; N Murphy for Walsh; D Kavanagh (0-01) for O'Connor; E Cotter for Shields; J Hayes for Goulding

CAVAN: F Reilly; M Brides, D Sheridan, M Hannon; M Cahill, J McCutcheon, A Clarke; C Galligan, N Walsh; E McGuigan, G Smith, R Flanagan (0-02); P Brady, S Johnston (0-01), M Brennan
Subs: M McKeever for Brady; C Mackey (0-01) for Brennan; D O'Dowd for Brides; T Corr for Flanagan

REFEREE: S Doyle (Wexford)

OFFALY 0-15 0-10 WATERFORD

10 July 2010

Niall McNamee fired five points as Offaly claimed back-to-back All-Ireland Senior Football Championship qualifier victories for the first time since 2003.

McNamee scored early on in Tullamore as Offaly edged ahead of Waterford. Conor McGrath and Gary Hurney kept the Déise in touch but Offaly were 0-09 to 0-06 to the good at half-time.

The Faithfuls pressed on and despite hitting a number of wides, including a Paul McConway goal miss, late points from Anton Sullivan and McNamee sealed the home win.

Offaly manager Tom Cribbin was forced to use five different free-takers in this match, before eventually settling on McNamee who slotted over two second-half points from placed balls.

It was Offaly who had the early breaks in the midfield sector but they failed to convert their early scoring chances, and it was Waterford who hit the front through McGrath in the sixth minute.

However, this was the only time that John Owens' charges led during a hard-fought opening half. Pre-match favourites Offaly strode ahead by kicking four unanswered points between the ninth and 17th minutes.

Graham Guilfoyle got the hosts off the mark. Team captain Karol Slattery made a lung-bursting run from 45 metres out, before laying off the ball to Guilfoyle who slotted over from close range.

A brace of scores from McNamee pushed Offaly 0-03 to 0-01 ahead in the 15th minute, and the scoring chances were coming quick and fast for Cribbin's men.

With a goal on the cards in the 16th minute, Brian Connor was denied by a superb save from Waterford stopper Tom Wall, but Ciaran McManus pushed his side three points clear from the resulting '45'.

Guilfoyle had a good opportunity to extend the home side's lead to four soon after, but Waterford full-back Tomás O'Gorman stood firm.

The Déise suddenly found their stride in attack, knocking over four of the next six points through Patrick Hurney, McGrath, Gary Hurney and Shane Briggs.

Slattery was forced off with a hamstring injury, in a significant blow for Offaly, but the Faithfuls recovered well to tag on points from McNamee, Scott Brady and Ken Casey before half-time.

Offaly started the second half in strong fashion, winning the opening exchanges at midfield, with scores from McManus and Guilfoyle extending their advantage to five points – 0-11 to 0-06.

Gary Hurney pegged a point back for the visitors, with two goal-scoring opportunities arriving for his side in a two-minute spell.

A 47th-minute effort off the ground from Patrick Hurney finished in the hands of Offaly goalkeeper Alan Mulhall, before a McGrath shot was blocked out by McManus and Michael Donnelly failed to convert the resulting '45'.

Gary Hurney cut the gap to three by registering his third point of the contest as the game entered the final quarter, but Offaly had the better of the closing stages to book their place in the third-round draw.

OFFALY: A Mulhall; B Darby, S Brady, S Pender; N Darby, R Brady (0-01), K Slattery; R Dalton, J Coughlan; G Guilfoyle (0-02), B Connor (0-01), C McManus (0-03); K Casey (0-01), A Sullivan (0-02), N McNamee (0-05)
Subs: P McConway for Slattery; J Reynolds for Guilfoyle; S Ryan for Coughlan; A McNamee for Casey

WATERFORD: T Wall; M O'Gorman, T O'Gorman, K Connery; N Hennessy, S Briggs (0-01), J Phelan; M Aherne, K Power; W Hennessy, C McGrath (0-02), B Wall, M Donnelly (0-01); G Hurney (0-05), P Hurney (0-01)
Subs: C Phelan for Connery; L O'Lionain for W Hennessy; S Cunningham for P Hurney; J Hurney for N Hennessy; C O'Keefe for McGrath

REFEREE: A Mangan (Kerry)

Offaly's Niall McNamee is tackled by Maurice O'Gorman and Shane Briggs of Waterford

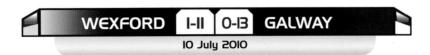

WEXFORD I-II 0-I3 GALWAY

10 July 2010

Ciaran Lyng's stoppage-time winner sent Galway crashing out of the All-Ireland Senior Football Championship at Pearse Stadium.

Another demoralising defeat brought an end to Joe Kernan's first season in charge of the Tribesmen, while Jason Ryan's men are looking to put together another big run along the back door route.

Lyng was the hero of the battle, finishing with a 1-06 tally.

Veteran Galway attacker Pádraic Joyce was also in sparkling form, hitting six points, but his leadership was not enough to save the men from the west in front of their own supporters in the disappointing crowd of 2,330.

Joyce produced the old magic in the early stages, hitting four points in the opening eight minutes to give his side a platform.

Wexford were under serious pressure due to the dominance of Niall Coleman and Joe Bergin at midfield, but they turned it around, principally through hard work and determination.

Ciaran Lyng and Mattie Forde narrowed the gap and as the Leinster men swept forward with Brian Malone and Adrian Flynn always willing to press from the back, they stepped up the threat.

Wexford almost had a goal in the 20th minute when Shane Roche sent Redmond Barry in, but Adrian Faherty kept the shot out with his left foot.

Jason Ryan's men coped better with the greasy conditions and drew level in the 23rd minute, with Lyng converting a free before Colm Morris finished off a sweeping move.

Galway went 15 minutes without scoring, before Matthew Clancy and substitute Cormac Bane rediscovered the range, but at the break they were clinging on to a flimsy one-point lead, 0-06 to 0-05, after Lyng clipped over his third from a tight angle.

Sean Armstrong set up a point for Bane and added a superb effort himself, but Wexford stayed very much in touch through Lyng and Eric Bradley, who turned over possession and galloped through the middle for a point.

Bane added another couple of scores to repay the faith shown in him midway through the opening half by manager Kernan, but Wexford took the lead in the 53rd minute when Darren Mullahy was penalised for a foul on Bradley, and Lyng tucked away the penalty.

But Galway's response was positive: Bane, Joyce and Gary O'Donnell belted over points to restore their two-point cushion.

However, Wexford stepped it up again, hitting the final three points of the game, including Lyng's glorious winner.

GALWAY : A Faherty; D Reilly, F Hanley, A Burke; G Bradshaw, K Fitzgerald, G O'Donnell (0-01); J Bergin, N Coleman; G Sice, F Breathnach, M Clancy (0-01); O Concannon, P Joyce (0-06), S Armstrong (0-01)
Subs: C Bane (0-04) for Concannon; Darren Mullahy for Reilly; P Conroy for Clancy

WEXFORD : A Masterson; J Wadding, G Molloy, B Malone; A Flynn (0-01), D Murphy, A Doyle; E Bradley (0-01), D Waters; C Morris (0-01), R Barry (0-01), S Roche; C Lyng (1-06), M Forde (0-01), PJ Banville
Subs: B Brosnan for Roche; B Doyle for Waters; P Naughter for Morris

REFEREE: J White (Donegal)

Galway captain Joe Bergin and Brendan Doyle of Wexford

89

DOWN | **1-14** | **1-10** | **LONGFORD**

10 July 2010

Longford's giant-killing heroics ended at Páirc Esler as Down did the business in this All-Ireland second-round qualifier.

Down made hard work of it in the second half, having established a 0-09 to 0-03 half-time lead. Martin Clarke pointed three times for the Mourne men in the opening 35 minutes, with Longford goalkeeper Damien Sheridan making two superb saves.

The home side managed to stay ahead during a second half that saw Kalum King and Shane Mulligan sent off, and Clarke and Longford's top scorer Francis McGee both found the net.

Down lined out with Dan Gordon as a makeshift full-back, filling in for the injured Brendan McArdle, and Longford hit the front in the third minute through the impressive McGee.

But by the midpoint of the first half, James McCartan's men had broken into a 0-04 to 0-02 lead. Mark Poland, Benny Coulter, John Clarke and Danny Hughes, who saw plenty of ball, all struck points.

In very wet conditions, McGee accounted for Longford's opening three points – direct from frees – but Down were finding scores from play far easier to come by.

They were also negating the threat of Paul Barden, with Declan Rooney doing a fine man-marking job and Ambrose Rogers acting as a sweeper to aid his defence in keeping the dangerous Brian Kavanagh out of the game.

At the other end, Longford net minder Sheridan was playing a blinder. He kept his team in the hunt with two inspirational stops in the fifth and 28th minutes. However, Poland and Hughes both doubled their tallies and Martin Clarke collected his third point in injury-time to leave six between the sides at the break.

There was a scuffle involving a number of players and officials as the second half got underway. A late challenge on Coulter seemed to spark it, and when tempers cooled, referee Martin Higgins gave yellow cards to Shane Mulligan and Danny Hughes.

Longford substitute Noel Farrell and Hughes swapped frees but the visitors were beginning to improve, as evidenced by Barden's point from the sideline for a 0-10 to 0-05 scoreline.

Down were quick to respond, however, and defender Rooney broke upfield to point after a quick passing movement involving five players. And when Clarke stuck his penalty effort away in the bottom-left corner, after a harsh foul awarded against Dermot Brady, the home side had a 1-11 to 0-06 lead. Brady had been whistled up for what looked a legitimate shoulder-led challenge on King.

Down's Daniel Hughes battles Longford's Diarmuid Masterson

Longford's scoring maestro on the night, corner-forward McGee, put the game back in the melting pot with a quick 1-01, his goal coming after his initial shot had been blocked by goalkeeper Brendan McVeigh.

McGee took his tally to 1-06 as Longford cut the gap to three points and Down lost King for his second bookable offence. Longford wing-back Mulligan was also dismissed, shortly afterwards, for his second yellow card.

It was now 14 players apiece, but Down had done enough to maintain the difference on the scoreboard, Hughes notching the insurance point in injury-time as Longford's summer campaign ground to a halt in soggy Newry.

DOWN: B McVeigh; D O'Hagan, D Gordon, D Rafferty; D Rooney (0-01), J Colgan, C Garvey; A Rogers, K King; D Hughes (0-03), M Poland (0-03), C Maginn; B Coulter (0-01), J Clarke, M Clarke (1-05)
Subs: K McKernan for Garvey; C Laverty for J Clarke; P Fitzpatrick for Poland; A Carr for Maginn

LONGFORD: D Sheridan; D Brady, B Gilleran, D Reilly; S Mulligan, E Williams, S Hannon; D Masterson, B McElvaney; P Dowd, P Barden (0-02), K Mulligan; F McGee (1-07), B Kavanagh, S McCormack
Subs: N Farrell (0-01) for Hannon; P Kelly for K Mulligan

REFEREE: M Higgins (Fermanagh)

DERRY 0-13 | 1-07 WESTMEATH

10 July 2010

Fourteen-man Derry held on to book their place in the third round of the All-Ireland Senior Football Championship qualifiers with a three-point win in Mullingar.

Westmeath's Ger Egan passes under pressure

Despite losing Joe Diver to a second booking, the Oak Leafers held on to win by three.

They led by six points midway through the second half, but had to dig deep to survive as substitute Martin Flanagan pulled back a goal for the home side.

The greasy conditions were in part responsible for the 13 yellow cards flashed by Sligo referee Michael Duffy in what was never a dirty contest.

Dessie Dolan and Paul Bannon exchanged early points with Mark Lynch and Eoin Bradley.

Westmeath, with Dolan and Denis Glennon both operating in withdrawn roles, had to live off scraps in the midfield area, where Joe Diver's fielding provided the launch-pad for Oak Leaf attacks.

Michael Ennis averted a dangerous situation with a perfectly timed tackle on Bradley, before venturing upfield to shoot a Westmeath point.

However, the sides were level for the fourth time moments later when full-forward Mark Lynch squeezed over a point from a tight angle in the 24th minute.

Despite losing captain and centre-back Gerard O'Kane to injury, the Ulster men stepped up the tempo.

Lynch's power was posing problems for John Gaffey, and his third score was the pick of five on the spin which eased the Oak Leafers into a double-scores lead, 0-08 to 0-04, by the 32nd minute.

David Duffy's long range score ended a 16-minute barren spell for the home side, who trailed by 0-08 to 0-05 at the break.

The northerners powered on early in the second half for Lynch and Kielt to land long-range frees, before Raymond Wilkinson hammered over a wonderful effort from play from wide on the right.

They appeared to be cruising at 0-11 to 0-05, but Westmeath got themselves right back into it when substitute Martin Flanagan punched home Paul Greville's cross off the underside of the crossbar.

Dolan clipped over a free, and suddenly just two points separated the sides, with Derry now a man down following the second-booking dismissal of Diver.

Dolan hit the target again, but Kielt and Bradley brought their personal totals to five to seal it for the Oaks.

WESTMEATH: G Connaughton; F Boyle, J Gaffey, K Maguire; M Ennis (0-01), J Keane, D Harte; D Duffy (0-01) P Bannon (0-01); K Martin, C Lynam, G Egan; P Greville, D Dolan (0-04), D Glennon
Subs: M Flanagan (1-00) for Lynam; C McCormack for Keane; D O'Donoghue for Maguire; I Coffey for Egan

DERRY: B Gillis; B Óg McAlary, K McGuckin, D McBride; M Craig, G O'Kane, C Kielt; J Diver, E Muldoon; C McKeever, J Kielt (0-05), B McGoldrick; E Bradley (0-02), M Lynch (0-05), R Wilkinson (0-01)
Subs: D Mullan for O'Kane; SL McGoldrick for McKeever; B McGuigan for Mullan

REFEREE: M Duffy (Sligo)

ARMAGH 0-11 0-07 FERMANAGH

11 July 2010

Steven McDonnell missed a penalty but still kicked a match-winning haul of 0-06 as Armagh advanced to the third round of the All-Ireland Senior Football Championship qualifiers.

Fermanagh gave their Ulster rivals quite a test in Enniskillen, with free-taker Seamus Quigley kicking five points and Brian Cox and Tommy McElroy also on target.

But the Orchard men, who led 0-04 to 0-01 early on and by 0-06 to 0-04 at half-time, always seemed to have enough in the tank. Jamie Clarke, Gareth Swift and Charlie Vernon completed the visitors' scoring.

Fermanagh brought Devenish's Martin O'Brien in at full-back and moved Ryan McCluskey to centre-back in an attempt to tighten up a defence that leaked 21 points against Monaghan.

Team captain James Sherry had Ryan Jones for company in midfield, and Fermanagh manager Malachy O'Rourke added Brian Cox, Seamus Quigley and Ciaran Flaherty to the attack.

Armagh boss Paddy O'Rourke brought Joe Feeney in at wing-forward in place of Anto Duffy, who dislocated his shoulder against Donegal.

Armagh signalled their intent as the in-form Jamie Clarke shot wide when presented with a glimpse of goal after just 16 seconds. Although Quigley converted a free for the opener, Clarke got his side level by jinking

Armagh's Jamie Clarke with Fermanagh's
Niall Bogue, Ryan McCluskey, Niall McGovern
and Daniel Ward

93

inside his marker to score in the sixth minute.

Two Steven McDonnell points and a single effort from Charlie Vernon had Armagh 0-04 to 0-01 ahead by the 26th minute, but Fermanagh had missed a gilt-edged goal-scoring chance during that spell.

Net minder Paul Hearty blocked a Ryan Carson shot, and Paul Ward opted to pass when an attempt on goal was the better option. Daryl Keenan could not get a foot to the pass and Armagh cleared the danger.

Quigley and McDonnell traded points before the Fermanagh marksman kicked two superb frees off the ground, from 48 and 52 metres respectively, to reduce the arrears for his determined side to 0-05 to 0-04.

McDonnell ended what had been an error-strewn half with a final point in injury-time, with both sides guilty of poor passing and some lacklustre shooting.

One of the busiest men on the pitch during the opening 35 minutes had been referee Derek Fahy, who booked five players.

Armagh almost made a dream start to the second half when they won a penalty, awarded after Fermanagh full-back O'Brien hauled down Malachy Mackin as he was

about to shoot. McDonnell stepped up to take it, but Fermanagh goalkeeper Ronan Gallagher pulled off a fantastic save as he diverted the ball around a post.

Tommy McElroy gave the Ernesiders real hope as he pointed to make it 0-06 to 0-05, but Armagh quelled any thoughts of an upset as Clarke and McDonnell extended the visitors' lead back to three.

On two occasions, a Quigley-inspired Fermanagh managed to get it back to a two-point game, and even Marty McGrath, who had been troubled by injury, made an appearance off the bench.

But there was no denying that Armagh were the better side and Vernon, McDonnell and Swift wrapped up the win – albeit with Clarke being denied a late goal by another excellent save from Gallagher.

For Malachy O'Rourke, the result brought to an end his third year in charge of the Fermanagh panel.

O'Rourke was 'delighted with how the players did themselves justice' with regards to work rate, intensity and will to win, especially after the poor showing against Monaghan. But he was non-committal over his future in the Erne hot-seat.

FERMANAGH: Ronan Gallagher; N Bogue, M O'Brien, B Mulrone; D Ward, R McCluskey, T McElroy (0-01); J Sherry, R Jones; D Keenan, R Carson, B Cox (0-01); P Ward, S Quigley (0-05), C Flaherty
Subs: N McGovern for Mulrone; M McGrath for Jones; O'Brien for Ward; Rory Gallagher for Flaherty

ARMAGH: P Hearty; A Mallon, B Donaghy, V Martin; P Duffy, C McKeever, K Dyas; C Vernon (0-02), M Mackin; J Feeney, A Kernan, F Hanratty; G Swift (0-01), S McDonnell (0-06), J Clarke (0-02)
Subs: F Moriarty for Dyas; B Mallon for Feeney; K Toner for Swift

REFEREE: D Fahy (Longford)

Final

MEATH	1-12	1-10	LOUTH

II July 2010

Joe Sheridan scrambled home a sensational and highly-controversial winning goal in the fourth minute of stoppage time to give Meath a first Leinster Senior Football Championship title since 2001, defeating Louth 1-12 to 1-10.

The end of this game will live long in the memory for all the wrong reasons, however, as Louth's anger at the decision to allow Sheridan's goal to stand spilled over after the final whistle and culminated in referee Martin Sludden being physically confronted by irate Louth fans as he left the field accompanied by gardaí.

In front of a crowd of 48,875 at Croke Park, Peter Fitzpatrick's men took control of the game in the second half, and were just seconds from glory when a goalmouth scramble ended with Sheridan's goal being given after the referee had consulted with an umpire.

Louth missed two glorious goal chances in a first half that took its cue for long spells from the edge given to Meath in midfield by Brian Meade and Nigel Crawford.

The first of the goal chances fell to JP Rooney in the opening minute, when he almost caught the Royal defence cold but drilled his shot just wide.

And on 20 minutes, Shane Lennon was sent in by Colm Judge, but from a tight angle rolled his effort away at the far post.

In between, Meath enjoyed a productive spell late in the first quarter, when they reeled off four points, through Graham Reilly, Stephen Bray and Cian Ward.

Rooney and Paddy Keenan had earlier struck Louth points, and they rediscovered the range when Brian White drilled over a couple of frees to bring the sides level on 19 minutes.

But Meath clicked into another gear, hitting four of the last five points of the half.

Reilly was on fire, bringing his tally to four, and Crawford also powered through the

Kevin Reilly of Meath with Shane Lennon of Louth

middle for a point.

Meath led by 0-08 to 0-05 at half-time, but Louth dominated the early stages of the second half, closing the gap with two White efforts, one of them stroked over on the end of an excellent move.

Keenan and White were now getting more out of the midfield battle, and the attack profited, with Judge splitting the posts for a 43rd-minute leveller.

A sublime sidestep and finish from Adrian Reed had the Wee County ahead soon afterwards, but Meath responded with scores from Ward and Anthony Moyles.

Louth went ahead in the 63rd minute when Mark Brennan's delivery was fumbled by Brian Meade before Rooney nipped in to

Meath's Joe Sheridan scores the controversial winning goal in the final minute of added time

Shane Lennon of Louth with Kevin Reilly and Eoghan Harrington of Meath

Meath's Eoghan Harrington and JP Rooney of Louth

Joe Sheridan scores a controversial goal for Meath in injury time to win the game

98

Louth players appeal to the referee after Meath's Joe Sheridan scores the winning goal in the final minute of added time

collect the ball and blast a superb finish past Brendan Murphy.

Meath responded with a couple of frees from Ward but as the final minute approached it looked like it would not be enough for the Royals. That was, of course, until a bizarre denouement which ended with Meath captain Nigel Crawford lifting the Delaney Cup and the Croke Park air thick with the fumes of controversy.

Postscript
Throughout the week after the game the debate raged countrywide about whether Louth should be offered a chance to replay the game. Television replays clearly showed that Meath's Joe Sheridan had illegally carried the ball over the Louth goal-line. The decision on a replay was left up to the Meath players. Feeling that the referee's decision was final, they declined to offer a replay.

MEATH: B Murphy; C O'Connor, K Reilly, E Harrington; A Moyles (0-01), G O'Brien, C King; B Meade, N Crawford (0-01); S Kenny, J Sheridan (1-00), G Reilly (0-04); C Ward (0-04), S O'Rourke, S Bray (0-02)
Subs: C McGuinness for Moyles; P Byrne for O'Rourke

LOUTH: N Gallagher; E McAuley, D Finnegan, R Greene; R Finnegan, M Fanning, J O'Brien; P Keenan (0-01), B White (0-04); A McDonnell (0-01), M Brennan, A Reed (0-01); C Judge (0-02), S Lennon, JP Rooney (1-01)
Subs: S Fitzpatrick for Greene; A Hoey for Fanning; P Smith for Lennon; D Byrne for Reed

REFEREE: M Sludden (Tyrone)

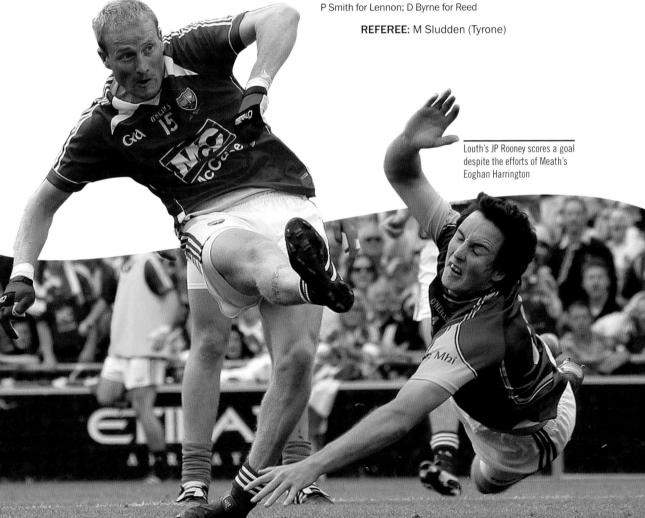

Louth's JP Rooney scores a goal despite the efforts of Meath's Eoghan Harrington

DUBLIN	0-14	0-11	ARMAGH

17 July 2010

Dublin passed another test of their championship mettle as they battled past Armagh at Croke Park.

Brogan, the nine-point hero, was the shining light once again as the Dubs booked their place in the fourth round of the All-Ireland Senior Football Championship qualifiers.

Rory O'Carroll turned in a man-of-the-match display, marking Armagh captain Steven McDonnell out of the game for long stretches.

Dublin's defence certainly looked more composed than it has done this summer, but too much hand-passing and not enough direct football from the Orchard men played into the winners' hands, allowing them to keep their structure throughout.

Dublin's greater mobility and the addition of some power off the bench – Darren Magee and Eamonn Fennell saw second half action – gave them a deserved win in the end.

But their over reliance on Bernard Brogan for scores will cause concern. Armagh, the National Football League Division 2 champions, could not stop the St Oliver Plunkett's/Eoghan Ruadh clubman from wielding his influence on proceedings.

In front of a 25,947-strong crowd, poor shooting blighted what was a much-anticipated clash, the counties' first in the championship since Armagh won in the 2003 qualifiers.

A territorially dominant Armagh seized the initiative, breaking into a 0-03 to 0-01 lead. Defender Ciaran McKeever pointed the opener on an overlapping run, and Steven McDonnell and Aaron Kernan landed a free each, as against Bernard Brogan's first point from play.

Brogan combined once again with his older brother, Alan, to chalk up Dublin's second point, following a good dispossession by

Armagh's Finnian Moriarty and David Henry of Dublin

midfielder Michael Dara MacAuley. Armagh's laboured build-up was seemingly playing into Dublin's hands.

The match struggled to catch fire until Armagh strung together three points in quick succession. Jamie Clarke dodged through to fire over a well-taken point from play, Brian Mallon finished off a powerful run with a point off his right and then Malachy Mackin casually broke forward to wallop over from the left wing.

Trailing by 0-06 to 0-02, Dublin needed to up their game and they did so, with a Bernard Brogan free ending a 17-minute scoreless spell for them. Eoghan O'Gara's decoy run created the space for Brogan to close the gap to two and Niall Corkery managed to put Brogan through for his fifth point of the encounter, with marker Andy Mallon clearly struggling.

Dublin finished the first half in fine fettle, with Corkery having an injury-time shot blocked out for a '45' which goalkeeper Stephen Cluxton converted to make it 0-06 apiece at the break.

Gilroy's charges continued to find scores as the second half got underway, outscoring the Orchard men by four points to one to take a 0-10 to 0-07 lead. Brogan and McDonnell traded points, before Brogan, substitute Kevin McManamon and Philip McMahon kicked successive points for last year's Leinster champions.

The best of the lot was defender McMahon's score as he sprinted down the left to provide support to McManamon and took a quick pass to register an inspirational point.

It was Armagh's turn to enjoy a spell of dominance as they turned possession into points, three in all which brought them back level at 0-10 apiece.

McDonnell collected his third point, with a free from close range, and succeeded in fisting over under pressure from Cluxton as a Gareth Swift point attempt dropped short.

Alan Brogan hit Dublin's eighth wide before McDonnell brought his tally to 0-05 with the 58th minute leveller.

It was all set up for a grandstand finish, but the quality of general play and finishing was lacking and a succession of frees took any momentum out of the game.

Dublin showed plenty of fight and spirit to get the necessary scores, in the end, with Bernard Brogan and Corkery also going close to notching a goal at the Hill 16 end.

Substitute Darren Magee set up an attack which saw Bernard Brogan point Dublin back in front. Finnian Moriarty put his name to Armagh's ninth wide as Paddy O'Rourke's men tried to hit back.

They almost got in for a goal in the 62nd minute. Brian Mallon's shot beat Cluxton but the covering Philip McMahon did brilliantly to get back and clear the ball away from the goal-line.

Injury doubt Paul Flynn came on to pop over a much-needed point, following some good recycling of possession, and a Brogan free suddenly made it 0-13 to 0-10.

Substitute Joe Feeney brought it back to a two-point game for Armagh, but with McDonnell misfiring a long-range free and Brogan easily finding Eamonn Fennell, from a sideline ball, for the insurance point in injury-time, Dublin had done enough to maintain their All-Ireland challenge.

DUBLIN: S Cluxton (0-01); M Fitzsimons, R O'Carroll, P McMahon (0-01); K Nolan, G Brennan, B Cahill; MD MacAuley, R McConnell; D Henry, A Brogan, B Cullen; N Corkery, B Brogan (0-09), E O'Gara
Subs: K McManamon (0-01) for O'Gara; E Fennell (0-01) for Corkery; P Flynn (0-01) for Henry; D Magee for McConnell; P Andrews for Cullen

ARMAGH: P Hearty; A Mallon, B Donaghy, V Martin; P Duffy, C McKeever (0-01), F Moriarty; C Vernon, K Toner; M Mackin (0-01), A Kernan (0-01), G Swift; B Mallon (0-01), S McDonnell (0-05), J Clarke (0-01)
Subs: J Feeney (0-01) for Toner; J Lavery for Mackin; T Kernan for Vernon; F Hanratty for Mallon

REFEREE: J McQuillan (Cavan)

DOWN 1-12 1-10 OFFALY

17 July 2010

Martin Clarke led the way for Down with five points as they got the better of a determined Offaly side in Tullamore to book their place in Round 4 of the All-Ireland Senior Football Championship qualifiers.

Ken Casey's second-minute goal helped Tom Cribbin's charges build a 1-06 to 0-06 half-time lead, before Aidan Carr netted for Down, three minutes after the restart.

Offaly battled back with the sides tied at 1-08 apiece at the end of the third quarter, however Down finished strongly to progress in championship 2010.

The Mourne men had to dig deep to record this hard-fought win at O'Connor Park as Offaly, inspired by Casey's early strike, led for 38 minutes.

Casey lit the touchpaper for the Faithfuls, bagging 1-01 inside the opening five minutes as Offaly got an early grip on midfield.

Ciaran McManus booted the ball into Niall McNamee who whipped it out of the sky to leave a Down defender in his wake and feed Casey for a crisply struck finish to the net.

Casey added a point three minutes later, after a tremendous intercept by Ross Brady, with Offaly oozing early confidence.

John Clarke opened Down's account in the sixth minute, and centre-forward Mark Poland followed up by slotting over a quick-fire score to cut the deficit to two points.

McNamee and McManus restored Offaly's lead to four, but Martin Clarke then took centre

Niall Darby of Offaly tries to block Paul McComiskey's shot at goal

stage with two excellent frees from long range to show Down's ability from placed balls.

It was nip and tuck up to half-time as Anton Sullivan and defender Ross Brady kept Offaly ahead. A '45' from Clarke saw Down end the opening 35 minutes in good stead.

Three points adrift, Down showed great attacking form on the resumption of play and were well rewarded for their efforts.

James McCartan's charges began to force the issue in centrefield, with Ambrose Rogers impressive. Poland fired over his second point with just 45 seconds played in the second half, before Aidan Carr netted Down's goal in the 38th minute.

It was a high quality score which would have made his father, former Down boss Ross Carr, proud. Collecting a pass from Poland, Carr sent a thunderbolt of a shot to the back of the Offaly net, giving goalkeeper Alan Mulhall little chance.

Carr's goal moved Down into the lead for the first time, and Clarke's fourth point made it 1-08 to 1-06 in the 40th minute.

Following the introduction of John Coughlan in midfield, Offaly got back on track but misfired on two occasions before John Reynolds eventually opened their second half account in the 48th minute.

This was the start of a good patch for the home side who put together back-to-back scores, with McManus tying the game for the first time in the 50th minute, 1-08 apiece.

Scores from substitute Daniel Hughes and Martin Clarke nudged Down two points clear with 15 minutes remaining, but Offaly showed no signs of wilting.

With ten minutes left on the clock, Niall McNamee tried to put McManus through for a score from the tightest of angles, but the roaming Benny Coulter made a superb block to launch another attack for the visitors.

Down had better luck in the scoring stakes during the second half, and a first from play for Poland opened up a three-point gap between the sides for the first time.

Offaly tried hard from defence to attack in the closing minutes, although there were some bad misses for McManus and Reynolds late on.

Down had a late Poland free ruled wide by the referee, despite the umpire raising the white flag, but this mattered little as they held out for a two-point victory.

Offaly's Ciaran McManus and Mark Poland of Down

OFFALY: A Mulhall; B Darby, S Brady, S Pender; N Darby, R Brady (0-02), P McConway; R Dalton, B Connor (0-02); G Guilfoyle, C McManus (0-02); A Sullivan (0-01); K Casey (1-01), J Reynolds (0-01), N McNamee (0-01)
Subs: S Ryan for McConway; J Coughlan for Dalton; A McNamee for McManus; D Egan for Casey.

DOWN: B McVeigh; D Rooney, D Gordon, D Rafferty; D O'Hagan, J Colgan, C Garvey; A Rogers, K King; P McComiskey, M Poland (0-03), A Carr (1-00); J Clarke (0-02), B Coulter (0-01), M Clarke (0-05)
Subs: D Hughes (0-01) for Carr; K McKernan for Colgan; R Sexton for McComiskey; R Murtagh for J Clarke, A Brannigan for Garvey

REFEREE: M Duffy (Sligo)

KILDARE	2-17	1-09	DERRY

17 July 2010

Kildare's season took another positive turn at Celtic Park, where they handed out a heavy defeat to Derry to book their place in the last 12 of the All-Ireland Senior Football Championship.

This resounding 11-point qualifier win leaves Derry in turmoil, with manager Damian Cassidy set to reflect on his position.

While the Lilywhites displayed a selfless work ethic, and had outstanding performances from Dermot Earley, John Doyle and Eamon Callaghan, the Oak Leafers were left to try and work out how they fell apart with the wind at their backs in the second half.

They got a perfect start with an early goal and led by five points, but failed to build on that impressive opening, allowing the Leinster men to boss the game and win at a canter.

The game was just over a minute old when Raymond Wilkinson pounced to drill the ball to the roof of the net from close range after the Kildare defence failed to clear when Eoin Bradley's free dropped short.

Bradley added a point, and James Kielt converted a free for a 1-2 to 0-0 lead. Kildare didn't get their first score until the 12th minute when Doyle was on target from a free, but they were building slowly and confidently, and the team captain added three more scores from placed balls, and hit a point from play to give Kildare the lead for the first time in the 23rd minute.

Centre-back Emmet Bolton pushed forward to knock over a score, and as Kildare defended with discipline, Derry struggled to create openings, and went 20 minutes without adding to that early scoring blitz.

Declan Mullan and Bradley got them back level, and they could have had a second goal when Mark Lynch crossed from the left to Wilkinson, but his shot was blocked by Andrew MacLochlainn.

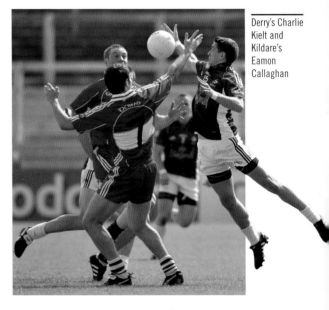

Derry's Charlie Kielt and Kildare's Eamon Callaghan

Padraig O'Neill's point sent Kildare into the break with a 0-08 to 1-04 lead. Although Derry got their noses in front briefly early in the second half, their challenge died.

Callaghan regained the lead for Kildare, before Padraig O'Neill's second point saw them take a two-point advantage into the final quarter.

Substitute Eoin O'Flaherty stretched the advantage and full-back Hugh McGrillen also drove forward to score.

Earley was a dominant figure at midfield, and Kildare killed the game off with Callaghan's 60th-minute goal.

And they made it a landslide win with a second goal from Alan Smith two minutes from the end.

Derry's Joe Diver closed down by Kildare's Daryl Flynn and Morgan O'Flaherty.

DERRY: B Gillis; B Óg McAlary, K McGuckin, D McBride; D Mullan (0-01); G O'Kane, C Kielt; J Diver, E Muldoon (0-01); C McKeever, J Kielt (0-02), B McGoldrick; E Bradley (0-03), M Lynch (0-02), R Wilkinson (1-00)
Subs: Patsy Bradley for C Kielt; SL McGoldrick for Wilkinson; M Craig for McKeever; R Convery for Diver

KILDARE: S McCormack; P Kelly, H McGrillen (0-01), A Mac Lochlainn; M O'Flaherty, E Bolton (0-01), B Flanagan; D Flynn, D Earley; J Kavanagh, P O'Neill, T O'Connor (0-01); J Doyle (0-08), R Sweeney (0-02), E Callaghan (1-04)
Subs: A Smith for O'Connor; E O'Flaherty for Sweeney; D Lyons for Bolton; D White for B Flanagan

REFEREE: M Duffy (Sligo)

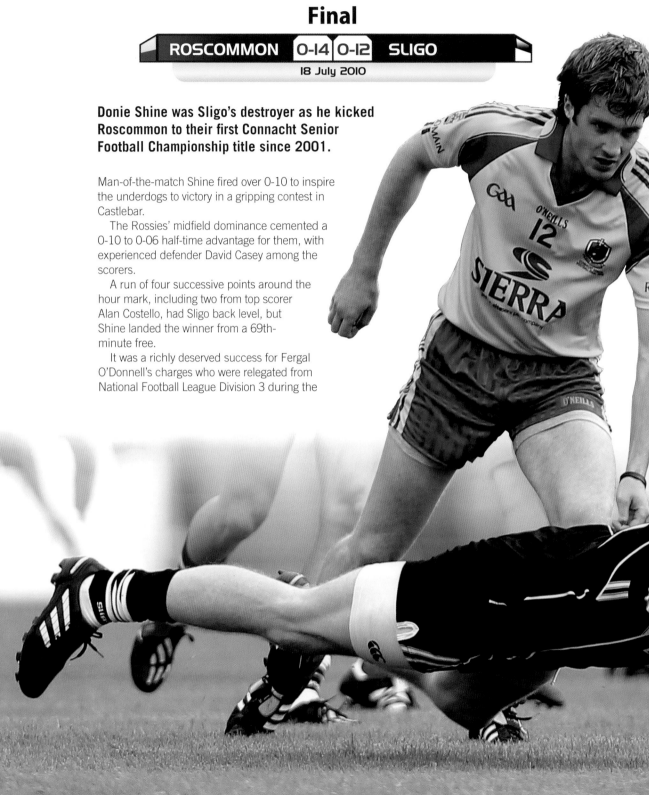

Final

ROSCOMMON	0-14	0-12	SLIGO

18 July 2010

Donie Shine was Sligo's destroyer as he kicked Roscommon to their first Connacht Senior Football Championship title since 2001.

Man-of-the-match Shine fired over 0-10 to inspire the underdogs to victory in a gripping contest in Castlebar.

The Rossies' midfield dominance cemented a 0-10 to 0-06 half-time advantage for them, with experienced defender David Casey among the scorers.

A run of four successive points around the hour mark, including two from top scorer Alan Costello, had Sligo back level, but Shine landed the winner from a 69th-minute free.

It was a richly deserved success for Fergal O'Donnell's charges who were relegated from National Football League Division 3 during the spring and given little chance of becoming Connacht champions at the outset.

But wins over London and Leitrim spread confidence throughout the panel; this performance saw them take the game to Sligo right from the off.

There was no sense of panic from O'Donnell's young guns when Costello pointed Sligo ahead after just 20 seconds. They hit back with two blockbuster scores from Shine, one a curling free after Ger Heneghan was fouled and the second a meaty '45' after Heneghan had a shot blocked.

Casey, who has had a cruel run of luck with knee injuries, raided forward to kick Roscommon's third point in the ninth minute, and the free-flowing football continued as Costello sliced superbly through the ball for his second. Shine then edged over his first from play, wide out on the left.

Shine, the scorer of 1-16 against London and Leitrim, was not just deadly accurate from placed balls, he was a menace in open play too, proving a handful for Sligo full-back Noel McGuire. Most of the traffic was towards the Sligo goal, so much so that their key forward David Kelly hardly touched the ball in the opening 20 minutes.

In between misses from Shine and Stephen Gilmartin, Cathal Cregg created enough space to smack over a fine point off his left and make it 0-05 to 0-02. Mark Breheny and Colm McGee steadied Sligo somewhat, but scores from David Keenan, Shine and David O'Gara had the Rossies

comfortably ahead at 0-10 to 0-04.

The pick of those scores came in the 21st minute when Cregg dinked a clever ball through for Shine to collect, turn and point in an instant.

Sligo, who brought on Eugene Mullen for Taylor, earned some much-needed scores in first half injury-time. Eamonn O'Hara hand-passed for Adrian Marren to score and the latter then popped over a free, awarded against Sean McDermott, to cut the gap to four points at the break.

The windy conditions played havoc with shooting at times, and both sides fluffed their lines as the second half started. McGee and Karol Mannion kicked wides, Sligo substitute Mullen also watched his effort get caught by the breeze and the energetic Jonathan Davey dropped another shot short of the posts.

Marren though showed his increasing influence by stroking over off his left, five minutes in, and the deficit was down to three. So it stayed as another textbook free from Shine was replied to by an inspirational score from Sligo captain Charlie Harrison.

Sligo boss Kevin Walsh turned to his bench in an attempt to wrestle back control of the game, making four changes by the hour mark. But Shine, the nerveless 21-year-old, continued to drive his side closer to the Nestor Cup. Another great turn and point pushed Roscommon's lead to 0-12 to 0-08.

The DCU student missed a kickable free in the 54th minute, for one of his few wayward attempts on goal, and Sligo really raised their game over the next 10 minutes.

Kelly got past McDermott's challenge, close to the end-line, and forced Roscommon goalkeeper Geoffrey Claffey into a point blank save. Claffey infringed as he grappled for the loose ball, and Breheny sent over the resulting free.

O'Hara played his part in setting up Costello for a lovely score, and the former Mayo player repeated the trick just moments later, getting away from Casey to pull the trigger from distance.

The sides were level for only the second time – at 0-12 apiece – when substitute Sean Davey rifled over in the 63rd minute. Roscommon

Sligo's Tony Taylor and Cathal Cregg of Roscommon

Roscommon's Cathal Cregg
and Ross Donovan of Sligo

Eamonn O'Hara and David
Keenan of Roscommon

Sligo's Sean Davey and
John Rogers of Roscommon

109

were suddenly struggling to get past midfield and there was evidence that they were tiring as Sligo got on top.

Davey missed a chance to put his side ahead, registering their seventh wide, and Shine coolly kicked Roscommon back in front in the 66th minute, nudging a free over from the left.

It looked like being a shootout between Shine and Costello when the Sligo wing-forward, a real star of their championship run, thumped over another terrific point from play – his fifth in all – to square things up again.

The questions were being asked and Roscommon, written off by many beforehand, showed that they had the answers. Shine, once again, stepped up to the mark.

He went into double figures in his first Connacht Senior Football Championship final when converting a free from the left. A subsequent wide from substitute Davey was the closest Sligo came to an equaliser.

Injury-time came and went and Roscommon, 20-point losers to Mayo at this venue last year, stood firm to make one of the biggest waves of the 2010 championship.

Their 20th Connacht senior title, and probably the sweetest of them all. The Connacht Under-21 trophy was also won earlier this year by the Rossies, emphasising that this should not be a false dawn. It is easy to imagine one of the county's favourite sons, the late Dermot Earley snr, smiling approvingly from above.

Roscommon's Michael Finneran contests a high ball with Eamonn O'Hara and Tony Taylor of Sligo

ROSCOMMON: G Claffey; S McDermott, P Domican, S Ormsby; S Purcell, C Dineen, D Casey (0-01); M Finneran, K Mannion; D Keenan (0-01), D O'Gara (0-01), C Cregg (0-01); J Rogers, D Shine (0-10), G Heneghan
Subs: K Higgins for Rogers; J Dunning for O'Gara; P Garvey for Dineen; C Garvey for Casey

SLIGO: P Greene; C Harrison (0-01), N McGuire, R Donavan; K Cawley, B Phillips, J Davey; T Taylor, S Gilmartin; A Costello (0-05), M Breheny (0-02), E O'Hara; C McGee (0-01), A Marren (0-03), D Kelly.
Subs: Eugene Mullen for Taylor; K Sweeney for McGee; S Davey (0-01) for Gilmartin; N Ewing for Phillips; S Coen for Breheny

REFEREE: J White (Donegal)

Final

TYRONE	1-14	0-07	MONAGHAN

18 July 2010

Tyrone retained the Ulster Senior Football Championship title with a comfortable win over Monaghan at Clones.

The Farney men, seeking their first provincial title since 1988, failed to rise to the occasion in front of 34,634 fans on their own home patch.

The vastly experienced Red Hands controlled the game once they got through a closely fought opening 20 minutes.

Yet they needed two stunning saves from Pascal McConnell to keep them in front in the first half.

Ten different players scored for the defending champions, with the Cavanagh brothers leading the way, Sean on three points, and Colm with the only goal of the game in the 65th minute

McConnell rescued Tyrone with two brilliant first half saves from the Freeman brothers.

First he denied Tommy in the fourth minute, when the Magheracloone attacker got in behind to collect a long delivery from Owen Lennon.

And in the dying moments of the half, he pulled off what will surely be a contender for save of the season, diving full length to keep out a stinging shot from wing-back Damien.

In between, the sides were level on four occasions, before the Red Hands pulled away as the interval approached.

Tommy Freeman and Paul Finlay were on target for the Farney men, with Tommy McGuigan and centre back Conor Gormley responding with Tyrone points.

All of the Red

Monaghan's Darren Hughes with Colm Cavanagh of Tyrone

Monaghan's Darren Hughes
with Sean Cavanagh and Brian
Dooher of Tyrone

Monaghan's Paul Finlay with Conor Gormley of Tyrone

Monaghan's Paul Finlay tackles Conor Gormley of Tyrone

113

Tyrone's Conor Gormley and Monaghan's Paul Finlay

Hands half-backs registered points in the first half, with Davy Harte and Philip Jordan also venturing forward to score.

It was Jordan who brought the teams level in the 22nd minute at 0-04 each, and the defending champions reeled off three points, through Sean Cavanagh, Kevin Hughes and Harte to go in at the break with a 0-07 to 0-04 cushion.

Martin Penrose and Sean Cavanagh stretched the advantage as gaps began to open up in the Farney defence early in the second half.

Monaghan suffered a further blow when full-back JP Mone was stretchered off on 45 minutes.

Tyrone used their vast experience to squeeze their opponents out of the game. Monaghan went 40 minutes without registering a score, until Conor McManus tapped over a 13-metre free in the 59th minute.

But that wasn't enough to spark a revival. The defending champions turned the screw and Colm Cavanagh charged through to drill home a brilliant goal.

Tyrone clinically finished the job off with late points from Harte, Penrose and Hughes.

TYRONE: P McConnell; C McCarron, Justin McMahon, R McMenamin; D Harte (0-01), C Gormley (0-01), P Jordan (0-01); C Cavanagh (1-00), K Hughes (0-02); B Dooher (0-01), S Cavanagh (0-03), Joe McMahon (0-01); M Penrose (0-02), T McGuigan (0-01), O Mulligan **Subs:** C McCullagh for Mulligan; P Harte for McGuigan, D Carlin for McCarron; B McGuigan for Dooher; S O'Neill for D Harte

MONAGHAN: S Duffy; D McArdle, JP Mone, C Walshe; D Freeman, D Hughes, G McQuaid; D Clerkin (0-01), O Lennon; S Gollogly, P Finlay (0-01), K Hughes; R Woods (0-01), C McManus (0-02), T Freeman (0-01) **Subs:** H McElroy for JP Mone; C Hanratty for Gollogly; D Mone (0-01) for Finlay; M McElroy for Hughes; N McAdam for McQuaid

REFEREE: D Coldrick (Meath)

CORK	0-12	0-05	WEXFORD

18 July 2010

Wexford were well beaten on their home patch this afternoon as Cork's All-Ireland crusade continued with a seven-point football qualifier win.

The Rebels could afford to score just one point in the closing 30 minutes at Wexford Park as they coasted into the fourth round.

Daniel Goulding and Paddy Kelly struck two points apiece as the visitors, helped by a huge wind, took a 0-07 to 0-03 interval lead.

The 6,700-strong crowd watched Matty Forde and substitute Ben Brosnan point for Wexford after the break, but Cork were never troubled.

Wexford manager Jason Ryan was forced into a late change as Collie Byrne took PJ Banville's place in the attack, and Shane Roche moved to top of the left.

Cork lined out unchanged from their facile win over Cavan and with the elements behind them, they quickly left Wexford in their wake.

Wexford turned over possession on a number of occasions in the opening quarter and Cork needed no second invitation. Daniel Goulding opened the scoring from a counter attack in the second minute, and both Paddy Kelly and Goulding kicked frees

Eric Bradley of Wexford with John Miskella and Ray Carey of Cork

115

for a 0-03 to 0-00 lead by the fourth minute.

Team captain Graham Canty switched positions to right half-back and provided plenty of leadership for his side, particularly when Wexford tried to turn the tide at the start of the second half.

The Model men, conquerors of Galway last time out, threatened on the break in the early stages but had nothing to show for their efforts, with Ciaran Lyng going closest.

They were putting the Cork defence under a good deal of pressure – Michael Shields and Ray Carey picked up early yellow cards – but scores from Canty and Walsh, after Colm Morris and Redmond Barry had coughed up decent ball, eased Conor Counihan's charges 0-05 to 0-00 ahead.

Some patient build-up play set up wing-back Adrian Flynn for Wexford's opening point in the 18th minute, only for Cork to cancel that out through full-forward Ciaran Sheehan, who profited from Colm O'Neill's quickly taken sideline ball.

Kelly converted a free after a foul on O'Neill, and it was clear that the mobility of Cork's full-forward line was causing problems for the hosts. The loss of late call-up Byrne through injury was another blow, but Brendan Doyle was a more than adequate replacement.

This was a scrappy encounter, dominated by the wind and rain, but Wexford's attacking play improved considerably coming up to half-time. Their hard-working half-backs supplied the platform for Eric Bradley and Lyng to tag on late points, closing the gap to 0-07 to 0-03 for half-time.

If Wexford could maintain that scoring run into the second half, it was a definite case of 'game on'. Unfortunately for the home support, Cork effectively put the game beyond Wexford's reach when they kicked four points in quick succession, between the 36th and 44th minutes.

Kelly and Goulding shared out three frees, with substitute Nicholas Murphy prominent, and John Miskella also broke forward from his defensive station to point on the run.

Matty Forde, who was well-shackled throughout, kicked Wexford's fourth point before a barren spell ensued for both sides, amid heavy rain showers.

Cork continued to create chances, Goulding went wide from a free, Canty drove a goal-scoring chance wide and substitute Paul Kerrigan, recovered from a hamstring injury, also blazed wide when trying to find a way past Wexford net minder Anthony Masterson.

A point from substitute Ben Brosnan in injury-time made it a six-point game, but Cork still managed to have the final say, with Sheehan's second point completing a solid day's work from the Munster men.

WEXFORD: A Masterson; J Wadding, G Molloy, B Malone; A Flynn (0-01), D Murphy, A Doyle; E Bradley (0-01), D Waters; C Morris, R Barry, C Byrne; C Lyng (0-01), M Forde (0-01), S Roche
Subs: B Doyle for Byrne; P Naughter for Waters; PJ Banville for Roche; D Carter for Wadding Brosnan (0-01) for A Doyle

CORK: A Quirke; R Carey, M Shields J O'Sullivan; G Canty (0-01), J Miskella (0-01), P Kissane; A O'Connor, A Walsh (0-01); P Kelly (0-04), P O'Neill, F Goold; D Goulding (0-03), C Sheehan (0-02), C O'Neill
Subs: P Kerrigan for Goold; N Murphy for O'Connor; N O'Leary for Kissane; J Hayes for C O'Neill; F Lynch for P Kelly

REFEREE: G Ó Conamha (Galway)

KILDARE	1-15	1-11	MONAGHAN

24 July 2010

Kildare qualified for the All-Ireland Senior Football Championship quarter-finals for the third successive season with a four-point win over Monaghan at Croke Park.

A dominant second-half display saw Kieran McGeeney's men secure their place in the last eight and underline their reputation as back-door specialists.

Once again Dermot Earley was a hugely influential figure in midfield for the Lilywhites, and while John Doyle had an off-day up front, James Kavanagh stepped up to the mark with five excellent points.

But McGeeney will be somewhat concerned by the manner in which his side allowed a nine-point lead to be trimmed back to four in the closing stages.

Monaghan were 0-04 to 0-01 ahead after 20 minutes confounding those who said they would be unable to lift themselves following a

Colin Walshe of Monaghan with Ken Donnelly and James Kavanagh of Kildare

117

Monaghan's Owen Lennon and
Damien Freeman with Kildare's
Dermot Earley

heavy Ulster final defeat to Tyrone six days earlier.

Tommy Freeman and Ciaran Hanratty were on target inside the opening two minutes. Conor McManus and Owen Lennon added further points in reply to James Kavanagh's Kildare opener.

Despite the Trojan efforts of Dermot Earley and Daryl Flynn in midfield, the Lilywhites were repeatedly frustrated by poor finishing, with ace marksman John Doyle the chief culprit.

Doyle hit six wides in the first half, but Monaghan's wayward passing denied them the opportunity to take full advantage of their opponents' attacking failings.

Finally, it started to happen for Kieran McGeeney's side in the last five minutes of the first half, when they hit four unanswered points to go in front.

Substitute Eoghan O'Flaherty scored with his first touch and set up a point for Eamon Callaghan. Another sublime effort from Kavanagh levelled the game before Doyle broke his duck with an injury-time free kick to give his side a one point advantage at the break.

The Lilywhites made their push for home in the early stages of the second half, with the in-form Kavanagh banging over three points. Eoghan O'Flaherty and Alan Smith also hit the target.

Monaghan managed just two points in the third quarter, through Paul Finlay and Darren Hughes, and their challenge was effectively killed off when substitute Ronan Sweeney punched Doyle's right-wing cross to the net in the 52nd minute.

Doyle extended the advantage to nine points but, to their credit, Monaghan staged

Eamon Callaghan of Kildare with Kieran Hughes of Monaghan

a strong finish.

Finlay, Damien Freeman and Stephen Gollogly all landed points, before Hugh McElroy slid home a late consolation goal as Monaghan bowed out of the championship for 2010.

KILDARE: S McCormack; P Kelly, H McGrillen, A Mac Lochlainn; M O'Flaherty; E Bolton (0-01), B Flanagan; D Flynn (0-01), D Earley; J Kavanagh (0-05), P O'Neill, A Smith (0-01); J Doyle (0-02), K Donnelly, E Callaghan (0-02)
Subs: E O'Flaherty (0-02) for K Donnelly; R Sweeney (1-01) for P O'Neill; G White for D Earley; K Cribben for E Bolton; D Whyte for M O'Flaherty

MONAGHAN: P McBennett; D McArdle, D Mone, C Walshe; D Freeman (0-01), D Hughes (0-01), G McQuaid; O Lennon (0-01), D Clerkin; K Hughes (0-01), P Finlay (0-03), C Hanratty (0-01); R Woods, C McManus (0-01), T Freeman (0-01)
Subs: S Gollogly (0-01) for Hanratty; F Caulfield for Clerkin; H McElroy (1-00) for Walshe; M McElroy for McManus; K Duffy for McArdle

REFEREE: J White (Donegal)

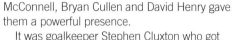

DUBLIN 2-14 | 0-13 LOUTH

24 July 2010

Dublin moved back into mainstream championship football, booking their place in the All-Ireland Senior Football Championship quarter-finals with a 2-14 to 0-13 win over Louth.

Eoghan O'Gara's two first-half goals took the wind out of the Wee County's sails as they tried to recover from the nightmare that was the Leinster final against Meath.

It was another day of agony at Croke Park for Peter Fitzpatrick's men, but this time they were fairly and comprehensively beaten.

The Dubs are building game by game, and will feel they have made progress during their trip through the back door, but once again they failed to convince.

However, the fact that they managed a healthy 2-14 despite the relative ineffectiveness of star attacker Bernard Brogan will have encouraged boss Pat Gilroy.

Louth defender John O'Brien enjoyed a triumphant afternoon as Brogan's marker, restricting him to just one point from play, and that scored in the final minute of the 70.

In front of a crowd of 47,738, Dublin established an early dominance around midfield, where Michael Dara MacAuley, Ross

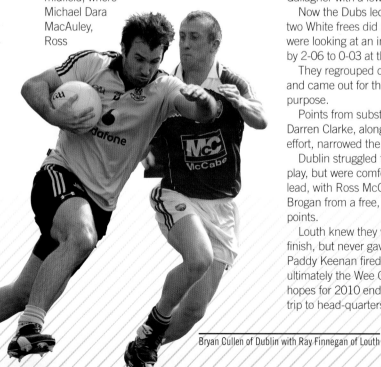

McConnell, Bryan Cullen and David Henry gave them a powerful presence.

It was goalkeeper Stephen Cluxton who got them going with the first of his two first-half '45' conversions, and points quickly followed from the Brogan brothers.

In the 11th minute O'Gara drilled home his first goal, drifting past two tackles before unleashing a shot that took a deflection to trick goalkeeper Neil Gallagher.

Louth could only manage three points, all from Brian White frees, in the opening 35 minutes, the first of which lifted the siege temporarily at the beginning of the second quarter.

Cullen charged through to hammer over a couple of points, Cluxton kicked his second '45' between the posts, and on 33 minutes, full-forward O'Gara struck again.

He collected Alan Brogan's pass out on the right, turned marker Dessie Finnegan and beat Gallagher with a low, angled finish.

Now the Dubs led by 11 points, and while two White frees did reduce the deficit, Louth were looking at an impossible situation, trailing by 2-06 to 0-03 at the break.

They regrouped during the interval, however, and came out for the second half with renewed purpose.

Points from substitutes Declan Byrne and Darren Clarke, along with an Andy McDonnell effort, narrowed the gap to five.

Dublin struggled to get any fluency into their play, but were comfortably able to protect their lead, with Ross McConnell, O'Gara, Bernard Brogan from a free, and Cullen all tagging on points.

Louth knew they were gone long before the finish, but never gave up. Both Clarke and Paddy Keenan fired over late scores but ultimately the Wee County's championship hopes for 2010 ends with another disappointing trip to head-quarters.

Bryan Cullen of Dublin with Ray Finnegan of Louth

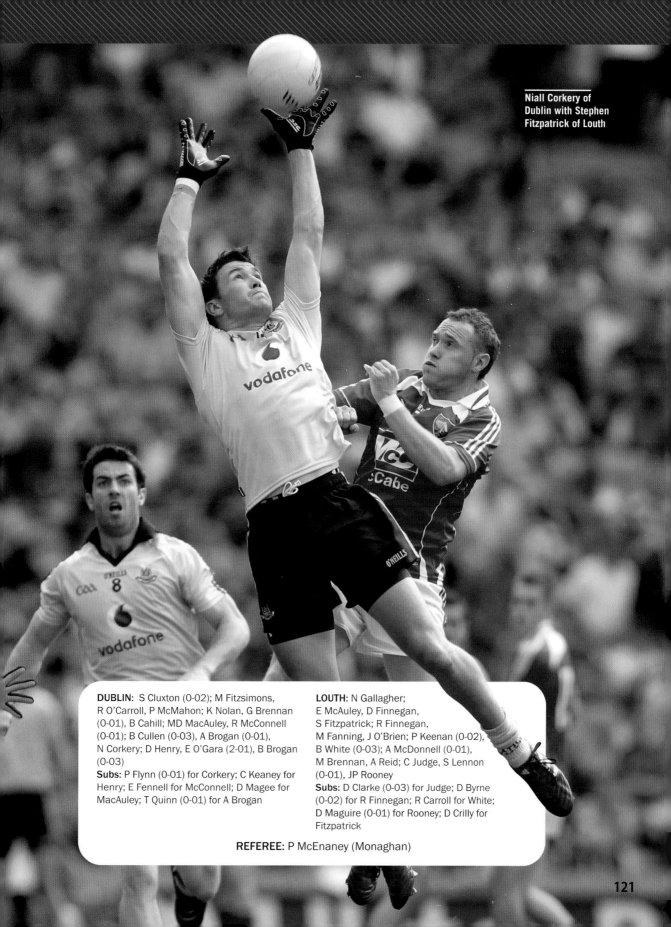

Niall Corkery of Dublin with Stephen Fitzpatrick of Louth

DUBLIN: S Cluxton (0-02); M Fitzsimons, R O'Carroll, P McMahon; K Nolan, G Brennan (0-01), B Cahill; MD MacAuley, R McConnell (0-01); B Cullen (0-03), A Brogan (0-01), N Corkery; D Henry, E O'Gara (2-01), B Brogan (0-03)
Subs: P Flynn (0-01) for Corkery; C Keaney for Henry; E Fennell for McConnell; D Magee for MacAuley; T Quinn (0-01) for A Brogan

LOUTH: N Gallagher; E McAuley, D Finnegan, S Fitzpatrick; R Finnegan, M Fanning, J O'Brien; P Keenan (0-02), B White (0-03); A McDonnell (0-01), M Brennan, A Reid; C Judge, S Lennon (0-01), JP Rooney
Subs: D Clarke (0-03) for Judge; D Byrne (0-02) for R Finnegan; R Carroll for White; D Maguire (0-01) for Rooney; D Crilly for Fitzpatrick

REFEREE: P McEnaney (Monaghan)

DOWN 3-20 0-10 SLIGO

24 July 2010

Down went through to the All-Ireland Senior Football Championship quarter-finals after an impressive 3-20 to 0-10 win over Sligo in Kingspan Breffni Park.

Beaten Connacht finalists Sligo were thoroughly outplayed by Down and trailed from early on. John Clarke's first-half goal helping the Ulster men into a 1-10 to 0-06 interval lead.

The Mourne men didn't ease up after the restart as team captain Ambrose Rogers grabbed his side's second goal and substitute Ronan Murtagh also netted, leaving an off-colour Sligo simply shattered.

Traffic congestion forced the throw-in to be delayed by ten minutes and it was Kevin Walsh's Sligo side who looked unsettled, as they tried to bounce back from their Connacht final defeat to Roscommon.

Down made an ominous start to this fourth-round qualifier, winning possession straight from the off and when John Clarke was found, he showed great pace to convert the first score inside 15 seconds.

The recent wins over Longford and Offaly had James McCartan's charges brimming with confidence.

They were all over Sligo in the opening stages, with the Clarke brothers, Martin and John, and midfielder Rogers involved in a superb fist passing move in the third minute.

Rogers laid off for Paul McComiskey to try his luck for a goal, but his effort was brilliantly stopped by Sligo goalkeeper Philip Greene.

Martin Clarke converted the resulting '45' and although Sligo seemed to settle thereafter, the Yeats men were afforded little time and space to create scores.

Rogers showed great leadership, adding his weight to the attack while also making some stunning blocks in defence, with David Kelly denied in the opening five minutes.

Adrian Marren got Sligo off the mark in the eighth minute, landing the first of his three first-

Sligo's David Kelly and
Daniel Hughes of Down

half points from placed balls, but Down continued to find holes in the westerners' defence.

Mark Poland and Daniel Hughes pointed either side of a Stephen Coen score, as Down went 0-05 to 0-02 ahead in the 11th minute.

Sligo hit a purple patch in terms of possession and scoring opportunities in the middle third of the opening half, as they began to find a foothold in the midfield sector.

But once again Down gave little away at the back, and Sligo's only reward for a dominant 12-minute spell was a Kelly point from play in the 17th minute.

Down responded by finding another gear before the interval, with John and Martin Clarke again in sparkling form. John fired home a 30th minute goal after Benny Coulter laid off a pass, to push his side 1-08 to 0-03 clear.

Sligo claimed three of the final five points of the first half with Marren and Kelly on target, but Down were still well in command and led by seven points at the break.

Any hopes Sligo had of staging a comeback were dashed when Down went on a scoring spree as the second half resumed, stringing together 1-02 inside five minutes.

Kevin McKernan and Rogers were on target for points, and the Down skipper then palmed the ball to the net after his initial shot was blocked by Sligo goalkeeper Philip Greene.

Marren pegged a point back for Sligo, but this was a mere blip in an otherwise dominant period from McCartan's men.

The Down boss opted to substitute the unusually quiet Coulter, but it was actually an inspired change. In the round 3 win over Offaly, Daniel Hughes scored within three minutes of his introduction. This time it was Ronan

Sligo's Brian Kennedy and Kalum King of Down

Murtagh who achieved a similar feat, staking a claim for a starting berth in the quarter-final.

Murtagh replaced Coulter in the 45th minute, and immediately showed his worth by scoring three superb points from play as Down cantered into a 2-15 to 0-08 lead.

By this stage, Sligo were well beaten and the Ulster side showed no signs of slipping up, with Conor Garvey, Damian Rafferty and Daniel McCartan among those performing strongly in defence.

Murtagh also showed no mercy by adding a 66th-minute goal to his tally.

Substitute Colm McGee tagged on a late brace of points for Sligo, but Hughes and substitute Peter Fitzpatrick cancelled out those scores to ensure a 19-point win for Down and a disappointing end to a summer which began so brightly for Sligo.

DOWN: B McVeigh; D McCartan, D Gordon, D Rafferty; D Rooney, K McKernan (0-01), C Garvey (0-01); A Rogers (1-01), K King; D Hughes (0-03), M Poland (0-02), P McComiskey (0-01); B Coulter, J Clarke (1-01), M Clarke (0-04)
Subs: R Murtagh (1-05) for B Coulter; D O'Hagan for D Rafferty; P Fitzpatrick (0-01) for K King; R Sexton for P McComiskey; J Brown for M Clarke

SLIGO: P Greene; C Harrison, N McGuire, R Donavan; K Cawley, B Kennedy, J Davey; E Mullen, S Davey; A Costello, M Breheny, E O'Hara; S Coen (0-02), A Marren (0-04), D Kelly (0-02)
Subs: P McGovern for J Davey; S Gilmartin for S Davey; K Sweeney for Costello; C McGee (0-02) for Breheny; F Quinn for O'Hara

REFEREE: M Deegan (Laois)

CORK	0-16	1-11	LIMERICK

24 July 2010

Cork stuttered into the All-Ireland Senior Football Championship quarter-finals as Limerick fell away in extra-time at the Gaelic Grounds.

A late penalty from Ger Collins and point from substitute Conor Fitzgerald got Limerick level at 1-09 to 0-12, but extra-time points from substitute Donncha O'Connor, Paddy Kelly and Daniel Goulding shot the Rebels through.

Limerick elected to play against a slight wind in the opening half, and corner-forward Collins latched onto a breaking ball to clip over the first point after 48 seconds.

Cork survived a fifth minute scare when Aidan Walsh seemed to drag down John Galvin as the big Limerick midfielder looked to create enough space for a shot on goal.

A penalty seemed the likely conclusion, but referee Padraig Hughes stunned most of the watching crowd by awarding a free out to the visitors.

The television replays showed that it was a clear penalty and Cork were let off the hook again, seven minutes later, when Limerick captain Seanie Buckley rattled a rising shot off the crossbar.

A superb pacey attack, initiated by Stephen Lucey set Buckley racing towards goal. The Limerick attacker's shot had goalkeeper Alan Quirke beaten, only for the woodwork to come to Cork's rescue.

Collins followed up with another free to increase the lead to three, a gap Cork soon set about whittling away.

Kavanagh stepped off his right and away from Galvin to open the Rebels' account in the 14th minute, and Goulding floated his first free over soon after.

Cork had registered four wides by the time Limerick wing-back Stephen Lavin burst onto a half clearance and raided through the middle of the Cork defence for a polished score.

But Mickey Ned O'Sullivan's men could only manage one further point before half-

Limerick's Stephen Lavin and Paul Kerrigan of Cork

time, through Stephen Kelly in the 32nd minute.

Cork were gradually getting to grips with the game, particularly around the half-back and midfield areas, and Limerick's poor distribution in to their two-man full-forward line certainly let them down.

Points from Goulding and Colm O'Neill, sandwiching Kelly's effort, brought the sides level for the second time as half-time approached. The quality of football improved somewhat in the second half and Ray Carey added his weight to the Cork attack, just after the restart, helping Aidan Walsh to nudge Cork 0-06 to 0-05 ahead. Goulding kicked a long-range free for a two-point lead, but Limerick managed to close that gap with points from Lavin and James Ryan. The talismanic Galvin was involved in both moves.

However, the Shannonsiders failed to score for the next 21 minutes and Cork moved into what looked to be a match-winning lead of 0-12 to 0-07.

Counihan's charges did not perform like All-Ireland contenders, but they were doing just enough to deserve their lead. Goulding brought his personal haul to six points, teenage full-forward Ciaran Sheehan added his name to the scoresheet and a crossfield ball from Colm O'Neill teed up substitute Alan O'Connor for a 65th-minute point.

Pearse O'Neill and substitute Nicholas Murphy, two of Cork's top performers in past years, were influencing proceedings and not even the most fervent of Limerick supporters could have envisaged what would happen next.

Collins kicked a free from a tight angle to kick-start an inspired late spell from Limerick.

In the second minute of injury-time, James Ryan lobbed a free towards the Cork square in the hope of nabbing a goal. Referee Hughes spotted a push by Alan O'Connor on Jim O'Donovan and the home side had a lifeline – a penalty.

Collins brilliantly tucked it away in the bottom left corner of the net, away from the diving Quirke.

With just one point in it and time running out, Limerick went in desperate search of the equalising point.

Their desire and belief in themselves was rewarded when Quirke produced a poor kickout, and the ball was worked towards the unmarked substitute Conor Fitzgerald who lofted over a point to tie the game at 1-09 to 0-12.

The floodlights were switched on for extra-time and although Limerick started brightly, their early endeavour led to a wide from James Ryan.

Goulding also shot wide twice before Collins failed to punish the Rebels for some slack defending, after a brilliant block by Padraig Browne at the other end.

It was left to Cork substitute Donncha O'Connor to provide some scoring inspiration. He converted two chances – one from play, and the other from a late free – to move the visitors 0-14 to 1-09 ahead by the end of the first period of extra-time.

Neither side were able to push on in the second half. Limerick roused themselves with a terrific tight-angled free from goalkeeper Brian Scanlon.

But their play lacked composure and direction at crucial times, and when Paddy Kelly burst into space to pop over a timely point off his right, Cork's two-point margin was restored.

Ian Ryan flicked a free over off the left-hand post in injury-time to jangle Cork's nerves. However, the Rebels had the final say at the end of this hard-fought battle. Limerick's Lavin was sent off for a second bookable offence and top-scorer Goulding sent the resulting free through the uprights to keep Cork's drive for the Sam Maguire Cup alive and dash Limerick's hopes once again.

LIMERICK: B Scanlon (0-01); M O'Riordan, J McCarthy, A Lane; S Lavin (0-02), S Lucey, P Ranahan; J O'Donovan, J Galvin; P Browne, J Ryan (0-01), S Buckley; G Collins (1-04), I Ryan (0-01), S Kelly
Subs: S Gallagher for McCarthy; C Mullane for O'Riordan; E Joy for Browne; C Fitzgerald (0-01) for Buckley; S Gallagher for Lucey; E O'Connor for I Ryan; J Mullane for O'Donovan; P Browne for Ranahan; S Buckley for Joy; J Mullane for Collins

CORK: A Quirke; R Carey, M Shields, J O'Sullivan; N O'Leary, G Canty, P Kissane; D Kavanagh (0-01), A Walsh (0-01); P Kerrigan, P O'Neill, P Kelly; D Goulding (0-07), C Sheehan (0-01), C O'Neill (0-02)
Subs: D O'Connor (0-02) for Kerrigan; N Murphy for Walsh; A O'Connor (0-01) for Kavanagh; F Goold for Kelly; P Kelly (0-01) for Goold; E Cotter for Shields; P Kerrigan for Sheehan; F Goold for A O'Connor

REFEREE: P Hughes (Armagh)

Quarter-Final

DOWN	1-16	1-10	KERRY

31 July 2010

Down shocked Kerry with a deserved 1-16 to 1-10 win in their Senior Football Championship quarter-final clash at Croke Park.

The Kingdom were flattered by the extent of this six-point defeat, with their goal coming deep into stoppage time from a penalty.

The Mourne men, who plotted an impressive course through the qualifiers, displayed passion and skill from start to finish, and in Martin Clarke they had a player of vision and creativity who played an immense role in this massive victory.

Clarke controlled the game for long stretches, contributing to many of his side's scores and posting a 0-04 tally himself.

Down, now with five wins from five championship meetings with Kerry, never showed any fear of their opponents, who looked disjointed and lacking in leadership.

Down stunned the Sam Maguire Cup holders with a goal after just 52 seconds.

Micheal Quirke was caught in possession, Paul McComiskey slipped the ball quickly to Mark

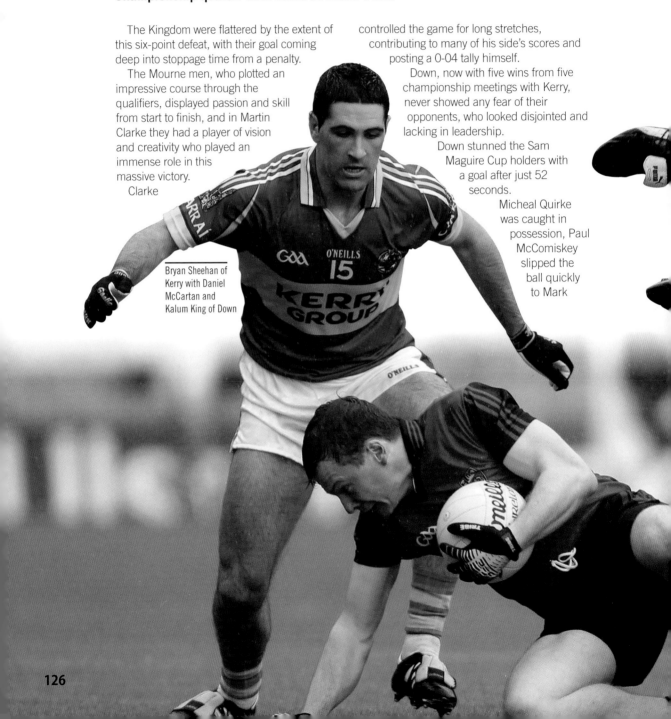

Bryan Sheehan of Kerry with Daniel McCartan and Kalum King of Down

126

Poland, and the centre-forward gave Brendan Kealy no chance with a rasping drive.

Down maintained that dazzling offensive, adding points through Benny Coulter, Ambrose Rogers and McComiskey to lead a shell-shocked Kerry side by 1-03 to no score after just 10 minutes.

Bryan Sheehan eventually got Kerry's first score in the 14th minute, and they steadied the ship, winning breaking ball around midfield to set up three further scoring chances which Colm Cooper executed.

And they had the ball in the net in the 23rd minute when Cooper and Donnacha Walsh combined to send Killian Young in to blast past Brendan McVeigh. Walsh, however, was penalised by referee Joe McQuillan for an illegal hand-pass.

Down went 17 minutes without scoring, but with Clarke orchestrating things, they played their way back into the game and banged over four points, two each from Clarke and Poland.

And former Aussie Rules star Clarke inspired his colleagues further by drifting back to make a superb interception as Walsh tried to release Cooper.

Down led by 1-07 to 0-04 at the break. Kieran Donaghy moved to midfield for the second half with Declan O'Sullivan, but Down pair

Ronan Murtagh of Down with Anthony Maher of Kerry

Ambrose Rogers and Kalum King continued to dominate in that sector.

Cooper and Sheehan pulled back points for Kerry as they cut the deficit to four, and they had a let-off when Down had a McComiskey goal disallowed.

The Kingdom were reduced to 14 men in the 45th minute when Donnacha Walsh picked up a second yellow card, but nevertheless they crafted a couple of goal chances, only to see Brendan McVeigh pull off two stunning saves from Donaghy.

Down grew in confidence once more, and a volley of superb points from Benny Coulter and Ronan Murtagh saw them kill the game off.

Kerry pulled back a late goal when David Moran netted a penalty after Donaghy had been fouled. Scant consolation for a side unaccustomed to exiting the championship before the third Sunday in September.

DOWN: B McVeigh; D McCartan, D Gordon, D Rafferty; D Rooney, K McKernan, C Garvey; A Rogers (0-01), K King; D Hughes, M Poland (1-02), P McComiskey (0-03); B Coulter (0-03), J Clarke, M Clarke (0-04)
Subs: C Maginn (0-01) for J Clarke; R Murtagh (0-01) for P McComiskey; P Fitzpatrick (0-01) for K King; R Sexton for M Poland

KERRY: B Kealy; M Ó Sé, T Griffin, T O'Sullivan; A O'Mahony, M McCarthy, K Young; S Scanlon, M Quirke; Darran O'Sullivan, Declan O'Sullivan, D Walsh; C Cooper, (0-07) K Donaghy, B Sheehan (0-03)
Subs: D Moran (1-00) for M Quirke; B J Keane for S Scanlon; K O'Leary for D O'Sullivan; D Bohane for K Young; A Maher for B Sheehan

REFEREE: J McQuillan (Cavan)

Quarter-Final

DUBLIN	1-15	0-13	TYRONE

31 July 2010

Dublin stunned Ulster champions Tyrone by 1-15 to 0-13 to reach the All-Ireland Football Championship semi-finals.

Bernard Brogan's nine-point haul and an Eoghan O'Gara goal saw off Tyrone in a gripping encounter.

It was Tyrone who led narrowly at half-time, but the Dubs finally got over the psychological barrier, and hit form in the second half.

Having lost heavily to Kerry and Tyrone at the quarter-final stage in the past two seasons, Dublin, under Pat Gilroy, have succeeded in becoming sufficiently competitive at the business end of the championship.

It was a compelling game that hung in the balance until five minutes from the end, when O'Gara grabbed the only goal of the game.

Dublin got off to a flying start, with Bernard Brogan converting two frees, before Bryan Cullen made it 0-03 to no score.

And they crafted a goal chance when they broke from defence, but Eoghan O'Gara's pass was just too heavy for Brogan.

The Dubs succeeded in closing down their opponents virtually every time they got some attacking momentum going, and Tyrone managed just one point in the opening 15 minutes, a Martin Penrose free.

Penrose, with a superb long-range effort, reduced the deficit, but with full-back Rory O'Carroll winning his personal battle with Sean Cavanagh, the Dubs looked safe and confident at the back.

And they restored their three-point cushion when goalkeeper Stephen Cluxton stepped up to send a '45' sailing between the posts.

Brogan and Penrose swapped frees, after tempers had flared briefly at the canal end.

Tyrone finally began to play with some fluidity late in the half, when Penrose and Owen Mulligan posted scores to narrow the gap.

Sean Cavanagh's move from the inside line to take up a deeper role had a positive effect for the Ulster men.

He won the frees which Penrose and Mulligan converted as the Red Hands went in front for the first time through wing-back Philip Jordan.

A long-range point from corner-back Philip McMahon brought the Dubs level again, but Tyrone missed a glorious goal chance when Penrose was sent clear by Brian McGuigan, only to send his shot crashing against the crossbar. A Penrose free sent Tyrone in at the break with a narrow 0-08 to 0-07 lead.

Jordan's second point, and another from the in-form Mulligan stretched the Tyrone lead, but a cameo from the Brogans saw them hit two delightful scores from play to tie it up at 0-10 each on 46 minutes.

Bernard Brogan was in scoring form and he launched three wonderful points from play to put his side in the driving seat.

Tyrone were labouring, but pegged back scores through Brian McGuigan and Penrose to stay in touch.

However, they kicked a succession of wides during a period of dominance, and were punished when full-forward O'Gara banged in the decisive goal after a Paul Flynn effort had come back off a post.

DUBLIN: S Cluxton (0-01); M Fitzsimons, R O'Carroll, P McMahon (0-01); K Nolan, G Brennan, B Cahill; M D MacAuley (0-01), R McConnell; B Cullen (0-01), A Brogan (0-01), N Corkery; D Henry, E O'Gara (1-00), B Brogan (0-09). **Subs:** C O'Sullivan for B Cahill; P Flynn for D Henry; E Fennell for N Corkery; C Keaney (0-01) for A Brogan; A Brogan for B Cullen

TYRONE: P McConnell; C McCarron, Justin McMahon, R McMenamin; D Harte, C Gormley, P Jordan (0-02); C Cavanagh, K Hughes; B Dooher, B McGuigan (0-01), Joe McMahon; M Penrose (0-05), S Cavanagh, O Mulligan (0-05). **Subs:** D Carlin for C McCarron; S O'Neill for D Harte; E McGinley for K Hughes; P Harte for M Penrose

REFEREE: D Coldrick (Meath)

Dublin's Eoghan O'Gara and
Joe McMahon of Tyrone

MICHAEL LYSTER

I still remember getting the phone call. I was working in radio sport when one of the producers of the *Sunday Sport Scene* television programme rang over to see would I be interested in doing some television work (at that time the television and radio sports departments were in different parts of the RTÉ complex).

An opportunity to work on television was something I thought might come somewhere down the line so I said: 'Sure, when were you thinking about?'

'How about next Sunday?' he said.

You would think that my first reaction would be 'great, a breakthrough into the world of the small screen – fame and fortune to follow!'

In fact my first reaction was far more practical – I just wondered if I had a clean shirt to wear. Being a single man at the time and living in digs, sweaters and T-shirts were just fine for presenting sports bulletins on radio; shirts and ties were for businessmen working in offices.

Anyway, I reckoned I could source a clean shirt somewhere and so accepted the offer to make my television debut on 22 January 1984. The main presenter of *Sunday Sport Scene* was Fred Cogley but the programme producers had decided to introduce a second presenter to handle some of the other sports stories of the day.

So, there I was on Sunday night at 10.30pm sitting in Studio 6 with Fred Cogley, caked in make-up and wondering what I was doing there. Fred was being very supportive but there were fellows making strange signals at me in some kind of secret code and I had no clue what it all meant. Any kind of training was obviously an optional extra that no-one was bothered with.

The difference between television and radio work is like chalk and cheese. Radio is very much a one-on-one experience, you and the microphone, and is best suited to people with a very strong personality who can make that connection with an audience who can't see them.

Television is all about camera angles and floor managers, stage managers, graphics, leading into things and out of things and 'For God's sake camera

three, hold your shot steady!' You can hear half a dozen different conversations in your ear-piece and you don't know whether you should try to listen to them all or try and ignore them all and just carry on.

In any event that first night must have gone okay because I was asked back for the duration of the series and I gradually began to get the hang of this television stuff. I didn't realise at the time that there was another reason why I had been asked to try out as a second presenter – and it also explained the short notice of it all. Television sport was looking for a new presenter for its summer GAA championship coverage on *The Sunday Game* and thought that I might be worth a look.

And so it came to pass that, in the spring of 1984, I was offered the presenter's chair for *The Sunday Game* and, without realising it at the time, had my career mapped out for me for the next twenty-five years – and, thankfully, counting!

When I sat down in studio that night on 6 May I was aware of how popular *The Sunday Game* was with viewers, but I had no idea how it was going to impact on my life. I wasn't the first presenter of the programme; Mick Dunne, Jim Carney and Seán Óg Ó Ceallacháin had been there before me. But for the next quarter of a century I was to be strapped into the cockpit and shot out onto the airwaves holding the controls of RTÉ's most consistently popular television sports programme.

Indeed, 1984 was to be an amazing year to take over as the programme's presenter. This was the Centenary Year of the GAA and, as part of the commemorations we had the Centenary Cup competitions to start off the summer. Cork won the hurling but, more significantly, Meath won the football with a fledgling Sean Boylan as manager – little did we know the impact Sean and Meath would have on football in the coming years.

Later that summer the All-Ireland hurling final was staged in Thurles, Cork beating Offaly in the final. RTÉ Sport decamped to 'The Home of Hurling' for the weekend and let's just say we engaged fully with the heady atmosphere of the occasion.

In the early days of *The Sunday Game* I had the fantastic experience of travelling around Ireland by helicopter. In those days there were no live matches and no satellite links so the tapes had to be brought back physically to RTÉ. If the venue was too long a drive, Killarney, Castlebar, Clones etc. then a helicopter was used and if the chopper was going to the match it made sense that myself and the analysts would go with it.

So, there we'd be, myself and Eamon Cregan or Enda Colleran or whoever it would be, descending on the Gaelic Grounds or Páirc Uí Chaoimh on big match days and stepping out of our chopper amidst the hoards of fans – we had it all sussed pre-Celtic Tiger!

I fell in love with helicopter flying and even had a go at flying lessons myself. If you've never flown in a chopper then you should mark it down as one of those things to do before you get too old. I came to despise whoever introduced satellite links into the national broadcaster.

Mind you, it wasn't all roses in the garden and in my first year on the programme I also learned the downside of getting a break on television and of stretching yourself too far. Apart from presenting *The Sunday Game* we also had a special *Monday Game* series to reflect on the centenary of the GAA. It was an excellent series wonderfully put together by our editor Maurice Reidy, who had dug out a lot of rare and unseen footage of games with football and hurling heroes from an age past.

The only problem with all this was that the powers that were in radio sport at the time didn't want me doing any of this television work in the first case. This went back to a long-standing conflict between the two sections, where radio objected to television sport coming in and, as they saw it, poaching its presenters.

It was agreed to release me for television work provided I carried out all my radio commitments as well. This meant that, on Sundays and Mondays I worked with television sport and from Tuesdays to Friday with radio sport. That didn't leave a lot of time for a social life, but I was still single at the time and I realised I was getting an opportunity I couldn't pass up.

Later that summer I got another TV opportunity – and a further complication in the radio/television dual life. 1984 was an Olympic year, Los Angeles, and as part of RTÉ's coverage the station decided to dip its toe into the water of breakfast television, which was just taking off in Britain. The programme was *Daybreak LA* and it was presented by myself and Moya Doherty (later of Riverdance fame) with reports from LA by the late, great, Vincent Hanley. It should have been a wonderful experience; it was a new venture and therefore very exciting and Moya, whom I knew from radio, was very talented and so easy to work with.

But even before the Olympics started I was in meltdown. A few days before our first morning broadcast I went for a walk on Killiney beach to clear my head but collapsed and had to be taken to a doctor. Apart from medication his other prognosis was 'a month off work and then we'll see how you are'.

My response was; No can do, doc. Opportunity knocks and I need to be in front of a television camera 8am Monday morning!

Victor, who became our family doctor for many years afterwards, understood, so for the duration of the coverage I reckon I was on more prescribed stuff than all the Olympic athletes put together (and given that it was LA '84 that's really saying something!). I never did get that month off!

In 1985 I knew I couldn't do it all again and so began the process of my release from radio duties to concentrate fully on television work and an association with a programme that has become, in many ways, almost like another family member. I know that, at the time, RTÉ brought me in as the 'new face' of its gaelic games coverage. It's a bit strange but now I am very happy to be the 'older face' of *The Sunday Game* (new faces form an orderly queue – I'm not done yet).

Over the years *The Sunday Game* has adapted to reflect the changing audience and the different demands. But the truth is, the core values of the programme remain the same; to cover the big matches the best we can and to give the viewer, hopefully, some insightful and entertaining analysis from our regular panellists – even if they do cause some people mild apoplexy at times.

It's been an amazing journey; I didn't know where it was heading all those years ago and perhaps I still don't. But at least I know I should have a clean shirt every weekend!

ANTRIM 2-18 3-12 CARLOW

3 July 2010

Antrim scored three late points as they came from behind to beat a gallant Carlow by 2-18 to 3-12 in their All-Ireland Senior Hurling Championship qualifier at Casement Park.

The Ulster champions' crucial scores came from Karl Stewart, Karl McKeegan and substitute Eddie McCloskey in this hard-fought game.

Craig Doyle's two-goal tally had Carlow dreaming of a famous Belfast win as early as half-time when they led by 2-06 to 0-07.

Kevin Ryan's charges got the better of neighbours Laois the previous weekend and travelled with renewed confidence to a venue where they were edged out on a 1-11 to 2-07 scoreline in the National League in February.

Antrim also came into this clash on a high, following their easy 4-22 to 1-12 dismissal of Down in the Ulster Hurling Championship final.

The early exchanges went the Barrowsiders'

way, with wing-forward Doyle hitting the net with his second attempt on goal after Antrim failed to clear their defensive lines.

Antrim's response was swift as McKeegan, Stewart and Shane McNaughton cracked over points, however Doyle's second goal gave Carlow a huge boost, facing into a stiffening breeze. Free-taker Paudie Kehoe, Mark Brennan and Doyle landed some well-taken points to give Carlow a 2-06 to 0-03 lead.

Dinny Cahill's charges were living off scraps of possession and Brennan, who was deployed in midfield, was winning plenty of puck-outs for the Leinster men. Cahill reacted by introducing Simon McCrory and dropping PJ O'Connell back into midfield, and the switches had the desired effect.

Antrim's Liam Watson and Carlow's Des Shaw

Liam Watson, going for goal, squeezed a shot over the crossbar for Antrim's first score in 15 minutes, and the home side enjoyed their best spell coming up to half-time as three further points followed.

Neil McManus put his name to all three points. The Cushendall clubman also went close to testing Carlow goalkeeper Frank Foley, only to be dispossessed at the last second and he had an earlier effort ruled out for a square ball.

While Carlow's defending had been particularly effective during the opening 35 minutes, Antrim did hit eight wides and the worry for Ryan was how would his side cope if the Saffrons went on a scoring run?

Again though, Carlow made a whirlwind start on the resumption. After initial points from McManus and Shane McNaughton, Kehoe rasped home a third goal to end a scoreless run for Carlow which stretched back to the 26th minute.

A real turning point arrived for Antrim just three minutes later when they won a penalty which Watson powered to the net, putting three points between the sides at 3-06 to 1-09. Kehoe steadied Carlow with a free, before McKeegan blazed over the bar when a goal looked on.

Defender Richard Coady got forward to tee up a lovely point from Doyle. Antrim's long ball tactic paid off when Ciaran Herron's drive was won by McManus, who set up corner-forward O'Connell to ripple the net from close range.

Doyle, comfortably Carlow's best forward in open play, jinked his way through to score from 35 metres and keep the underdogs on course at 3-09 to 2-10. Points from Shane McNaughton and McManus brought the Saffrons level before Kehoe and John Rogers replied to set up a nail-biting final ten minutes.

Antrim's Sean Delargy and Carlow's Craig Doyle

McCrory pointed to put one between them at 3-11 to 2-13 and Antrim were back on terms when McKeegan crashed a shot over off the woodwork. The reliable Kehoe provided Carlow's response, but Antrim dominated the final five minutes.

McCrory, a central figure in Antrim's comeback, laid off for McKeegan to slot over the leveller in the 69th minute (2-15 to 3-12). Carlow were suddenly struggling for possession and some neat build-up play, again involving McCloskey, allowed Stewart to point off his left.

Carlow's brave bid wilted as the busy McCloskey helped himself to a deserved point and that was enough to see Antrim hold out for a character-building victory.

ANTRIM: C O'Connell; K McGourty, C Donnelly, S Delargy; P Shiels, J Campbell, C Herron; S McNaughton (0-03), K Stewart (0-03); C McFall, N McManus (0-05), T McCann; PJ O'Connell (1-00), L Watson (1-01), K McKeegan (0-04) **Subs:** S McCrory (0-01) for C McFall; B McFall for McCann; E McCloskey (0-01) for O'Connell

CARLOW: F Foley; A Corcoran, S Kavanagh, D Shaw; E Coady, E Nolan, R Coady; J Hickey, D Byrne; C Doyle (2-03), M Brennan (0-01), HP O'Byrne (0-01); A Gaule, D Murphy, P Kehoe (1-06) **Subs:** J Rogers (0-01) for Hickey; R Foley for Murphy; E Byrne for E Coady; A McDonald for D Byrne

REFEREE: A Stapleton (Laois)

TIPPERARY 3-24 0-19 WEXFORD

3 July 2010

Wexford's championship challenge petered out at Semple Stadium as hosts Tipperary comfortably took a 3-24 to 0-19 win in a one-sided All-Ireland Senior Hurling Championship phase 1 qualifier.

Tipperary coasted into a 0-15 to 0-07 half-time lead and added second half goals from Lar Corbett and substitute Darragh Egan to put the result beyond any doubt.

The sides' first championship meeting since Wexford's 2007 All-Ireland quarter-final triumph began with an off-the-ball skirmish involving Tipperary full-back Declan Fanning and Wexford full-forward Stephen Banville.

Blood was seen coming from Fanning's ear after his helmet was ripped off him, with Banville also emerging from the tussle without his headgear. Referee James McGrath brandished a yellow card to both, and the Tipp defender had to be replaced by Paul Curran.

The opening ten minutes were evenly contested before Liam Sheedy's men added some cushion to their lead, without hitting third gear. Corbett pointed the dethroned Munster champions ahead in the first minute, quickly followed by wing-back David Young's first score at this level.

Good work by Eoin Quigley preceded Colm Farrell's opener for Wexford and as Tipperary hit their stride, an athletic catch and point on the turn from Noel McGrath took their tally to 0-03. The Premier County were finding scores easier to come by and in between pointed efforts from Banville and Harry Kehoe, Corbett, Gearóid Ryan and Young fired over at the other end.

An arcing run from Shane McGrath ended with a rising shot which Wexford goalkeeper Noel Carton deflected out over the line. Tipp captain Eoin Kelly sent the resulting '65' over the bar to give his side a three-point lead.

Wexford then failed to clear their lines, allowing Noel McGrath to swoop on the ball and score a fine point on the run. Soon after Tipperary's defence was under threat when Rory Jacob darted around Curran and lashed a one-handed shot towards goal. Net minder Brendan Cummins stood up well to force it wide, and Peter Atkinson converted the '65' for Wexford's fifth point of the game..

Tipperary opened up a six-point gap as Seamus Callanan, Kelly and Corbett collected successive points. Wexford responded through Colm Farrell and Tomás Mahon, but they could not prevent Kelly, Patrick Maher and Young from bolstering the home side's lead to eight points at half-time.

The game was effectively over as a contest just three minutes into the second half. Kelly grabbed a quick brace of points from play before Corbett cracked home his two goals in the space of one minute.

The pacey full-forward flicked home his first after taking a hand-pass from Noel McGrath

Gearóid Ryan of Tipperary with Darren Stamp and Colm Farrell of Wexford

Darragh Egan of Tipp scores his side's third goal

and riding two challenges. Moments later he latched onto a through ball to blast home his second with an angled drive to the roof of the net.

Points from Atkinson and the impressive Harry Kehoe reduced the arrears to 2-17 to 0-09 but Wexford continued to struggle with Tipperary's dominance for the remainder of the game.

The Jacob brothers, Rory and substitute Michael, caused some problems for Cummins and his defenders however the Model men could not get the goals they craved.

Kelly took his haul to 0-08 before being called ashore twelve minutes from the end, and Tomás Waters was fortunate to get away with a stamp on a prone Conor O'Mahony as frustration got the better of him. O'Mahony however, picked up a yellow card for his retaliation.

Wexford goalkeeper Noel Carton reacted smartly to deny Patrick Maher as he raced through unchallenged and a terrific catch and point from Ryan, following Brendan Maher's diagonal delivery, made it 2-20 to 0-10.

Patrick Maher notched his second point and Ryan added his third as Tipp edged towards the 30-point mark. Wexford put in a final spurt, during which Mahon, Rory Jacob, Farrell and substitute Jim Berry landed points, as Tipp switched off slightly.

Ryan registered his fourth point before the winners mustered their final goal in the 67th minute. Wexford were caught for numbers through the middle and although Noel McGrath's kicked effort bounced back off the bar, substitute Egan finished clinically to the net after a great piece of first time control.

TIPPERARY: B Cummins; M Cahill, D Fanning, C O'Brien; D Young (0-03), C O'Mahony, Padraic Maher; B Maher, S McGrath; G Ryan (0-04), S Callanan (0-01), Patrick Maher (0-02); N McGrath (0-03), L Corbett (2-03), E Kelly (0-08)
Subs: J O'Brien for Callanan; S Hennessy for E Kelly; D Egan for S McGrath; S Maher for B Maher; M Heffernan for Ryan.

WEXFORD: N Carton; P Roche, K Rossiter, C Kenny; R Kehoe, D Stamp (0-01), D Redmond; C Farrell (0-03), H Kehoe (0-03); P Atkinson (0-02), T Waters, E Quigley; R Jacob (0-03), S Banville (0-02), T Mahon (0-02)
Subs: L Prendergast for Quigley; J Berry (0-03) for Atkinson; M Jacob for Banville; S Banville for Waters; T Dwyer for Redmond; B Kenny for Roche

REFEREE: J McGrath (Westmeath)

Final

| KILKENNY | 1-19 | 1-12 | GALWAY |

4 July 2010

Kilkenny's dominance of Leinster hurling continued at Croke Park this afternoon as they pulled clear of first-time finalists Galway during a disappointingly one-sided second half.

The Tribesmen played well below par as the Cats won a record sixth successive Leinster Senior Hurling Championship title, with top scorer Henry Shefflin contributing 1-07.

Shefflin and Damien Hayes traded goals as Kilkenny claimed a 1-08 to 1-05 half-time lead, in front of 31,376 spectators.

A swirling wind played havoc with both sides' attacking play, eventual winners Kilkenny hitting an uncharacteristic 17 wides.

But, most tellingly, Galway got their tactics badly wrong, withdrawing top scorer Damien Hayes to midfield and opting to play long balls in, which were meat and drink to the Kilkenny backs.

Kilkenny half-backs Tommy Walsh, JJ Delaney and first-half substitute John Tennyson mopped up a huge amount of possession and the westerners' main attacking threat, Joe Canning, was isolated for most of the opening hour.

Canning hit two late points, including a trademark sideline cut, but the damage had been done by that stage.

Galway hit the front after just 12 seconds, Aonghus Callanan playing the ball through for Aidan Harte to slot over from the right wing.

Wides from Michael Fennelly and Shefflin got Kilkenny off to an inauspicious start.

Their first threat on goal came when Eoin Larkin flicked the ball around advancing Galway goalkeeper Colm Callanan, but it beat everyone, including the lurking Martin Comerford to harmlessly cross the end line.

A brace of frees from Shefflin got Kilkenny off the mark and the championship's record scorer teed up TJ Reid for a third, from play.

It was a cagey opening from both sides, pockmarked by wides at either end. Kilkenny goalkeeper PJ Ryan was not his usual reliable self, failing to clear his lines, when Harte and Hayes came sniffing for goal and causing concern in the Kilkenny square.

Kilkenny feed off early goals and one duly arrived in the 13th minute.

Shefflin drifted menacingly in behind the corner-back on the left, getting onto a breaking ball to stick it into the bottom right corner of the net, giving Callanan little chance.

The Cats sandwiched a Ger Farragher free with two scores from play from Michael Rice, the second after a quickly won puck-out.

Crucially, Galway kept in touch through a 19th minute goal from Damien Hayes. Noel Hickey and Ryan failed to clear a Farragher delivery, it diverted through the goalkeeper's legs and Hayes scrambled home.

The pace of the match quickened as Eddie Brennan pointed from near the sideline and Iarla Tannian responded for Galway to make it 1-06 to 1-03. Shefflin and Farragher

Kilkenny's Martin Comerford

136

exchanged points from placed balls before Richie Power nabbed another point from play to stretch Kilkenny's lead to four points.

General play was lacklustre and the intensity was non existent, leaving little for the supporters to get their teeth into.

Galway closed out the first half's scoring, Joe Canning winning a right-sided free which Farragher converted for a 1-08 to 1-05 scoreline.

John McIntyre's charges were very much still in the running at this stage, as Farragher's fourth free cancelled out a Shefflin opener at the start of the second half.

But Galway's first Leinster final appearance went into freefall thereafter, Kilkenny scored seven unanswered points before substitute Kevin Hynes registered the Tribesmen's third point from play, in the 58th minute.

The contest went flat as Shefflin, TJ Reid, Power and substitutes Richie Hogan and Aidan Fogarty sent a succession of scores over Callanan's crossbar.

Both sides wides' tally hit double figures, and Galway tired somewhat, looking lethargic after two hard-fought games against Offaly.

As the league champions struggled to win their own puck-outs, Kilkenny's midfield duo of Rice and Fennelly combined well with their all-conquering half-backs to control that area of the park.

The Cats, showed signs of their attacking class as young substitute Hogan danced away from Galway captain Shane Kavanagh to score a skilful point soon after his introduction. Rice's drilled pass set up another new man in, Fogarty, for a point and a comfortable lead at 1-14 to 1-06.

Slack marking allowed Shefflin to play a free short to Reid who picked off his third point from play. Wides from Hayes and substitute Eoin Lynch did little for Galway's dwindling confidence.

John Dalton of Kilkenny with Iarla Tannian of Galway

A soccer-style dribble from Rice, after he lost his stick, showed Kilkenny's ease on the ball as they continued to punish their rivals.

Hayes' first point was quickly cancelled out by a third from Power, Fogarty doing the hard graft to create the score for the full-forward.

The remaining minutes saw the pace slacken as the result became painfully obvious for the first-time finalists.

Credit to Galway, they kept hunting for scores but it was goals they needed and subsequent points from Lynch, after a delightful flick from Joe Canning, substitute Cyril Donnellan and Canning himself mattered little in the end.

Kilkenny were operating in a low gear and playing well within themselves; they could afford to. Larkin and Shefflin closed out the champions' scoring and they cruised into the All-Ireland semi-finals with a galling degree of comfort.

KILKENNY: PJ Ryan; J Dalton, N Hickey, J Tyrrell; T Walsh, B Hogan, JJ Delaney; M Rice (0-02), M Fennelly; TJ Reid (0-03), E Brennan (0-01), E Larkin (0-01); M Comerford, R Power (0-03), H Shefflin (1-07)
Subs: J Tennyson for B Hogan; A Fogarty (0-01) for Comerford; R Hogan (0-01) for Brennan; J Mulhall for Power.

GALWAY: C Callanan; D Joyce, S Kavanagh, O Canning; D Barry, T Óg Regan, D Collins; G Farragher (0-04), A Cullinane; A Callanan, A Harte (0-01), A Smith; D Hayes (1-01), J Canning (0-02), I Tannian (0-01)
Subs: E Lynch (0-01) for Cullinane; C Donnellan (0-01) for Callanan; K Hynes (0-01) for Farragher; J Gantley for Smith

REFEREE: M Wadding (Waterford)

Joe Canning of Galway
with Noel Hickey of
Kilkenny

Henry Shefflin of
Kilkenny with Ollie
Canning and Damien
Joyce of Galway

Kilkenny's Noel Hickey with Damien Hayes of Galway

DUBLIN 2-22 0-15 CLARE
10 July 2010

All-Star midfielder Alan McCrabbe struck eight points as Dublin accounted for Clare's young guns at a rain-soaked Croke Park.

McCrabbe's haul included two superb sideline cuts, but the turning point was a speculative 45th-minute goal from Dublin's Peter Kelly whose long delivery in was missed by goalkeeper Donal Tuohy.

The Clare net minder's mistake saw the Dubs move back into a four-point lead at 1-14 to 0-13 and they never looked back; a second goal from substitute Simon Lambert put the seal on the Metropolitans' first ever All-Ireland Senior Hurling Championship qualifier win.

Having opened up a 0-14 to 0-07 lead at half-time, Clare came hard at Anthony Daly's men with a rousing display in the early part of the second half. Points from Colin Ryan, Nicky O'Connell, Darach Honan and Fergal Lynch whittled the gap down to the minimum and it was anyone's game.

Unfortunately for Clare, Tuohy's lapse allowed Dublin to regain control and with David O'Callaghan and McCrabbe being afforded too much space, the contest was over with that second goal in the 66th minute.

Up to the 18th minute, the sides seemed evenly matched. Locked level at 0-04 apiece, Dublin had opening points from McCrabbe, O'Callaghan and Stephen Hiney, while Clare's scores arrived from the hurleys of John Conlon, Fergal Lynch, Colin Ryan and Sean Collins.

Clare were struggling to garner possession from puck-outs, Joey Boland claiming a couple of notable balls for Dublin, and Declan O'Dwyer also impressed when setting up team captain Hiney's point on the quarter-hour.

Dublin went on to dominate the remainder of the first half, scoring nine points in succession before Clare got a chance to reply.

McCrabbe started the run, taking a pass from the prominent Liam Rushe, and O'Dwyer, operating in a deeper role, added another for a 0-06 to 0-04 lead.

The best of the lot was wing-forward Peter Kelly's inspirational catch and point from 100 yards out. With Pat Vaughan's presence clearly missed, the Clare backs struggled to keep tabs on O'Callaghan and Rushe and scores followed from O'Callaghan, Shane Durkin and McCrabbe. 'Dotsy' had six on the board by half-time.

O'Callaghan's sixth was sandwiched by late Clare scores from John Conlon, who snaffled his side's first point in 16 minutes, substitute Nicky O'Connell and Jonathan Clancy.

Seven points adrift at half-time, Clare had a mountain to climb but credit to the younger players, including eight from last year's All-Ireland Under-21 winning side, they mustered a terrific response.

Colin Ryan kicked things off with a free and points from play from O'Connell and Honan, who broke onto a loose ball to bat over off his left, confirmed Clare's improvement. They were winning more puck-outs and a second Fergal Lynch point had the Dubs' lead down to three.

Dublin goalkeeper Gary Maguire stood firm to deflect a rasping shot from Darach Honan out for a '65' which Ryan duly pointed. Centre-forward Conlon tagged on his third point to increase the pressure on Daly's side at 0-14 to 0-13.

But when Touhy misjudged the flight of Kelly's delivery in towards the Clare square and the ball cleared everyone to nestle in the back of the net, Dublin got back in the groove. McCrabbe showed his class with a textbook sideline cut from the right and followed up with his sixth point of the encounter.

When Maurice O'Brien finished a good run with a point, Dublin's seven-point advantage had been restored. Lambert and McCrabbe, with his second sideline cut, cancelled out a Clancy effort for Clare. O'Callaghan's impish run and batted pass set up Lambert for a powerful 66th minute shot to the net and it was a case of game over.

Rushe and Brendan Bugler added their names to the scoresheet before Maguire bravely stooped low to save a stinging goal-bound shot from Clancy. Dublin had the final say in injury-time, as McCrabbe pulled first time on a breaking ball to point from play and Hiney added another in less spectacular fashion.

The end of summer hurling for this young Clare side, but one Banner man was happy leaving head quarters as his charges advanced with confidence to a phase 3 meeting with Antrim.

DUBLIN: G Maguire; N Corcoran, T Brady, O Gough; S Hiney (0-02), J Boland, M O'Brien (0-01); J McCaffrey, S Durkin (0-01); P Kelly (1-01), L Rushe (0-01), A McCrabbe (0-08); P Carton, D O'Dwyer (0-01), D O'Callaghan (0-06)
Subs: L Ryan for O'Dwyer; S Lambert (1-01) for Durkin; M Carton for P Carton; K Flynn for Rushe; S Ryan for O'Callaghan

CLARE: D Tuohy; P Vaughan, C Dillon, C Cooney; B Bugler (0-01), D McMahon, P Donnellan; B O'Connell, D O'Donovan; S Collins (0-01), J Conlon (0-3), J Clancy (0-02); F Lynch (0-02), D Honan (0-01), C Ryan (0-3)
Subs: N O'Connell (0-02) for Vaughan; A Markham for Collins; G Quinn for Donnellan; D Barrett for Ryan

REFEREE: J Sexton (Cork)

Fergal Lynch of Clare with Joey Boland of Dublin

OFFALY	1-19	1-13	LIMERICK

10 July 2010

Four unanswered points in the closing seven minutes gave Offaly victory against Limerick and a shot at Tipperary in phase 3 of the Senior Hurling Championship qualifiers.

Offaly's Shane Dooley and Limerick goalkeeper Tadhg Flynn

For long stretches of this Tullamore clash Offaly looked to be on course for the win. However, they were met with a late onslaught from Justin McCarthy's young Limerick side who bagged 1-02 inside a five-minute spell cutting the deficit to two points with just eight minutes remaining.

But closing scores from Cathal Parlon, Shane Dooley and Joe Bergin dashed any hopes of a major championship upset at O'Connor Park.

Offaly led by 1-08 to 0-07 at half-time, thanks to a 12th-minute Derek Molloy goal, with Thomas O'Brien and James V O'Brien keeping Limerick in touch.

Limerick had gained the early initiative with fine points by the aforementioned O'Briens, getting the underdogs off to a solid start.

Both sides were producing fast flowing hurling despite the heavy underfoot conditions. Offaly responded to the visitors' early burst with scores from Dooley and Parlon to tie the contest at 0-02 apiece

Indeed, the hosts were unlucky not to snatch a fifth-minute goal, but Limerick keeper Tadhg

Flynn pulled off a fine save from a Joe Bergin shot.

Offaly did bulge the net, seven minutes later, when Bergin's initial shot was blocked by Limerick defender Kieran O'Rourke, and Molloy pounced on the resulting break to slot to the net from 13 metres out.

Offaly strung together some fine scores from play from Parlon, Molloy and Brendan Murphy to claim a 1-08 to 0-05 lead by the 32nd minute.

Thomas O'Brien bagged his fifth point inside two minutes of the restart, but Offaly were beginning to win the breaking ball at midfield, and capitalised with Brian Carroll hitting two points from play to push 1-10 to 0-08 ahead in the 40th minute.

Thomas O'Brien and substitute Cathal Mullane cut the deficit to a goal with 12 minutes remaining, but Offaly hit back with four unanswered points, seemingly doing just enough to keep ahead.

As the showers turned to glorious sunshine, the game suddenly upped in intensity, with points from Nicky Quaid and substitute Peter Russell either side of Thomas O'Brien's goal. The midfielder did well to create enough space for himself to fashion a shot beyond the reach of goalkeeper James Dempsey. There was now just two points in it with eight minutes remaining.

But Offaly dug deep with Parlon, Dooley and Joe Bergin pointing them home and into phase 3 of the qualifiers.

OFFALY: J Dempsey; D Franks, P Cleary, J Rigney; D Kenny, R Hanniffy, D Morkan; D Hayden, B Murphy (0-02); B Carroll (0-03), J Brady (0-01), D Molloy (1-02); C Parlon (0-05), J Bergin (0-01), S Dooley (0-05)
Subs: K Brady for Hayden; G Healion for Molloy

LIMERICK: T Flynn; S O'Neill, C Hayes, K O'Rourke; L O'Dwyer, B O'Sullivan, P Browne; T O'Brien (1-07), D Moore; J O'Brien, JV O'Brien (0-02), N Quaid (0-01); R McKeogh, A Owens, G Mulcahy (0-01)
Subs: C Mullane (0-01) for Moore; A Brennan for J O'Brien; M Noonan for McKeogh; P Russell (0-01) for Owens

REFEREE: J Owens (Wexford)

Final

WATERFORD	2-15	2-15	CORK

11 July 2010

Waterford's evergreen defender Tony Browne tucked away an injury-time goal to send this closely fought Munster Senior Hurling Championship final to a replay.

Trailing by 2-15 to 1-15 in the fourth minute of injury-time, the Deise's hopes hinged on a close range free from Eoin Kelly. His driven shot was stopped on the line by Cork goalkeeper Donal Óg Cusack and his defenders, but the ball rebounded out for the onrushing Browne to thread it home through a crowded square.

Cork had time to respond and substitute Michael Cussen, one of their best players in the second half, will be kicking himself that he sent a last-gasp shot to the right and wide.

Kelly and John Mullane had done most of the damage – nudging Waterford into a 0-07 to 0-06 half-time lead – and the pair shared out the first three points on the resumption,

with Cork struggling to recapture the form that saw them oust last year's champions Tipperary.

The Rebels' patience paid off when they hit two hugely inspirational goals through Aisake Ó hAilpín and Ben O'Connor to lead by 2-12 to 0-13, and suddenly it was Waterford's turn to look out of sorts.

In front of a 35,375-strong crowd, Davy Fitzgerald's men met Cork's challenge head on and their gutsy response including a cracking goal from top scorer Kelly and the late leveller from Browne, who turned 37 at the start of July.

In a feisty and fiery opening, a terrific catch and burst forward from Cork full-back Eoin Cadogan set the tone, and Shane

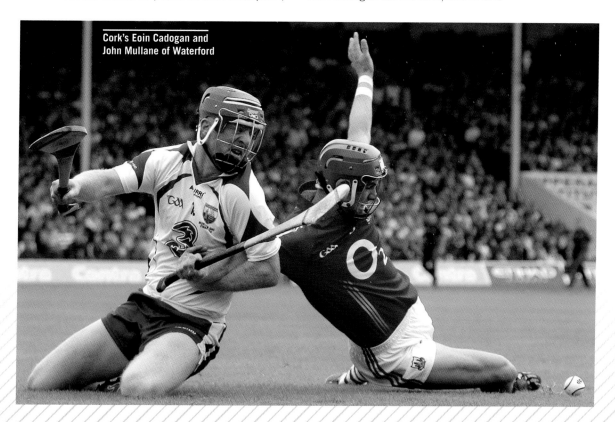

Cork's Eoin Cadogan and John Mullane of Waterford

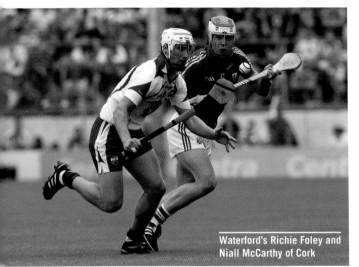

Waterford's Richie Foley and Niall McCarthy of Cork

O'Sullivan gave Waterford an early advantage by pointing to punish Sean Óg Ó hAilpín for a misplaced pass.

Cadogan had Mullane for company as the Deise danger man slotted in at full-forward, but the Cork attack got up to speed with Ben O'Connor teeing up Naughton for his side's opener. The pacey midfielder ran through the middle for a second point in the fourth minute.

Michael 'Brick' Walsh and Browne were involved in the build-up to Mullane's first point and after a tremendous sideline cut from Shane O'Sullivan, Mullane arced over a superb second from close to the left sideline for a 0-04 to 0-02 Deise lead.

Ben O'Connor, who failed to show his usual accuracy from placed balls, knocked over a quick brace to get Cork back on terms by the quarter hour mark, as scores were becoming increasingly hard to come by in such a tense encounter.

Cork's full-forward line of team captain Kieran Murphy, Aisake Ó hAilpín and Patrick Horgan were seeing very little ball and that had as much to do with their team-mates' failure to create an adequate supply, as Waterford's committed defending.

The red-helmeted Mullane was the pick of the bunch at the other end. He blazed a trail towards the Cork goal in the 17th minute,

but Stephen Molumphy's pass had forced him wide and his tame shot failed to trouble Cusack.

Kelly opened his account from a free and he added two more from placed balls to keep Waterford ahead for the break. Cork struggled to find their top gear, their best move seeing the advancing Kenny have a goal-bound shot blocked out by Waterford keeper Clinton Hennessy.

Defenders Sean Óg Ó hAilpín and John Gardiner scored Cork's final two points before the break, closing the gap to the minimum.

The intensity and quality of hurling improved significantly with Mullane darting into space to collect his third point, just 15 seconds after the restart. Kelly tagged on a free in his first effort from play to make it 0-10 to 0-06. Waterford were starting to ask some questions of their rivals.

But Cork did not fret and points from Kenny, Ben O'Connor and the ever influential Gardiner swamped a single effort from Kevin Moran as the margin was swiftly reduced to 0-11 to 0-10.

Another swashbuckling run and turn produced a fourth point for Mullane, before Ben O'Connor clipped over a free and set up a point for the unmarked Cussen. Suddenly the sides were level.

Kelly pointed a free to move the Deise back in front but Cork, with Cussen turning the screw in midfield, sent shockwaves through Thurles with a stunning two-goal blast.

Ben O'Connor broke the ball to Aisake Ó hAilpín who galloped through, shouldered Noel Connors out of the way and drilled a rising shot past Hennessy in the Waterford goal.

Waterford had hardly drawn breath when a hand-pass from Kieran Murphy invited Ben O'Connor to run into open space on the right. The wing-forward had Ó hAilpín free in the middle for a pass, but opted to solo through the Deise's crumbling defense and finish crisply to the net.

There was no sense of panic from Fitzgerald's charges, Stephen Molumphy had a point attempt blocked before Kelly registered a settling free. Kelly took centre stage coming up to the hour mark when he caught 'Brick' Walsh's diagonal ball in, shrugged off Shane O'Neill's challenge and planted a rocket of a shot to bottom right corner of the Cork net.

Now just 2-12 to 1-14 in arrears, Waterford brought the Shanahan brothers, Dan and Maurice, and Ken McGrath into the fray. Maurice was narrowly wide with his first-up shot and amid a breathless spell of end-to-end hurling, Brian Murphy and Niall McCarthy conjured up points for Cork.

Kelly took his tally to 1-08 from a '65' and when Cussen won a free in midfield, Ben O'Connor duly pointed what looked like the match-winning score. But, deep into injury-time Waterford got the lifeline of a 21-yard free and although Kelly's initial shot was saved, it was Browne who came to the rescue.

Cork's Shane O'Neill and Eoin McGrath of Waterford

CORK: D Óg Cusack; S O'Neill, E Cadogan, B Murphy (0-01); J Gardiner (0-03)R Curran, S Óg Ó hAilpín (0-01); T Kenny (0-01), C Naughton (0-02); B O'Connor (1-05), J O'Connor, N McCarthy (0-01); K Murphy, A Ó hAilpín, P Horgan
Subs: R Ryan for S Óg Ó hAilpín; M Cussen (0-01) for J O'Connor; P O'Sullivan for K Murphy; P Cronin for Horgan

WATERFORD: C Hennessy; E Murphy, L Lawlor, N Connors; T Browne (1-00), M Walsh, D Prendergast; S O'Sullivan (0-02), R Foley; K Moran (0-01), S Molumphy, E Kelly (1-08), J Mullane (0-04), S Walsh, E McGrath
Subs: S Prendergast for McGrath; J Nagle for Lawlor; D Shanahan for Moran; M Shanahan for Walsh; K McGrath for Foley

REFEREE: J Ryan (Tipperary)

Final

WATERFORD | 1-16 | 1-13 | CORK

17 July 2010 (replay)

In wet conditions in Thurles, Dan Shanahan blasted past Donal Óg Cusack in the second period of extra-time to confirm the Deise's first provincial success since 2007.

Waterford, helped by the introductions of Dan and Maurice Shanahan and Eoin McGrath, outlasted their great rivals in extra-time to earn the sweetest of victories in front of 22,763 spectators.

On the balance of play, Davy Fitzgerald's men deservedly pulled through to earn a place in the All-Ireland semi-finals and leave injury-hit Cork with just a week to regroup for an All-Ireland quarter-final clash with Antrim.

As expected, Sean Óg Ó hAilpín was unable to start due to a hamstring injury, so Shane Murphy was drafted into the defence and former footballer Michael Cussen replaced the injured Jerry O'Connor in the Rebels' attack.

Seamus Prendergast's inclusion in the forwards was Waterford's only change from the drawn game, Eoin McGrath the player to make way.

The first half was similar to last week's opening period, in that Waterford's economical approach helped them hit the front and have the better of the half. Eoin Kelly was on the mark on three occasions as the Deise opened up a 0-03 to 0-01 lead, with Cathal Naughton registering Cork's first point.

Cussen was moved to centre-forward and Seamus Prendergast switched into the right-corner on Brian Murphy, but Cork continued to struggle for scores throughout the opening 35 minutes. Indeed, by half-time, Naughton's opener was their only point from play.

Denis Walsh's side had the better of the exchanges in the half-backs and midfield, however they did not get the scores to show for it as Pat Horgan, Niall McCarthy and Aisake Ó hAilpín all failed to find the net.

The best of those goal chances came in the 18th minute when Horgan flicked the ball around the advancing Clinton Hennessy, only for Noel Connors to retrieve the situation for Waterford with a wonderful dive and clearance.

By that stage, John Mullane, who the Deise used as their furthest man forward, had landed his first point. It was a terrific score, with Michael 'Brick' Walsh and Declan Prendergast involved in the build-up. Cork responded with a free and a '65' from Ben O'Connor. John Gardiner then emulated his team-mate with another accurate shot from the 65-yard line, to close the gap to 0-06 to 0-04.

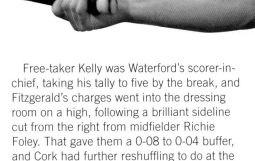

Free-taker Kelly was Waterford's scorer-in-chief, taking his tally to five by the break, and Fitzgerald's charges went into the dressing room on a high, following a brilliant sideline cut from the right from midfielder Richie Foley. That gave them a 0-08 to 0-04 buffer, and Cork had further reshuffling to do at the rear, with Ray Ryan coming in for the injured Shane O'Neill.

The use of Stephen Molumphy as an extra midfielder put pressure on Cork and the lack of balls in towards Ó hAilpín gave the young target man little chance. But the Rebels bounced back strongly at the start of the second half, with the dark and damp conditions making it the first ever floodlit Munster Senior Hurling Championship final.

147

After a Mullane shot had rebounded off the post, Cork raided forward for three successive points, two of them from lively substitute Paudie O'Sullivan. Ó hAilpín also increased his influence, laying off for Cussen to point and using his strength to create the second for O'Sullivan.

Kelly and O'Connor traded points before Foley struck Waterford's first wide in the 44th minute. That particular statistic showed the clinical nature of their play, but they could only watch aghast when O'Connor picked off Cork's only goal.

The Newtownshandrum clubman sent a flat, skimming shot – a right-wing free – that caught goalkeeper Clinton Hennessy off guard and nestled in the top left corner of the net. On the greasy surface, O'Connor's strike looked like a mishit but it certainly provided a crucial score for Cork.

It could have been a pivotal moment, but Waterford recovered quickly to lessen the blow. Substitute Brian O'Halloran, Kelly, Mullane and Shane Walsh scored four points in-a-row to give Fitzgerald's side a 0-13 to 1-08 lead.

Mullane's 53rd-minute effort was typical of the electric De La Salle forward. He showed great bravery to snaffle a catch and he then used his pace to race away from the cover and launch a stunning point from close to the left sideline. Walsh also delighted the Waterford fans with a rousing catch and point.

O'Connor stopped the rot for Cork with a free and Naughton pointed from midfield to leave the sides level for a second time at 1-10 to 0-13. Kelly pointed a free from a tight angle on the left to put Waterford in front again, only for Cork to win a 64th-minute penalty as the advancing Cussen was clumsily brought down by Foley.

Up stepped Gardiner, his shot straight and true and a combination of Hennessy and Shane O'Sullivan diverted the ball over the crossbar for the concession of a point.

That made it 1-11 to 0-14, a score that remained unchanged until the final whistle, despite some last-ditch attempts at the posts from Kelly.

Cork lost their third first choice defender to injury when Ronan Curran was deemed unfit to take part in extra-time. Under-21 star William Egan took his place and pointed with his first touch, replying to the opener from Kevin Moran that came after just 19 seconds of play. Dan Shanahan was involved in the build-up and already proving a worthy replacement for the injured Mullane.

As the rain got progressively heavier and handling conditions worsened, scores were really at a premium. Cussen sliced badly wide and on the cusp of half-time, defender Tony Browne, the goal-scoring hero from the drawn game, planted a long-range free between the posts to give Waterford a 0-16 to 1-12 advantage.

The game slipped from Cork's grasp, three minutes into the second period, when Eoin McGrath helped break the ball through for fellow substitute Shanahan to drill a well-placed shot beyond the reach of Cork stopper Cusack. Waterford had one hand on the trophy.

Cork never let their effort slip though and following an O'Connor free which reduced the arrears to three points, Waterford had to defend a number of balls played in towards Ó hAilpín and company before referee Brian Gavin brought this battle of wills to a close.

CORK: D Óg Cusack; S O'Neill, E Cadogan, B Murphy; J Gardiner (0-02), R Curran, S Murphy; T Kenny, C Naughton (0-02); B O'Connor (1-05); N McCarthy; M Cussen (0-01), K Murphy, A Ó hAilpín, P Horgan
Subs: R Ryan for O'Neill; P O'Sullivan (0-02) for Horgan; L O'Farrell for Murphy; W Egan (0-01) for Curran

WATERFORD: C Hennessy; E Murphy, L Lawlor, N Connors; T Browne (0-01), M Walsh, D Prendergast; S O'Sullivan, R Foley (0-01); K Moran (0-01), S Molumphy; E Kelly (0-08); J Mullane (0-03), S Walsh (0-01), S Prendergast
Subs: B O'Halloran (0-01) for Prendergast; M Shanahan for Walsh; J Nagle for Lawlor; D Shanahan (1-00) for Mullane; E McGrath for O'Halloran; K McGrath for Moran; S Casey for M Shanahan

REFEREE: B Gavin (Offaly)

MARTY MORRISSEY

I don't know whether it's because the GAA was founded in Hayes Hotel in Thurles in 1884 but this fine historic town in County Tipperary and the Munster Hurling Final day are inextricably linked and synonymous with one of the GAA's greatest occasions.

I was brought up on tales of heroes like Christy Ring, Mick Mackey, Jimmy Smyth and Jimmy Doyle. As a young lad watching on black and white pictures courtesy of RTÉ Television I saw for myself what it meant to the people of Limerick when Richie Bennis hit the sliotar between the posts in the last puck of the match in 1973 as Limerick finally beat Tipp on this hallowed ground.

I remember the great Cork three-in-a-row team of 1976–1978 that contained stars like Tim Crowley, Charlie Mc Carthy, Ray Cummins and Seanie O'Leary and they breaking my heart as they saw off the challenge of my own crowd, denying Seamus Durack, Ger Loughnane, Sean Stack, Sean Hehir, Colm Honan, Johnny Callinan, Martin McKeogh and others that elusive Munster medal.

Apart from the first Sunday in September in Croke Park, a Munster Hurling final in Thurles is the heartbeat of the hurling season. Its pulse rate emanates from the hallowed turf and reaches all corners of this island and abroad.

In a word - it's special.

Knowing I was assigned to the Munster final this year meant I kept a particularly close eye on the happenings down south. For the Cork v Tipperary match in Páirc Uí Chaoimh I was sideline reporter and for the Rebels' semi-final against Limerick I was upstairs in the commentary box. But where was I the day Clare played Waterford in Thurles? You'd never guess!

I was flying to Moscow for the European Boxing Championships. I was actually in Frankfurt on a three hour stop-over as the match was being played. The texts were flying in every minute and it seemed like the longest match ever played.

And so 11 July 2010 finally arrives!

I travel to Thurles early as Guinness have very kindly invited me to be MC on their gig rig in the middle of the town. Parked just above Hayes Hotel, where it all began in 1884, thousands gather to sample the atmosphere. Former Cork and Waterford stars Tomás Mulcahy, Diarmuid O'Sullivan, Paul Flynn and Dave Bennett participate in a question and answer session. The banter with the audience is great and there, amongst the thousands, asking the first question, is my colleague from RTÉ Rory O'Neill who happens to be there on his stag weekend! (Only a Cork man could plan his stag around supporting his team. Us poor Clare lads wouldn't dare plan that far ahead!)

When the Q&A is over, I walk with my good friend Dave Punch (who played in the 1981 All-Ireland Final against Galway) through the streets of Thurles and head down to Semple for the big game. For the last number of years he has travelled around Ireland with me, keeping me up to date on the game's crucial stats.

As we walk and talk, the familiar sights and sounds of Munster Hurling Final day fill the air. The distant sound of the accordion player clicking out his tunes, the fizzle and hiss of the chippers hard at work, the street vendors with their familiar cry of 'hats, flags and headbands' and the families happily lunching from the boot of the car.

When we get to the grounds my first port of call is the referee. Today it's Johnny Ryan and I discover it's his first Munster Hurling Final as well. He tells me who his umpires are and I wonder if he is nervous on this hugely historical day in our sporting calendar.

Next stop is the Cork dressing room where I meet Denis Walsh and Pat Buckley, 'no changes?' I ask.

'As selected' is the response.

I meet Donal Óg Cusack and Sean Óg out in the tunnel as they watch the Clare v Waterford minor final, which for the record, Clare won. Fully focused as usual we shake hands firmly and I wish them well. Down the corridor I get a warm welcome in the Waterford dressing room. Davy Fitzgerald tells me, 'It's all systems go. We are ready.'

Upstairs I meet Michael Duignan, my co-commentator for the match. I really enjoy Michael's company and jokingly he tells me 'to chill out' as he's done loads of these Munster Finals, 'it's easy'.

I tell him that there are new rules for this game, he can only talk during the commercial breaks.

So the slagging is good and the mood is relaxed but focused in the commentary box.

The first half of the 2010 Munster Final was rather poor. Defences dominated and generally speaking it was a disappointing start.

The second half however was totally different. Two cracking goals by Aisake Ó hAilpín and Ben O'Connor within a few minutes of each other seemed to set Cork on their way to victory.

But this Waterford outfit now have an inner belief and strength of character not really seen before. Two minutes into injury-time, the score-line reads Cork 2-15 Waterford 1-15 and the Decies get a debatable free on the 20-metre line.

Eoin Kelly shoots, his shot is saved, in rushes 37-year-old Tony Browne, he pulls first time and the sliotar hits the back of the Cork net. Drama in Semple yet again. Drawn game. Replay next Saturday evening. Six days later, on 17 July 2010 we all return to Thurles.

The evening of 17 July brought rain of unexpected proportions. And with it came a game worthy of the rich folklore of Munster Hurling. For the very first time a Munster Final was played under floodlights as over 22,000 rain-soaked supporters enjoyed an epic Munster Hurling Final replay. It also attracted one of the largest TV audiences of the year. Level again after 70 minutes the game went to extra time.

The dark clouds hung low when Dan the Man, better known as Dan Shanahan from Lismore, came off the bench to pull on a ground ball in the second period of extra time. The ball whizzed past Cork goalkeeper Donal Óg Cusack and as the ball hit the net, we all knew that Waterford had just won their 9th Munster title and Cork would be taking the scenic route through the qualifiers.

I visited the Waterford dressing room after the match and just inside the door stood the hero of the night Dan Shanahan.

'Welcome back Dan', I said to him and he replied with a massive grin on his face in that great Waterford accent he has, 'I never left Marty, I never left, I stuck with it, I knew it would come right. These lads are a great bunch of lads. I tell you one thing though Marty, I was glad to see the ball hit the net.'

Those who say the provincial system is old fashioned and dated cannot by-pass the Munster Hurling Championship. The people of Munster treasure it. Look at the thousands that ran on to the pitch that night and see the delight in their eyes.

All I can say is thank God for hurling, for Semple Stadium, for late equalisers for Tony Browne, for replays, for extra time.

I may have waited a long time to commentate on a but hey, I got to do two and a half in six days! You will forgive me then if I think 2010 was a vintage year!

Tony Browne

CLUB: Mount Sion

COUNTY: Waterford

AGE: 37

HEIGHT: 5' 11"

WEIGHT: 12st

OCCUPATION: Self-employed

Tony has enjoyed huge success with his club Mount Sion earning seven senior county medals throughout his long and illustrious club career. His inter-county career has also provided him with much success. Since making his debut in 1991 he has won two Munster titles and one National Hurling League title.

Although Tony has notched up many memorable scores throughout his 19 years playing wing–back with Waterford, possibly one of the most important and most dramatic came in this year's Munster Hurling Championship final against Cork when his injury-time goal earned his side a replay and ultimately another Munster title.

Tony has made 57 appearances and is, at 37 years of age, the oldest inter-county player left on the scene. He has played in six All-Ireland semi-finals, and one All-Ireland final, in 2008 – when Waterford lost to Kilkenny.

Tony is the most capped Waterford hurler of all time and is one of only eight players in the history of the GAA to have played more than 50 championship games for their county.

ANTRIM 1-17 | 0-19 DUBLIN

17 July 2010

Antrim caused something of an upset when they edged out Dublin by 1-17 to 0-19 at Croke Park to book a place in the All-Ireland Senior Hurling Championship quarter-finals.

Dublin's Maurice O'Brien with Neil McManus of Antrim

Midfielder Karl Stewart struck the decisive injury-time point as Antrim overcame a dithering Dublin.

The Dubs had a 0-18 to 1-09 lead with 20 minutes remaining, but the Saffrons rallied superbly to seal their first All-Ireland quarter-final appearance since 2004.

Indeed, this was Antrim's first ever championship victory over Dublin and a real shot in the arm for Dinny Cahill's under-rated side.

Free-takers Alan McCrabbe and Neil McManus led the scoring as the sides went in level at half-time, 0-10 to 1-07, with PJ O'Connell registering Antrim's goal.

Dublin ace McCrabbe added five more points to his tally, but the Ulster champions' never-say-die spirit got them over the finish line.

Dublin picked up where they left off against Clare, with centre-back Joey Boland breaking through to slot over the first score after just 20 seconds.

Karl McKeegan snatched an equaliser soon

after, and despite Dublin regaining the lead through McCrabbe's fourth-minute score, the sides were tied again at 0-02 apiece when McManus sent over the first of his five first-half points from placed balls.

In sunny conditions, the first half was reasonably free-flowing and evenly-contested, devoid of any major incident with referee Diarmuid Kirwan failing to show a yellow card in the opening 35 minutes.

Antrim were not fazed by the vastness of Croke Park, and quickly showed that their gutsy display in taking Offaly to extra-time earlier in the championship was not a flash in the pan.

The Saffrons delivered on their promise in the eighth minute when PJ O'Connell smashed the ball to the net from close range.

O'Connell got the better of two Dublin defenders to cut through from the right side and drill his shot past Dublin goalkeeper Gary Maguire. Cahill's charges then edged 1-03 to 0-02 clear thanks to a Liam Watson point.

Dublin's only clear cut goal opportunity of the opening half arrived in the 21st minute, with Peadar Carton feeding Alan McCrabbe, but Antrim goalkeeper Chris O'Connell smothered the ball.

However, McCrabbe converted from the resulting breaking ball to kick-start a dominant spell from the Dubs who fired over three unanswered points to level the tie at 0-08 to 1-05 in the 24th minute.

There was little to separate the sides before the break, scores from Carton and McCrabbe were sandwiched in between a brace from McManus to leave it all-square at the interval.

McCrabbe fired his fifth point inside two minutes of the restart, and Dublin were beginning to hit their stride when Simon Lambert pointed a free to make it 0-16 to 1-08 in the 47th minute.

Antrim net minder O'Connell pulled off a

superb block from Paul Ryan's goal-bound shot, after the Dublin substitute had galloped through on a solo run towards Hill 16.

McCrabbe slotted over the resulting '65' and when McNaughton and Lambert traded quick-fire points, Dublin were 0-18 to 1-09 to the good.

Dublin had been guilty of some wastefulness in front of goal – the substituted David O'Callaghan being one of the guilty parties - and those wides came back to haunt them during a lacklustre closing spell.

Antrim raised their game and as they held Dublin scoreless over an 11-minute spell, they strung together points from McManus, Watson and Karl McKeegan.

McCrabbe slotted over a much-needed Dublin point – his ninth of the contest – with a little over 10 minutes remaining. But Antrim looked the hungrier side at this stage, and it showed in the end.

The Ulstermen scored eight of the game's last nine points, with defender Sean Delargy claiming an inspirational point in the 61st minute. McManus continued to close the gap with his precision from frees.

Both sides had scoring opportunities in the closing minute of normal time. Agonisingly for Dublin, substitute Liam Ryan sent a blazing goal shot wide of the target in the 70th minute.

Antrim then turned the screw in injury-time. McNaughton equalised from a free a minute into injury-time, before Stewart's late winner sent the vocal Antrim support into raptures and left the pre-match favourites stunned.

Antrim's Simon McCrory and Barry McFall with Declan O'Dwyer of Dublin

DUBLIN: G Maguire; N Corcoran, T Brady, O Gough; S Hiney, J Boland (0-01), M O'Brien; S Lambert (0-03), S Durkin; P Kelly, L Rushe (0-01), D O'Dwyer; P Carton (0-03), D O'Callaghan (0-01), A McCrabbe (0-09)
Subs: P Ryan (0-01) for Durkin; M Carton for Kelly; D Treacy for O'Callaghan; L Ryan for Rushe; K Flynn for O'Brien

ANTRIM: C O'Connell; K McGourty, C Donnelly, S Delargy (0-01); P Shiels, J Campbell, C Herron; S McNaughton (0-02), K Stewart (0-01); S McCrory, N McManus (0-08), T McCann; PJ O'Connell (1-01), L Watson (0-02), K McKeegan (0-02)
Subs: B McFall for Shiels; E McCloskey for McCann; M Herron for McKeegan

REFEREE: D Kirwan (Cork)

TIPPERARY `0-21` `1-12` **OFFALY**

18 July 2010

Eoin Kelly claimed 11 points as Tipperary overcame Offaly in Portlaoise to book their place in the All-Ireland Senior Hurling Championship quarter-final.

Liam Sheedy's charges looked very impressive throughout and led by 0-14 to 0-05 at the interval, with seven of their players on target.

Tipperary pressed on and were 0-17 to 0-07 ahead by the 42nd minute, watched by 13,888 spectators.

A valiant Offaly side could not curb Kelly's influence, and Shane Dooley's injury-time goal was mere consolation. They also suffered the loss of substitute Kevin Brady to a late dismissal.

Tipperary hit the ground running at O'Moore Park, keen to kick on from their high-scoring win over Wexford in the first phase of the qualifiers.

They showed great precision in the opening half, converting 14 of their 18 scoring chances to move comfortably ahead on the scoreboard.

Free-taker Kelly was in good form from placed balls, knocking over four efforts. He was on target in the opening 10 minutes, along with Conor O'Mahony and Gearóid Ryan, as Offaly fell 0-03 to 0-00 behind.

Shane Dooley opened the Faithfuls' account in the 14th minute, but with a strong wind behind them, the Premier County side cantered ahead.

Scores from Kelly, Brendan Maher, Noel McGrath and Lar Corbett sent them 0-07 to 0-01 clear by the end of the opening quarter.

Offaly pressed hard through the likes of Joe Bergin, Dooley, Derek Molloy and Brian Carroll, but scores were at a premium for the midlanders.

A fourth point from the stick of Kelly opened up a 0-10 to 0-02 lead in the 23rd minute, before Offaly found some rhythm thanks to points from Molloy

Tipperary's Lar Corbett and Rory Hanniffy of Offaly

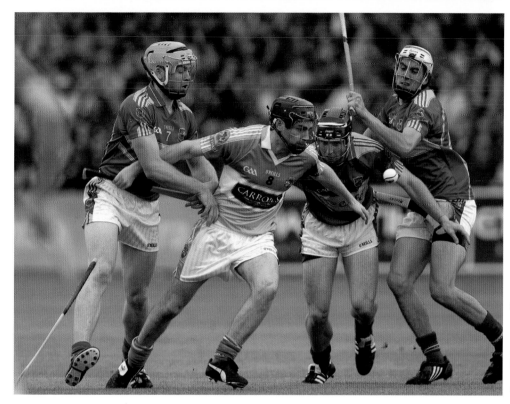

Tipperary's Pádraic Maher, Conor O'Mahony and Patrick Maher tackle Brendan Murphy of Offaly

and Dooley.

However, Tipperary gained the upper hand once more before the break, with Shane McGrath, Gearóid Ryan, David Young and Kelly on target to open up a nine-point gap.

Bergin collected his second point from two early Offaly attacks, as the second half took on a more even feel. But there was no sense of complacency from Tipperary as they claimed three of the next four scores.

Offaly manager Joe Dooley introduced both Ger Healion and Daniel Currams and the shake-up had the desired effect.

Midfielder Dylan Hayden set the Faithfuls off on this purple patch, connecting superbly for a rousing long-range point in the 46th minute.

Pointed frees from Dooley arrived either side of a Kelly score, leaving the score-line at 0-18 to 0-10 as the game entered the final quarter.

The high stakes saw the game get heated in the final stages, evidenced by an off-the-ball incident involving a number of players.

Offaly substitute Kevin Brady was barely five minutes on the pitch when he was picked out of the bunch by referee John Sexton and given a straight red card.

Kelly and Bergin swapped scores in the closing five minutes with Tipp's victory now beyond doubt. Offaly managed to sign off with the game's only goal, scored by corner-forward Dooley in the second minute of injury-time. The end of the road for Offaly, but for Tipperary the focus moves on to Galway in the quarter-finals.

TIPPERARY: B Cummins; P Stapleton, P Curran, M Cahill; D Fanning, C O'Mahony (0-01), Pádraic Maher; B Maher, D Young; G Ryan (0-03), S McGrath (0-01), Patrick Maher; N McGrath (0-01), L Corbett (0-02), E Kelly (0-11)
Subs: S Callanan for P Maher; P Bourke for N McGrath; C O'Brien for Young; J O'Brien for S McGrath

OFFALY: J Dempsey; D Franks, P Cleary, J Rigney; D Kenny, R Hanniffy, D Morkan; B Murphy, D Hayden (0-01); B Carroll, J Brady, D Molloy (0-01); C Parlon, J Bergin (0-03), S Dooley (1-07)
Subs: G Healion for Parlon; K Brady for Hayden; O Kealey for Molloy; D Currams for J Brady

REFEREE: J Sexton (Cork)

155

Quarter-Final

CORK	1-25	0-19	ANTRIM

25 July 2010

Cork will meet champions Kilkenny in the All-Ireland Senior Hurling Championship semi-final following their nine-point win over Antrim at Croke Park.

Manager Denis Walsh will, however, be looking for a vast improvement ahead of the clash with the Cats.

The Rebels often struggled against an eager but limited Saffron side that chalked up a big scoring tally.

Niall McCarthy's goal just before half-time provided a platform for the Munster men, but they failed to convince in a second half that saw them struggle to get on top of the Ulster champions.

Cork laid down a marker in the opening six minutes, flashing over four points through Paudie O'Sullivan, Cathal Naughton, Aisake Ó hAilpín and Ben O'Connor.

But when full-back Cormac Donnelly began to play with assurance, twice denying Ó hAilpín with well timed blocks, the Ulster men

Cork's John Gardiner and Liam Watson of Antrim

156

grew in confidence.

Neil McManus and Karl McKeegan found the target to reduce the deficit to a point, and full-forward Liam Watson knocked over a couple of excellent scores.

Cork's opening eight points all came from frees, and by the 25th minute, they had moved into a 0-11 to 0-06 lead.

But the Saffrons continued to battle bravely, and McManus and Watson added to their tallies.

However, gaps started to open up in the Antrim defence late in the half, allowing Tom Kenny and Kieran Murphy to take advantage and add points.

It was in the 35th minute that Ó hAilpín slipped the ball to Niall McCarthy, and he found the net from close range.

O'Connor tagged on a couple of frees, and the Rebels went in at the break with a 1-16 to 0-11 lead.

Ray Ryan and Eoin Cadogan had to be alert to snuff out a couple of Antrim raids early in the second half, but the Saffrons did narrow the gap through points from Watson and McManus.

A composed John Gardiner drove over two long-range frees but, once again, Antrim were able to pose a threat, and goalkeeper Donal Óg Cusack had to scramble to deny the combined effort of McManus and Karl Stewart.

O'Connor converted two more frees to bring his tally to six, while McManus continued to strike accurately on his way to a nine-point tally at the other end.

The Saffrons finished with 14 men after Watson was sent off for a second booking, and Cork finished the job with a late salvo of scores from Murphy, Cathal Naughton and substitute William Egan.

CORK: D Óg Cusack; S Murphy, E Cadogan, B Murphy; J Gardiner (0-03), R Curran, R Ryan; T Kenny (0-03), C Naughton (0-02); B O'Connor (0-06), M Cussen, N McCarthy (1-02); P O'Sullivan (0-03), A Ó hAilpín (0-01), K Murphy (0-04) **Subs:** P Horgan for Ó hAilpín; P Cronin for Cussen; W Egan (0-01) for McCarthy

ANTRIM: C O'Connell; K McGourty, C Donnelly, S Delargey; P Shiels, J Campbell (0-01), C Herron; S McNaughton (0-01), K Stewart; S McCrory, N McManus (0-09), T McCann; PJ O'Connell, L Watson (0-06), K McKeegan (0-01) **Subs:** J McKeague for Shiels; B McFall for McCann; M Herron (0-1) for McKeague; D Hamill for PJ O'Connell; E McCloskey for McNaughton

REFEREE: M Wadding (Waterford)

Quarter-Final

TIPPERARY 3-17 3-16 **GALWAY**

25 July 2010

Lar Corbett's stoppage time winner secured Tipperary's victory in an epic All-Ireland Senior Hurling Championship quarter-final at Croke Park.

A thrilling contest ebbed and flowed from start to finish, propelled by the passion and skill of two totally committed sides.

The scores were level on nine occasions before Liam Sheedy's men pushed on in the closing stages to take the win and set up a semi-final clash with Waterford.

A crowd of 27,864 was transported on a roller-coaster of twists and turns which produced half a dozen goals and heroism in spades.

Eanna Ryan gave the Tribesmen a massive boost in the tenth minute when he burst through a gap in the Tipp defence to fire home a goal.

It was a much-needed score, given what had gone before, with the Munster men easing ahead with points from Patrick Maher, Lar Corbett and two from Eoin Kelly.

Damien Hayes gave Galway the lead for the first time on 13 minutes, but Tipperary succeeded in keeping Joe Canning quiet. Corner-backs Paddy Stapleton and Michael Cahill were largely responsible for the Portumna ace's failure to score from play in the first half.

Canning did bring the sides level for the third time from a '65' midway through the first half, but Tipperary immediately struck for a goal, Kelly drilling past Colm Callanan from Maher's knock-down.

However, it was Galway who gained a fresh impetus from that score, scoring the next six points to go three clear.

Canning arrowed over a superb sideline cut, and tagged on a couple of frees. Damien Hayes, Iarla Tannian and Ger Farragher, with a huge effort were also on target for the tribesmen.

Excellent defending from Tony Óg Regan, Shane Kavanagh and David Collins kept Tipperary scoreless for 16 minutes, but they finished the half with a 1-02 salvo to take a four-point advantage into the break.

Kelly and Brendan Maher knocked over points, before Noel McGrath's flick sent substitute Seamus Callanan through for a stoppage time goal and a 2-08 to 1-09 lead.

Galway hit the front again with a sensational start to the second half. Damien Hayes took advantage of a rare Paul Curran error to get in for a goal, and points from Farragher and Canning made it 2-11 to 2-10.

Shane Kavanagh of Galway with Lar Corbett of Tipperary

Tipperary's Pádraic Maher competes for the dropping ball

A remarkable tie quickly took yet another twist, with Gearóid Ryan showing lightning pace to dart through for Tipp's third goal on 43 minutes.

Corbett gave them the relative comfort of a four-point lead, but inevitably there was to be yet another goal.

Joe Canning was fouled and smashed home the penalty himself, and when Damien Hayes and Kevin Hynes tagged on points, the Connacht men were back in front.

Hynes and fellow sub Aonghus Callanan added further points, but Tipperary refused to surrender, and late scores from John O'Brien, Ryan and Corbett saw them win a classic contest.

TIPPERARY: B Cummins; P Stapleton, P Curran, M Cahill; D Fanning, C O'Mahony, P Maher; B Maher (0-02), D Young; G Ryan (1-02), P Maher (0-01), S McGrath; N McGrath (0-01), L Corbett (0-03), E Kelly (1-07)
Subs: S Callanan (1-00) for Young; J O'Brien (0-01) for N McGrath; C O'Brien for Fanning; P Bourke for P Maher
GALWAY: C Callanan; D Joyce, S Kavanagh, O Canning; D Barry, T Óg Regan, D Collins; G Farragher (0-02), D Burke (0-01); E Ryan (1-01), K Hayes, A Smith; D Hayes (1-03), J Canning (1-05), I Tannian (0-01)
Subs: K Hynes (0-02) for K Hayes; A Callanan (0-01) for Ryan; J Lee for O Canning; N Healy for A Smith

REFEREE: J Owens (Wexford)

159

MARY HANNIGAN

It's Sunday afternoon on an island off the west coast of Donegal and the sun is beating down on the man perched on the roof.

'Any good,' he shouts.

'No,' comes the voice from the living room, 'nothing but snow, try turning it the other way.'

So, he inches the aerial clockwise, all the time beseeching the heavens above that he'll strike gold before kick-off.

'Well?'

'Still snowing. Keep going.'

'Is it heavy?'

'A blizzard.'

'Is there any sound?'

'Yeah, kind of like a torrential shower.'

'That'll be Pat Spillane.'

'Maybe, but you can't see him – keep turning.'

By now he's loudly cursing the winds of the night before, not so much because they lifted three more tiles off his already ailing roof, more because they robbed him of his television reception, leaving him facing the catastrophic prospect of missing the match.

Plan B would have him boating it to the port where the nearest pub would be showing the game on the big screen, but the last time he did that he had a heated debate with a holidaying Dub over who was the finer free-taker, Charlie Redmond or Manus Boyle. He'd argued that the Dub was asking for trouble when he provocatively suggested both players were rather good, insisting that such an opinion was an incitement to violence. His friends and family had urged him to watch matches at home from there on in.

Back on the roof the frustration is mounting, to the point where a leg is swung at the base of the aerial, the kick so accurate Manus (or Charlie) would have purred.

'THAT'S IT! WE HAVE LIFT-OFF,' comes the celebratory cry from below and with that the theme tune from *The Sunday Game* fills the Donegal air, scattering seagulls to the four winds. There's a stampede towards the living room, the gathering greeting the sight of Michael Lyster's smiling face as they would a set of winning Lotto numbers.

As is often the case with these things, the descent is more treacherous than the climb, especially when Joe Brolly is drowning out the pleas from the man on the summit that someone hold his ladder. It's a solo run then, his skilful sidestepping of the holes where tiles once lay akin to Peter Canavan jinking and weaving his way towards goal.

'Turn that down a minute,' he says.

'What?'

'Turn it down.'

'Why?'

'Listen.'

A dozen ears are cocked.

'Is Colm O'Rourke sitting next door or was that Derry fecker's telly working all along?'

'Well, he says since he bought the satellite dish off the fella in Ardara he hasn't lost his picture once.'

'AND HE WOULDN'T INVITE US IN?'

'The last time he invited you in you told him Derry were like the Ardara under-12 netball team.'

'Well, I apologised.'

'You did – to the Ardara under-12 netball team.'

Half-time in the minor match, the Armagh attack seriously malfunctioning.

Joe: 'That move there summed up Armagh's insouciance,'

Pat: 'Their what, Joe?'

Joe: 'I thought you were the Socrates of the GAA.'

Pat: 'If you can't convince, confuse. Can I use a big word?'

Michael: 'You can.'

Pat: 'Conundrum.'

Joe: 'It's not really that big Pat, that was an anti-climax.'

'What's insouciance mean anyway?'

'Couldn't hit a barn door with a banjo.'

'Really?'

'Yeah.'

On to senior matters. The panel are discussing the merits of the main contenders.

Colm O'Rourke: 'You could write the Meath tactics on the back of a postage stamp – just kick it up there. Some people would say it's bogman football.'

Joe: 'But you are bogmen.'

Colm: 'That's true.'

'Honest to God, that O'Rourke talks desperate nonsense.'

Soon after.

Pat: 'The foot has gone out of football, it's now a bastardised game of basketball.'

Colm: 'I love when you go off on this rant. I remember when you were playing with your team back in the 70s, you were the Harlem Globetrotters in disguise – if they'd painted you black you wouldn't have known if you were basketball or football players.'

'I always said it, O'Rourke is the only one on that panel who talks any sense at all.'

Cue roomful of rolling eyes.

The senior match. Not pretty, although the panel is gentle with its criticism at half-time.

Pat: 'Absolutely abysmal stuff.'

Joe: 'A near death experience.'

Colm: 'More or less as we expected: awful.'

The room, in a rare outbreak of harmony, nods as one.

By now the sun through the window has intensified, turning the television screen into a mirror. 'Cripes, Lyster is very red in the face.'

'That's not Lyster, that's you – you should have brought the Ambre Solaire with you up on the roof.'

The curtains are drawn, prompting a beach-bound football-a-phobe to note that they'd been whinging all week about the stormy weather and as soon as the sun comes out they're gathered around the telly complaining about the glare on the screen. The room shakes its head as one, some folk just don't understand. 'There's always one,' they agree.

Second half. The tension, like the wind outside, is beginning to rise.

When the goal comes there's a joyous roar from the Derry man's living room.

'I'm going in there.'

'SIT DOWN!'

It's not over yet, though. The fightback leaves only a point in it with a minute to go.

'Ref! Free!'

The air is sucked from the room by the collective intake of breaths. A light snow begins to fall. On the telly that is, not outside. 'Please God, no.' As the free-taker studies the posts the flurry thickens. As he steps up to the ball it's a blizzard again and the picture disappears. A dozen ears are cocked.

'NOOOOOOooooooo,' cries the Derry man next door.

'YEEEEeeessss,' cries the room, 'REPLAY!'

Off he heads for his boat, loudly whistling the theme from *The Sunday Game* as he passes the Derry man's door, the address for the fella in Ardara in his pocket. Enough with the insouciance, enough with the blizzards, there's a replay to be seen.

Tommy Walsh

CLUB: Tullaroan

COUNTY: Kilkenny

AGE: 27

HEIGHT: 5' 10"

WEIGHT: 12st

OCCUPATION: Bank Official

Tommy was born in 1983, the year Kilkenny beat their great rivals Cork in the All-Ireland final to claim their 19th title.

Tommy was only twenty when he embarked on his senior inter–county career in 2003 and in that year Kilkenny won the National Hurling league, the Leinster title and the All-Ireland Hurling final. 2003 also saw Tommy pick up his first All-Star award.

Tommy's versatility has seen him play in many different positions for the Cats; midfield in 2003, left-corner-back in 2004, left-half-forward in 2005, left-half-back in 2006. In recent years he has made the position of right-half-back his own, breaking the hearts of many of the country's finest forwards.

In 2009 Tommy won the Texaco Hurler of the Year, the All-Star Hurler of the Year and the GPA Hurler of the year. His place in hurling greatness is well-earned and most deserved.

Former Kilkenny great Eddie Keher believes Tommy is already established as one of Kilkenny's greatest ever hurlers: 'I don't think anyone makes the game look as effortless as he does. We've had many great half-backs but none were greater than Tommy.'

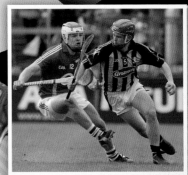

Quarter-Final

KILDARE	2-17	1-12	MEATH

I August 2010

Kildare put in a typically strong second-half performance to beat Meath by 2-17 to 1-12 and book an All-Ireland Senior Football Championship semi-final clash with Down.

Meath became the fourth provincial champions to crash out at the quarter-final stage at Croke Park.

The Lilywhites blossomed despite the loss of talisman midfielder Dermot Earley after just a minute, and systematically took the Royal defence apart with an irresistible display of positive, attacking football.

For the first time ever, no provincial title-holders will feature in the All-Ireland semi-finals, and Kildare will go into their last four eliminator against Down brimming with confidence following this hugely impressive display in front of a crowd of 47,016.

After the loss of Earley, Kildare fell six points behind inside the opening 12 minutes.

Cian Ward, Shane O'Rourke and Joe Sheridan all steered over points, Sheridan sent a screamer crashing against the crossbar and Brian Meade was fouled as he seized on the rebound.

Ward stepped up to take the penalty, goalkeeper Shane McCormack stopped the shot, but the greasy ball escaped his grasp and slipped over the line, and Meath led by 1-03 to no points.

This was the sort of start Kieran McGeeney and his men felt they must avoid, but they stuck to their task and got down to work.

Four points on the spin, from John Doyle, Eoghan O'Flaherty and James Kavanagh narrowed the gap, but Meath regrouped and

Kildare's Padraig
O'Neill and Eoghan
Harrington of Meath

went four ahead with a couple of sublime strikes from corner-back Chris O'Connor and the excellent Graham Reilly.

In the 29th minute, however, Kildare got themselves right back into the game with a James Kavanagh goal. He collected a searching delivery from Hugh Lynch and calmly stepped around goalkeeper Brendan Murphy before planting the ball in the net.

Once again, Meath's response was defiant, and another four-point salvo, including two mammoth Sheridan efforts, restored the four-point cushion.

But Kildare struck again in stoppage time, Padraig O'Neill's vision picking out Alan Smith at the far post, and the perfectly timed pass was finished with the fist past Murphy.

Meath led by 1-09 to 2-05 at the break, but it was a fired-up Lilywhite side that stepped up a gear on the restart.

Padraig O'Neill, Doyle and Emmet Bolton were all on target, before O'Flaherty fired over a couple of long-range efforts as they hit the front for the first time.

Shane O'Rourke floated over a long-distance special, Brian Meade and Jamie Queeney added points but those three scores were all they could muster in the second half.

Kildare swept forward in droves, growing in confidence with every passing minute, and O'Flaherty unveiled another aspect of his immense range of talents with a couple of superbly struck long-range frees.

Doyle was also on fire, hitting the target from play and frees on his way to an eight-point tally.

The pair reeled off six points without reply in the closing 10 minutes as the Royal effort faded away.

Meath's misery was compounded by the dismissal of wing-forward Seamus Kenny on a second yellow card two minutes from the end.

Brian Flanagan of Kildare with Joe Sheridan of Meath

Kildare's Dermot Earley and Nigel Crawford of Meath

KILDARE: S McCormack; P Kelly, H McGrillen, A Mac Lochlainn; M O'Flaherty, E Bolton (0-01), B Flanagan; D Flynn, D Earley; J Kavanagh (1-01), P O'Neill (0-02), E O'Flaherty (0-05); J Doyle (0-08), A Smith (1-00), E Callaghan
Subs: H Lynch for Earley; M Foley for Flanagan; R Sweeney for Callaghan; G White for Bolton; D Lyons for Kelly

MEATH: B Murphy; C O'Connor (0-01), K Reilly, E Harrington; A Moyles, G O'Brien, C King; N Crawford, B Meade (0-01); S Kenny, J Sheridan (0-03), G Reilly (0-02); C Ward (1-02), S O'Rourke (0-02), S Bray. **Subs:** C McGuinness for Moyles; J Queeney (0-01) for Ward

REFEREE: M Duffy (Sligo)

165

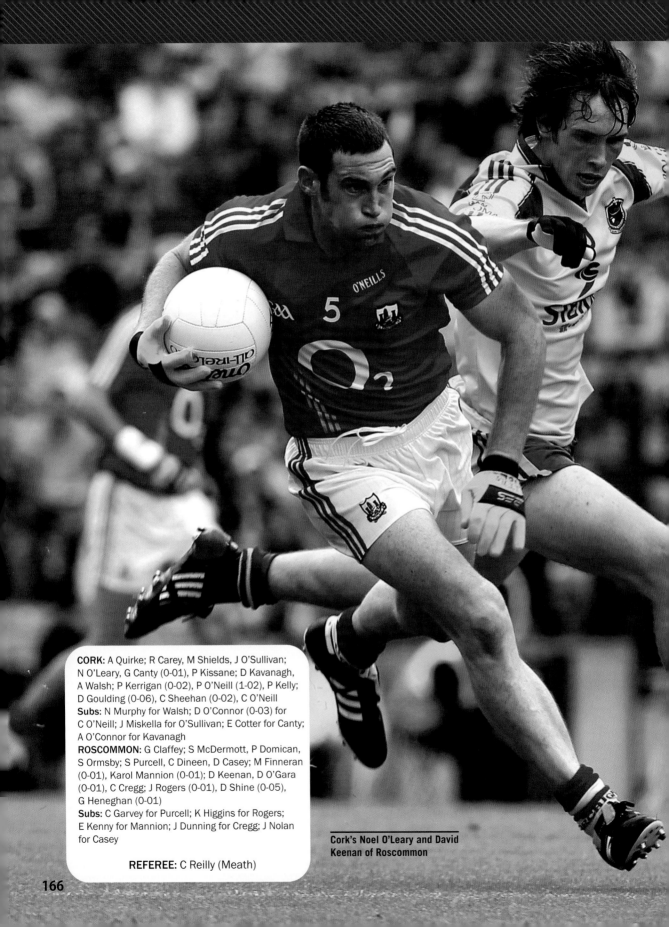

CORK: A Quirke; R Carey, M Shields, J O'Sullivan;
N O'Leary, G Canty (0-01), P Kissane; D Kavanagh,
A Walsh; P Kerrigan (0-02), P O'Neill (1-02), P Kelly;
D Goulding (0-06), C Sheehan (0-02), C O'Neill
Subs: N Murphy for Walsh; D O'Connor (0-03) for
C O'Neill; J Miskella for O'Sullivan; E Cotter for Canty;
A O'Connor for Kavanagh
ROSCOMMON: G Claffey; S McDermott, P Domican,
S Ormsby; S Purcell, C Dineen, D Casey; M Finneran
(0-01), Karol Mannion (0-01); D Keenan, D O'Gara
(0-01), C Cregg; J Rogers (0-01), D Shine (0-05),
G Heneghan (0-01)
Subs: C Garvey for Purcell; K Higgins for Rogers;
E Kenny for Mannion; J Dunning for Cregg; J Nolan
for Casey

REFEREE: C Reilly (Meath)

Cork's Noel O'Leary and David
Keenan of Roscommon

Quarter-Final

CORK 1-16 0-10 ROSCOMMON

1 August 2010

Cork booked an All-Ireland Senior Football Championship semi-final clash with Dublin after a 1-16 to 0-10 win over Roscommon at Croke Park.

But it was only in the second half that the Munster men showed glimpses of what they are capable of.

After a lacklustre first-half display, Cork led by just a point, and fell behind early in the second period to a courageous but limited Roscommon side.

The Rebels increased the tempo thereafter, with Pearse O'Neill turning on the style at centre-forward, and drilling home the only goal of the game in the 64th minute.

Manager Conor Counihan's half-time changes proved effective as Cork delivered a much improved second half display, marred only by the loss of captain Graham Canty, who limped off with a hamstring injury on 57 minutes.

Daniel Goulding found the range right from the outset, knocking over a 20-metre free, and adding a '45', before Roscommon's Donal Shine curled over a gem from far out on the left wing after taking David O'Gara's return pass.

The Rebels found it difficult to break down a hard-working Roscommon defence, and the willingness of their attackers to help out was highlighted by Cathal Cregg's wonderful block on Aidan Walsh.

However, midfielder Walsh helped the Munster men shade possession in the central area, and Goulding's fourth score was followed by a Paul Kerrigan point for a 0-05 to 0-01 lead in the 22nd minute.

O'Gara launched a massive point from almost 50 metres to lift Roscommon spirits, and when John Rogers slotted over a 27th-minute effort, just three points separated the sides.

Goalkeeper Geoffrey Claffey kept the Rossies very much in the game with a smart save from Pearse O'Neill, who connected first time when sent in by Walsh.

But the Connacht champions grew in confidence, with Michael Finneran and Karol Mannion stepping it up in the midfield battle and in a rousing finish to the half, Shine steered over two more points.

Had he not missed a couple of decent chances, Roscommon would have been in front at the break, rather than 0-06 to 0-05 behind.

They went ahead early in the second half. First Alan Quirke had to produce a brilliant save to deflect Ger Heneghan's shot over the bar, and then midfielders Mannion and Finneran both tagged on points.

Nicholas Murphy and Donncha O'Connor, who were among three subs introduced at half-time by Counihan, started to make an impact, and as Roscommon legs became heavy, the Rebels reeled off five points on the spin to go four clear.

Goulding, O'Connor, Ciaran Sheehan, Kerrigan and O'Neill were all on target, and it was O'Neill who fired in a 64th-minute goal to seal the win, after substitute Alan O'Connor had turned over possession.

Donncha O'Connor was content to tap a penalty over the bar as the Rebels cruised over the finish line.

David Casey of Roscommon with Jamie O'Sullivan and Michael Shields of Cork

167

Roscommon's Cathal Cregg and Aidan Walsh of Cork

Semi-Final

CORK	1-15	1-14	DUBLIN

22 August 2010

Cork came good right at the end to edge out Dublin and claim a place in the All-Ireland Senior Football Championship final with a one-point win in the semi-final clash at Croke Park.

The Rebels staged a second-half revival to turn a five-point deficit into a narrow one point win.

Bernard Brogan rocked Cork with a goal after just a minute, and it looked as if that early score was to be the platform for a day of glory for the boys in blue.

But Donncha O'Connor netted a 54th-minute penalty, and hit the three late frees that sealed the Rebels' place in the decider against either Kildare or Down.

Just a point separated the sides at the end of a riveting contest, and Pat Gilroy and his men will harbour grave regrets over a game that, with a little more composure in the closing stages, they would surely have won.

In front of a near-capacity crowd of 82,225, Gilroy's men stunned Cork with an early goal.

Barely a minute had elapsed when Niall Corkery's searching delivery found Bernard Brogan lurking behind Ray Carey, and he beat Alan Quirke with a low shot, planted in the corner of the net with power and precision.

Cork had points from Donncha O'Connor and Daniel Goulding, but had their supporters in despair with a series of bad wides.

Dublin corner-back Philip McMahon offered a lesson in finishing with an accomplished effort at the other end, and the Brogan brothers made it 1-03 to 0-02 by the 13th minute.

The Brogans were at it again, stretching the Dubs' lead to five on 18 minutes, and Cork's defending was at times haphazard and fraught with nerves and uncertainty.

Rebel confidence was further shaken by another volley of wides, although midfielder Aidan Walsh did execute an eye-catching score from Paul Kerrigan's crossfield pass.

Dublin responded with a Michael Dara MacAuley point and another sublime finish from Bernard Brogan, who in stoppage time at the end of the first half brought his mounting tally to 1-04.

Moments earlier Kerrigan had sent an angled shot crashing against the far post with goalkeeper Stephen Cluxton nowhere near it.

Dublin led by 1-08 to 0-07 at the break, and Cork's difficulties intensified when skipper Graham Canty, a pre-match doubt with a hamstring injury, was unable to return for the second half.

The Dubs' battling qualities were exemplified by Ross McConnell's success in turning over possession, and the big midfielder powered over his side's first score of the second half in the 42nd minute.

Kevin Nolan, Philip McMahon and substitute Barry Cahill defended quite superbly and closed out their opponents, who managed just one point, through Goulding, in the opening 15 minutes of the second half, despite dominating possession.

Meanwhile, Bernard Brogan continued to punish the Munster men with his unerring finishing, stretching the advantage to five.

But the lead was cut back to a point in the 54th minute when Donncha O'Connor slotted a penalty in off a post, after McConnell had hauled down substitute Colm O'Neill.

Dublin quickly restored their three-point advantage, but Paul Kerrigan's industry helped the Rebels rally once again, and O'Neill and Patrick Kelly landed points.

Cork continued to chip away at the lead, with O'Connor punishing indiscipline with his accuracy from placed balls, and he gave them the lead for the first time in the 70th minute after McConnell had been sent off for a rash challenge on Noel O'Leary.

Derek Kavanagh nailed on a point, and while Bernard Brogan brought his total to 1-07, the Dubs fell just short.

Cork's Aidan Walsh and Michael Dara MacAuley, Dublin

CORK: A Quirke; R Carey, M Shields, J Miskella; N O'Leary, G Canty, P Kissane; A O'Connor, A Walsh (0-01); P Kerrigan (0-01), P O'Neill, P Kelly (0-02); D Goulding (0-04), C Sheehan, D O'Connor (1-05)
Subs: E Cadogan for Canty; N Murphy for A O'Connor; C O'Neill (0-01) for Sheehan; D Kavanagh (0-01) for Miskella; F Goold for O'Leary

DUBLIN: S Cluxton; M Fitzsimons, R O'Carroll, P McMahon (0-01); K Nolan, G Brennan, C O'Sullivan; R McConnell (0-01), MD MacAuley (0-01); N Corkery, A Brogan (0-02), B Cullen (0-01); D Henry, E O'Gara, B Brogan (1-07)
Subs: B Cahill for O'Sullivan; P Flynn for Henry; E Fennell for Corkery; C Keaney (0-01) for O'Gara; D Bastick for O'Carroll

REFEREE: M Deegan (Laois)

Cork's Donncha O'Connor celebrates scoring a late free

Cork's John Miskella and David Henry of Dublin

173

Cork's Michael Shields and Dublin's Bernard Brogan

Cork's Donncha O'Connor celebrates scoring the point to give his side the lead late in the game

Cork's Alan O'Connor and Aidan Walsh with Ross McConnell of Dublin

175

Semi-Final

DOWN	1-16	1-14	KILDARE

29 August 2010

Down qualified for their first All-Ireland final since 1994 with a two-point victory over Kildare in a gripping contest at Croke Park.

But they had to survive a heart-stopping finish from Kieran McGeeney's men.

Down had gone seven points clear before Eamon Callaghan smashed in a 58th-minute goal, but the Ulster men held out in a frantic finale to set up a meeting with Cork in the decider, after Kildare sub Robert Kelly had sent a stoppage time free crashing against the crossbar.

It was a most dramatic finish to a memorable game, and the Lilywhites, who came so close to snatching it at the end, will reflect on what might have been had talisman Dermot Earley not been ruled out of the game through injury.

For Down's part, they will approach the decider on 19 September confident in the knowledge that they have never lost an All-Ireland final in five previous attempts.

In front of a crowd of 62,182, both sides contributed to the highly entertaining spectacle.

Kildare made a strong start, easing ahead through Eamon Callaghan, James Kavanagh and John Doyle.

Down were struggling for attacking momentum, but a touch of good fortune helped them explode into the game in the 12th minute with a controversial goal.

Benny Coulter appeared to have entered the square too early before he punched Marty Clarke's left-wing delivery to the net.

The goal stood and Down grew in confidence, pushing on with a couple of inspirational scores from centre-back Kevin McKernan and a Mark Poland free.

Doyle kicked accurately from frees, but with Peter Fitzpatrick and Kalum King

getting on top at midfield, Kildare were unable to stem Down's growing confidence.

Danny Hughes, Poland, Paul McComiskey and Clarke were all on target and McComiskey, with a little more composure, could have had a goal.

Coulter lifted Down's spirits further with a sublime point, sliced over off the outside of his right boot in stoppage time to send his side in with a 1-09 to 0-07 interval lead.

Hughes and Clarke maintained their industrious input, their energy and mobility providing Down with qualities that their opponents struggled to replicate.

Clarke's free kick stretched their lead to six points before centre-back Emmet Bolton punished sloppy defending with a fine point to end Kildare's 16-minute scoreless stretch.

Kildare came close to a goal when Eamon Callaghan sent a shot crashing against the post, and Down also had a golden opportunity, but were denied by a double save involving Morgan O'Flaherty and goalkeeper Shane McCormack.

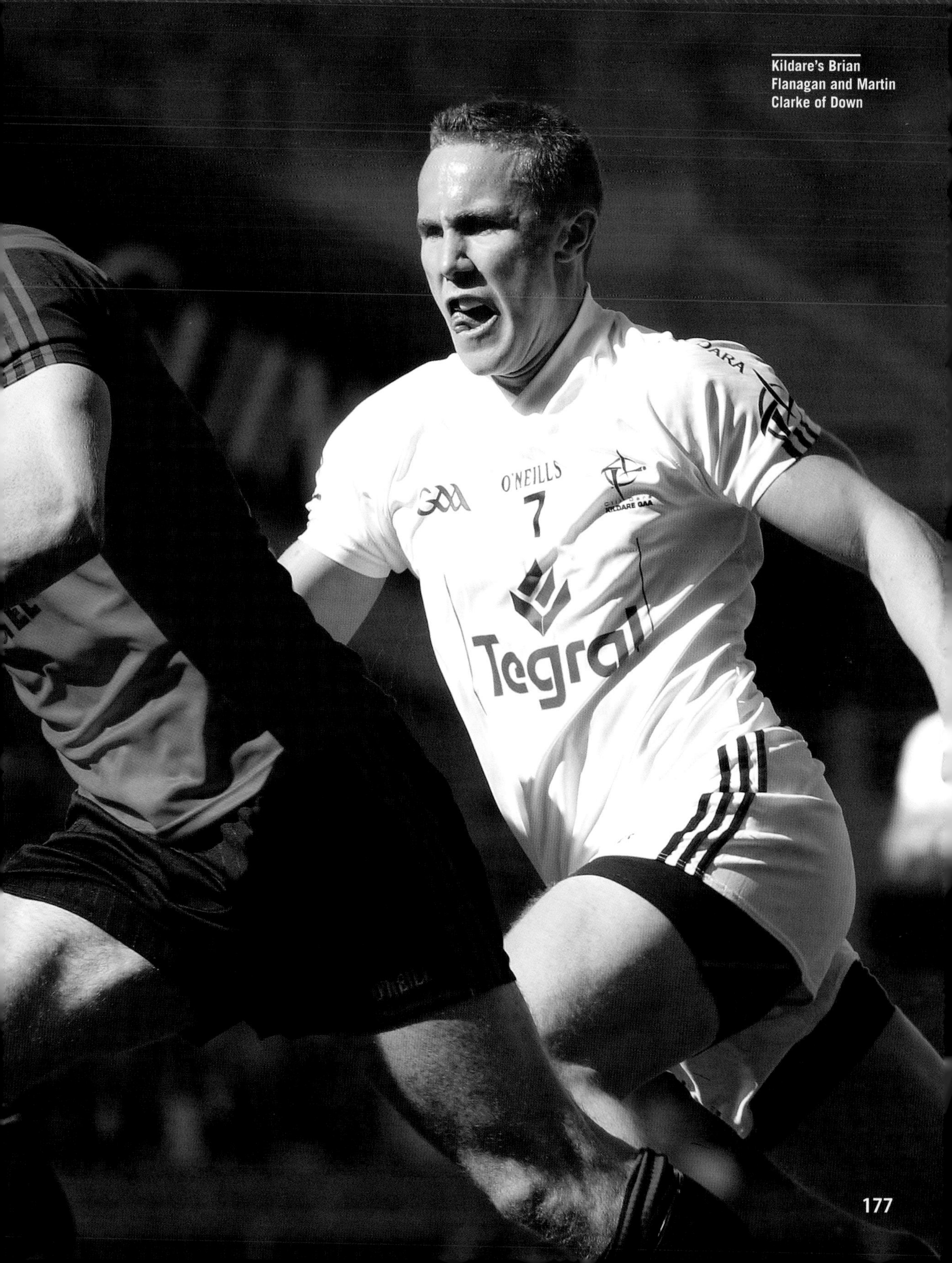

Kildare's Brian Flanagan and Martin Clarke of Down

Kildare's Morgan O'Flaherty and Danny Hughes of Down

The Down team scramble the ball away as Robert Kelly of Kildare takes a free in injury-time

Down's Dan Gordon and Kalum King with Daryl Flynn of Kildare

John Doyle of Kildare with
Conor Garvey of Down

Padraig O'Neill of Kildare with Declan Rooney of Down

John Doyle and Hugh Lynch of Kildare with Kalum King of Down

Down's Brendan Coulter scores a goal despite the efforts of Emmet Bolton and goalkeeper Shane McCormack of Kildare

Down never allowed the tempo to wane, defending in numbers and breaking at pace. After surviving a series of Lilywhite raids they restored their five-point cushion with Poland's third free.

Peter Fitzpatrick, from Clarke's perfect pass, had just opened up a seven-point lead when Eamon Callaghan broke through a gap in the Down defence to smash home a goal for Kildare.

Midfielder Hugh Lynch thumped over a couple of superb long-range points and, with five minutes to play, Kildare were within three points.

Doyle and David Lyons made it a one-point game and in the fourth minute of stoppage time, substitute Robert Kelly's thunderbolt free-kick deflected off the crossbar. The chance was gone, and with it went Kildare's dreams of returning to Croke Park on the third Sunday of September.

KILDARE: S McCormack; P Kelly, H McGrillen, A Mac Lochlainn; M O'Flaherty (0-01), E Bolton (0-01), B Flanagan; D Flynn, H Lynch (0-02); J Kavanagh (0-01), P O'Neill, E O'Flaherty; J Doyle (0-06), A Smith, E Callaghan (1-01) **Subs:** R Sweeney for Flynn; K Ennis (0-01) for M O'Flaherty; D Lyons (0-01) for M O'Flaherty; R Kelly for Smith; T O'Connor for Lynch

DOWN: B McVeigh; D McCartan, D Gordon, D Rafferty; D Rooney, K McKernan (0-02), C Garvey; P Fitzpatrick (0-01), K King; D Hughes (0-02), M Poland (0-03), P McComiskey (0-01); B Coulter (1-02), J Clarke, M Clarke (0-3) **Subs:** A Brannigan for Garvey; C Maginn (0-01) for J Clarke; R Murtagh (0-01) for McComiskey; J Colgan for Poland

REFEREE: P McEnaney (Monaghan)

Benny Coulter of Down celebrates at the final whistle

Donal
Shine

CLUB: Clan na Gael

COUNTY: Roscommon

AGE: 21

HEIGHT: 6'2"

WEIGHT: 14st 3lbs

OCCUPATION: Student

Donie Shine has been playing senior football for Roscommon since 2008. Back in 2006 he and his team-mates caused a huge upset when they beat Kerry in the All-Ireland Minor Final. The game went to a replay and six days after they'd drawn with Kerry in Croke Park they were celebrating an historic All-Ireland minor victory.

This year Donie added a Connacht Senior Football Championship medal to his collection. Despite being under-dogs Roscommon claimed their first provincial title since 2001 when they beat Sligo.

Donie was man-of-the-match in that game, scoring 10 of Roscommon's 14 points.

Donie's footballing hero is Maurice Fitzgerald of Kerry. His free-taking skills have been inspirational to the Clan na Gael man throughout his career.

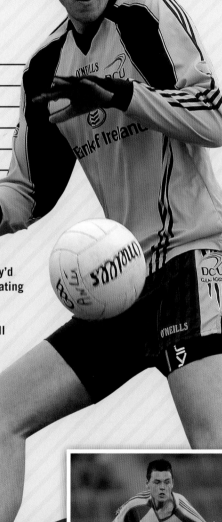

Semi-Final

KILKENNY	3-22	0-19	CORK

8 August 2010

Kilkenny cruised into the All-Ireland Senior Hurling Championship final with a 12-point win over Cork.

This semi-final was over long before half-time. The Cats controlled the game with a masterful performance, killing off the Cork challenge with goals from Eddie Brennan and Aidan Fogarty on their way to a 13-point interval lead.

Cork staged a revival in the second half with a string of well-taken scores from Pat Horgan and Ben O'Connor, but Kilkenny grabbed a third goal from Richie Power to end any faint hopes of a Cork comeback.

Power finished with a personal tally of 1-08, having taken over free-taking duties from Henry Shefflin who picked up a knee injury in the first half.

Cork made two pre-match changes, with Shane Murphy replacing injured corner-back Shane O'Neill, and Cian McCarthy coming in at wing-forward for Michael Cussen.

But it was Kilkenny who imposed themselves on the contest right from the outset in front of an attendance of 41,060.

Early scores from Aidan Fogarty and Shefflin set the tone, and while Cork drew level with two Ben O'Connor frees by the 15th minute, their challenge was simply taken apart by a ruthless Kilkenny side thereafter.

The Cats struck the first major blow in the 17th minute when Shefflin found space through the middle before offloading to Eddie Brennan for a clinical finish.

Five minutes later the Rebels were reeling after conceding a second goal, Aidan Fogarty hitting the net after the Cork defence had failed to clear James Ryall's long delivery.

Even the loss of injured pair Brian Hogan (shoulder, 17 mins) and Shefflin (knee, 22 mins) failed to halt the Kilkenny charge.

With JJ Delaney and Noel Hickey majestic at the back, and James 'Cha' Fitzpatrick and Michael Fennelly lording over the midfield battle, they swept forward relentlessly.

Kilkenny's James 'Cha' Fitzpatrick and Jerry O'Connor of Cork

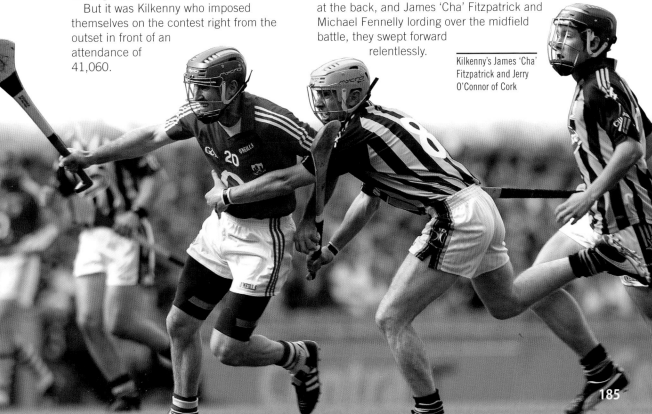

Fogarty, Michael Comerford and Eoin Larkin all fired over points, while Richie Power revelled in the role of free-taker in Shefflin's absence.

By the half-way stage, they led by 2-12 to 0-05, and refused to allow the tempo to wane after the restart.

The Cats dug their claws deeper into their wounded opponents, stretching the advantage with a string of points from Power, Brennan and Fitzpatrick, who became the ninth Kilkenny man to score.

Cork had fallen 17 points adrift by the time O'Connor gave them their first score of the second half, from a free.

Pat Horgan had a penalty deflected over the bar for a point, and added two more scores to raise Rebel spirits.

John Gardiner, and Horgan again, found the target as the Rebels sought to salvage some pride.

It appeared at that stage as if Kilkenny were content to defend a comfortable lead, but in the 62nd minute they exploded into spectacular action once again, for Power to blast home a goal.

Horgan landed another volley of delightful points at the other end, and O'Connor continued to strike accurately from frees, but the Rebels never threatened to win this one.

KILKENNY: PJ Ryan; J Dalton, N Hickey, J Tyrrell; T Walsh (0-01), B Hogan, JJ Delaney; J Fitzpatrick (0-02), M Fennelly (0-02); TJ Reid (0-01), H Shefflin (0-02), E Larkin (0-01); E Brennan (1-01), R Power (1-08), A Fogarty (1-02)
Subs: J Ryall for Hogan; M Comerford (0-02) for Shefflin; M Rice for Brennan; J Mulhall for Reid; D Lyng for Fitzpatrick

CORK: D Óg Cusack; S Murphy, E Cadogan, B Murphy; J Gardiner (0-02), R Curran, S Óg Ó hAilpín (0-01); T Kenny, C Naughton (0-01); C McCarthy, K Murphy, N McCarthy (0-01); P Horgan (0-06), A Ó hAilpín, B O'Connor (0-07)
Subs: W Egan for C McCarthy; P O'Sullivan for A Ó hAilpín; J O'Connor (0-01) for Murphy; M Cussen for Naughton, G Callanan for Kenny

REFEREE: B Gavin (Offaly)

Tempers flare off the ball during the game

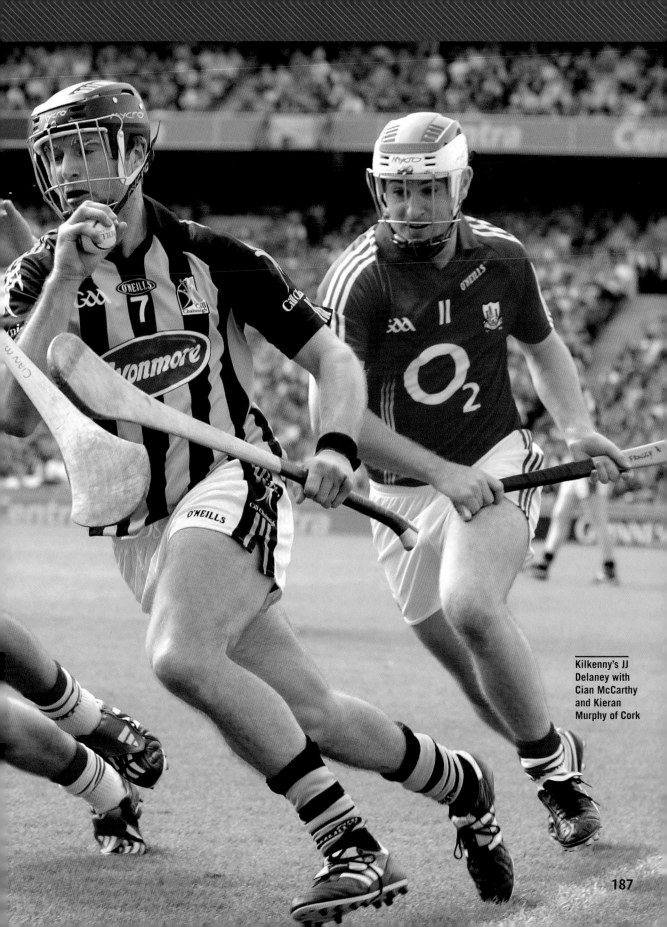

Kilkenny's JJ
Delaney with
Cian McCarthy
and Kieran
Murphy of Cork

Kilkenny's Michael Fennelly and James 'Cha' Fitzpatrick tackle Ben O'Connor of Cork

Waterford's Kevin Moran shoulders
Gearóid Ryan of Tipperary over the line

Semi-Final

TIPPERARY	3-19	1-18	WATERFORD

15 August 2010

Tipperary set up a repeat of last year's All-Ireland Hurling final with a comfortable seven-point win over Waterford in Croke Park.

The scene is now set for another meeting between Liam Sheedy's in-form side and a Kilkenny outfit gunning for a fifth successive title.

Eoin Kelly smashed in two second-half goals to add to Lar Corbett's three-pointer, and Waterford, who were always chasing the game, never looked like overhauling their Munster rivals.

In front of a Croke Park crowd of 49,754, there was nothing to separate the sides throughout an opening quarter that saw them level on five occasions. Noel McGrath, John O'Brien and Eoin Kelly all hit the target for Tipp, with Richie Foley, Eoin Kelly, Kevin Moran and John Mullane – with two splendid efforts – responding for Waterford.

But with Shane McGrath getting through an immense amount of work at midfield, Tipperary began to gain an edge.

McGrath steered over an inspirational long-range point, and in the 23rd minute they struck for a goal.

Pádraic Maher's searching delivery arrived in the danger area, where Lar Corbett beat Liam Lawlor to possession and directed a close-range shot past Clinton Hennessy.

Having handed a first championship start to teenager Brian O'Halloran, Davy Fitzgerald's gamble failed to pay off, and he was forced to withdraw the youngster after 21 minutes with Tipperary full-back Paul Curran having imposed himself on the personal duel.

And Liam Sheedy's men finished the half strongly, with Noel McGrath bringing his tally to 0-04.

They led by 1-11 to 0-08 at the break, with all but a point of their first-half total having come from play.

Mullane drifted deeper to win possession, and steered over a long-range point to add to those scored soon after the restart by Tony Browne and Eoin Kelly, both from frees.

Kelly's fifth free narrowed the gap to three after his Tipperary namesake had failed to find the target from a straightforward free.

And with Michael 'Brick' Walsh driving on from centre-back, Waterford looked a more potent force.

But their revival was cut short in the 53rd minute when Kelly

Kevin Moran of Waterford with
Conor O'Mahony and Brendan
Maher of Tipperary

showed his predatory instincts to smash home a goal with the Waterford defence failing to clear McGrath's sideline cut.

Tipperary now led by eight, and turned the screw to punish a flagging Waterford defence with a third goal on the hour.

It was the intuitive Corbett who slipped the ball inside for Kelly to beat Hennessy with a crisply struck finish, and it was all over for Waterford.

Veterans Ken McGrath and Mullane refused to admit defeat, and the latter brought a wonderful save from Brendan Cummins.

Substitute Eoin McGrath hit a consolation goal in the dying moments, but O'Brien set the seal on an impressive Tipperary win with his sixth point from play.

TIPPERARY: B Cummins; P Stapleton, P Curran, M Cahill; D Fanning, C O'Mahony, Pádraic Maher; B Maher, S McGrath (0-01); G Ryan, Patrick Maher, J O'Brien (0-06); N McGrath (0-06), E Kelly (2-04, 0-03), L Corbett (1-02)
Subs: S Callanan for G Ryan; P Bourke for Patrick Maher

WATERFORD: C Hennessy; E Murphy, L Lawlor, N Connors; T Browne (0-03), M Walsh, D Prendergast; S O'Sullivan, R Foley (0-01); K Moran (0-01), S Molumphy (0-01), E Kelly (0-05); J Mullane (0-03), S Walsh, B O'Halloran
Subs: S Prendergast (0-01) for O'Halloran; K McGrath (0-03) for Kelly; D Shanahan for Moran; T Ryan for Molumphy; E McGrath (1-00) for S Walsh

REFEREE: J Sexton (Cork)

Tipperary's John O'Brien rises highest in the square

Tipperary's Noel McGrath
runs past Jackie Tyrrell
and John Tennyson

Final

TIPPERARY	4-17	1-18	KILKENNY

5 September 2010

Tipperary's first All-Ireland hurling title since 2001 thwarted Kilkenny's bid for a fifth successive Liam McCarthy Cup triumph.

Liam Sheedy's heroes produced a devastating attacking display, embellished by a Lar Corbett hat-trick, as they swept to a 26th success.

Kilkenny's first championship defeat in 22 games was delivered in compelling fashion by the Munster men, who always believed in themselves, and in their capacity to avenge last season's painful defeat in the decider.

Brian Cody's gamble on attacker Henry Shefflin's famous knee did not come off, and the Kilkenny ace was forced to retire injured after just 12 minutes.

In front of a crowd of 81,765, Eoin Kelly had already swept over three frees when Tipp stunned the Cats with a Corbett goal in the tenth minute.

Shane McGrath's booming delivery was collected confidently by Corbett, who turned stumbling full-back Noel Hickey and planted the ball in the net from close range past PJ Ryan in one smooth movement.

Kilkenny crafted a goal chance of their own soon afterwards when Henry Shefflin sent TJ Reid through, but his shot was comfortably dealt with by Brendan Cummins.

The All-Ireland champions suffered another blow in the 12th minute when ace attacker Shefflin was forced to go off with problems to his damaged knee.

Nevertheless, they narrowed the gap, with Richie Power taking over the free-taking duties to plant one between the posts, and Aidan Fogarty guiding over a point.

Tipp were still calling the shots, however, and scores from Brendan Maher and Kelly saw them open out a 1-7 to 0-4 lead.

Even goalkeeper Brendan Cummins got in on the act with a point from a massive free, but with John Tennyson, JJ Delaney and Michael Fennelly leading by example and using their vast experience and know-how, Kilkenny set about dismantling that advantage.

Power was unerring from frees, and smashed home a brilliant 33rd-minute goal after Eoin Larkin had sliced through the Tipp defence.

Two more Power frees narrowed the gap to a single point, leaving

Tipperary ahead by 1-10 to 1-09 at the break.

Skipper TJ Reid's expertly executed sideline cut brought the sides level on 38 minutes, but Corbett's second goal set Croke Park alight,

He gave PJ Ryan no chance with a screaming shot after getting on the end of Noel McGrath's exquisite defence-splitting pass in the 42nd minute.

Two minutes later, Tipp had the ball in the net again, McGrath scrambling home from close range to open up a seven point advantage and leave the McCarthy Cup holders with a mountain to climb.

But with Jackie Tyrell and Tommy Walsh driving from the back, the Cats started to claw their way back.

Power and Reid added to their personal tallies, and it looked as if a raft of substitutions had started to work for Brian Cody.

But Liam Sheedy's decision to spring Seamus Callanan from the bench had an instant effect, with the big attacker sweeping over two magnificent points.

Fellow subs Benny Dunne and Seamus Hennessy also tagged on scores, and Pádraic Maher was in imperious form at the back for Tipp, repelling a series of Kilkenny attacks.

And deep into stoppage time, a sweet triumph was sealed when Corbett drilled home to complete his hat-trick.

Tipperary's Shane McGrath celebrates at the final whistle

TIPPERARY: B Cummins (0-01); P Stapleton, P Curran, M Cahill; D Fanning, C O'Mahony, Pádraic Maher; B Maher (0-02), S McGrath; G Ryan (0-01), Patrick Maher, J O'Brien (0-02); N McGrath (1-00), E Kelly (0-07), L Corbett (3-00)
Subs: C O'Brien for O'Mahony; S Callanan (0-02) for O'Brien; B Dunne (0-01) for S McGrath; S Hennessy (0-01) for B Maher

KILKENNY: PJ Ryan; J Dalton, N Hickey, J Tyrrell; T Walsh, J Tennyson, JJ Delaney; J Fitzpatrick, M Fennelly; TJ Reid (0-04), H Shefflin (0-01), E Larkin; E Brennan, R Power (1-09), A Fogarty (0-01)
Subs: M Rice (0-01) for Shefflin; M Comerford for Brennan; D Lyng (0-01) for Fitzpatrick; R Hogan for Fogarty; J Mulhall (0-01) for Reid

REFEREE: M Wadding (Waterford)

Lar Corbett of Tipperary grabs the sliotar ahead of Noel Hickey to score a goal

199

Kilkenny's Eoin Larkin is tackled by Conor O'Mahony and Paddy Stapleton of Tipperary

Richie Power of Kilkenny dejected at the end of the game

Tipperary's Eoin Kelly raises the Liam McCarthy Cup

EVANNE NÍ CHUILINN

'People don't realise camogie players, like footballers and hurlers, train six nights a week. We play club championship in between the All-Ireland semi-final and the All-Ireland final. We have no life. Absolutely no life other than camogie'

The words of Wexford centre-back, Mary Leacy, minutes after her team beat Galway by two points in the biggest game of the camogie calendar. Based on her performance, and that of her defensive colleagues, during the last 15 minutes of this year's senior final, one would be forgiven for thinking that Leacy literally does nothing but hook, block, and point from play all day long, from May until September.

Right on the hour mark, when Aislinn Connolly's free deceived even Mags D'Arcy to raise the green flag for Galway, Wexford were forced to show exactly just how bullish they could be. Just two points up, a dramatic climax meant that they had a minute of injury-time to ensure the ball came nowhere near D'Arcy again, and with the pendulum of momentum swinging steadily towards Galway, Wexford knew it was all or nothing.

'We didn't care what kind of game it looked like, we battled it out,' said Leacy in the immediate aftermath of the final. '[There was] a lot of hooking and blocking in the second half. We didn't care if we won by one point or 10 points – just the win was the main aim. It was body, head, legs, everything was going in. I think everyone gave 100 per cent.'

The favourites tag is something that doesn't always sit easily with teams, well-seasoned campaigners or otherwise. For four years, Brian Cody's Kilkenny squad learned how to deal with the innate pressure that comes hand-in-hand with the assumption of victory, but they were duly rendered mortal by a hungrier Tipperary team this year.

Wexford too went into their second All-Ireland final in four years, and their second national final of 2010, as firm favourites to land the O'Duffy Cup. The Model County, under the new stewardship of JJ Doyle, hassled and harassed their way through the championship, and cemented their reputation as the most physical and challenging of oppositions.

The round-robin format of the GALA All-Ireland Senior Camogie Championship was reinstated this year after a brief experiment with two groups of four in 2009. While the jury is still out in some quarters, the structure has been welcomed by the country's top players over the last number of years.

However, Kilkenny manager Ann Downey is on the record as expressing her reservations about the quick turnaround nature of the championship. Her concern is justifiable, in that injuries become part and parcel of the season. A hamstring strain picked up in round 1 can rule a player out for rounds 2 and 3. On the other hand, teams always have a second chance; one that Wexford relished this year. They were beaten by Galway in the round-robin stage, but made amends when it mattered.

This year, Cumann Camógaíochta na nGael revelled in the chance to claim total control over Croke Park on the second Sunday in September. The GAA's decision to remove the Under-21 Hurling final from the bill on that day was met with disappointment by some camogie fans, who had to make an extra journey to see both games.

However, the change represented a unique opportunity for the Camogie Association. Far from demoting the code, there was an increase in the number of camogie enthusiasts at Croke Park this year. Traditionally, the Under-21s have attracted a crowd of 26,000, with camogie deciders drawing about 15,000. On 12 September 2010 however, 18,000 boisterous fans made their mark on the Hogan Stand.

RTÉ's *Sunday Game* cameras were re-housed in the Cusack Stand, so that the full effect of a compact crowd was appropriately highlighted and promoted.

The added intrigue of the intermediate final, featuring the great Joachim Kelly's Offaly outfit, paid dividends as the junior and senior finalists benefited from more 'inherited' bums on seats. The first triple-header on All-Ireland final day saw six teams from five counties, and all four provinces represented. The competing counties also postponed all major hurling fixtures scheduled for the day, which was a welcome gesture from the GAA.

On the field, a review of the Senior Camogie Championship reveals an encouraging trend. Not only have we new National League Champions and new All-Ireland Champions, but the place occupied by Cork in recent years is suddenly under threat. Galway dismissed the Leesiders at the penultimate stage of this year's championship, but even that target was only met with a replay and an eventual one-point win.

Kilkenny, last year's runners-up, won all but one of their round-robin matches before being blitzed by Wexford's physicality. The Kittens, as a team, have an array of underage medals, and are an All-Ireland-winning team for the very near future.

Tipperary drew the short straw in finishing just outside the top four; Dublin continue to build steadily as real contenders, while Clare have caused a few upsets in recent seasons, and are emerging as the most likely banana skin for the big four.

And so, back to the inspiring post All-Ireland final thoughts of one Wexford woman: 'The Wexford supporters, they really do follow the women. I think women's sport in general, whether it's camogie, even rugby, swimming or soccer, is not thought of in the same way [as men's] by people. Even women don't follow women's sport. But the supporters in the Hogan Stand are the best supporters in the country.'

While her colleagues treated the Hogan dressing rooms as their own karaoke booth, Mary Leacy used the opportunity to send out a message through the assembled media. In explaining how camogie players force the respect from sports fans that her male counterparts often take as read, she pointed out the only difference between herself and an All-Ireland winning hurler.

Wexford rowed in behind their camogie players this year, just as they did in 2007. Their support often out-classed that of their male colleagues in the county that year, and thousands of people lined the streets of Gorey, Enniscorthy and Wexford town for the O'Duffy Cup homecoming once again this year.

For the code of camogie to continue with the strides it has made this year, and to repeat the highs of 2010 in 2011, the code's promoters and supporters would do well to take a trip to the sunny southeast.

Comhghairdeachas le foireann bhainistíochta agus imreoirí Loch Gorman. Le cúnamh Dé beidh Craobh Comórtas iontach iomaíoch againn arís an bhliain seo chugainn. Beidh sé do dhéanta aon srian a chur ar an bhfuadar a bheidh ós ár gcomhair amach i 2011.

2010 National League Champions – Wexford
2010 All-Ireland Senior Champions – Wexford
2010 All-Ireland Intermediate Champions – Offaly
2010 All-Ireland Junior Champions – Antrim

Wexford's Katrina Parrock celebrates scoring a goal

Final

DUBLIN	3-16	0-09	TYRONE

26 September 2010

Sinead Aherne shot the lights out at Croke Park as Dublin finally captured the TG4 All-Ireland Ladies' Senior Football Championship after three previous final defeats.

The Sky Blues ran out comprehensive 16-point winners against first-time finalists Tyrone in front of 21,750 spectators at Croke Park

Dublin lost against Cork in last year's decider and also finished runners-up against Galway in 2004 and Mayo in 2003.

But it was clear from the moment Aherne opened the scoring with 37 seconds on the clock that there would be no denying Dublin on this occasion.

Manager Gerry McGill and his players were left devastated last September when Cork won a final that Dublin had dominated until the closing stages.

The pain was even more acute for Aherne, who missed a first half penalty against Cork but the St Sylvester's All-Star produced a stunning performance against Tyrone to banish any lingering memories from the 2009 decider.

The full-forward was simply sensational and finished with a personal tally of 2-07 (2-04 from play) to claim the player of the match award.

Aherne's movement was too much for her direct marker Maura Kelly, a fine defender in her own right, to cope with, and overall this was a superb Dublin performance.

From goalkeeper Cliodhna O'Connor, who was spot-on with her pinpoint kickouts, through to left corner-forward Elaine Kelly, Dublin dominated proceedings and had this game wrapped up by half-time.

At the break, the Leinster champions – who were relegated from Division 1 of the Bord Gáis

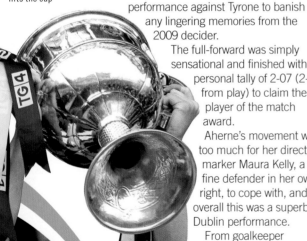

Denise Masterson lifts the cup

Energy National League earlier this year – led by 2-08 to 0-05.

There was no letting up in the second half as Dublin continued to display an incredible work-rate and appetite that Tyrone could not match.

Their full-back line was rock solid and, at midfield, captain Denise Masterson led by example with a display of boundless energy in both halves of the field.

In attack, five of Dublin's six starting forwards were on target from play and while Mary Nevin may not have got on the scoresheet, the experienced Na Fianna star put in one hell of a shift.

One of the survivors from the 2003, 2004 and 2009 defeats, Nevin was called ashore with eight minutes to go and the look of joy on her face as she embraced manager McGill was one of the images of the season.

Tyrone, meanwhile, had emerged as one of the stories of the year after bouncing back from their Ulster championship defeat to Armagh to make it all the way to Croke Park.

Along the way, the Red Hands hit a combined 11-42 against Leitrim and Sligo before accounting for Cork, who had won the last five All-Ireland titles, in a remarkable quarter-final.

Tyrone then shook off Kerry after a replay but, just when they needed it most, their form deserted them as stage-fright appeared to play a part in a below-par performance.

Midway through the first half, Tyrone were still in contention, trailing by 0-03 to 0-06, but Dublin then began to press home their superiority.

Their first goal arrived in the 16th minute, courtesy of hard-working centre-forward Amy McGuinness, who would not be denied after Kelly had kept out her initial effort with a fine block.

On the follow-up, Lyndsey Davey rattled a shot off the crossbar before McGuinness followed up to bulge the Tyrone net.

Prior to that Tyrone had lost full-forward Sarah Connolly to a broken finger and their day continued to deteriorate as Dublin dominated the game and finished the half with a superb 27th-minute goal from Aherne.

Sorcha Furlong's perceptive crossfield pass left Aherne one on one with Kelly and, after selling the full-back a dummy, Aherne slipped a shot beneath Shannon Lynch and into the net.

Within eight minutes of the restart, Dublin were 14 points clear as Aherne took a pass from Elaine Kelly and slotted home her second goal.

With 20 minutes remaining, Dublin led by 16 points against a shell-shocked Tyrone. That lead was retained right up until the final whistle and it could have been even more but for a fine save by Tyrone goalkeeper Lynch to deny Lyndsey Peat a fourth Dublin goal with two minutes remaining.

In the intermediate final Donegal held off valiant underdogs Waterford. It finished Donegal 2-12 Waterford 0-16.

Limerick produced a stunning second-half comeback to claim the ladies' junior title. They beat Louth 4-10 to 3-08.

Dublin's Amy McGuinness and Eimear Martin Celebrate after the game

DUBLIN: C O'Connor; R Ruddy, A Cluxton, M Kavanagh; S McGrath, S Furlong, G Fay (0-01); D Masterson, N McEvoy; M Nevin, A McGuinness (1-03), L Peat (0-01); L Davey (0-02), S Aherne (2-07), E Kelly (0-02)
Subs: B Finlay for Kelly; N Hyland for Nevin; N Healy for McGuinness; N McEvoy for N McEvoy; C Barrett for Fay

TYRONE: S Lynch; E Teague, M Kelly, S McLaughlin; M Donnelly, N Woods, L Donnelly; S Donnelly, S Quinn; C Donnelly (0-01), G Begley (0-04), A O'Kane; C McGahan, S Connolly, J Donnelly (0-03).
Subs: N Murphy (0-01) for Connolly; R Rafferty for Teague; M Gallagher for M Donnelly; O O'Neill for McGahan; C Scullion for A O'Kane

REFEREE: K Delahunty (Tipperary)

Final

CORK	0-16	0-15	DOWN

19 September 2010

Resurgent Cork won their first All-Ireland football title since 1990 with a one-point comeback win over Down at an emotion-filled Croke Park.

After so many setbacks, disappointments and false dawns, the Rebels finally got their hands on the Sam Maguire once again, but they had to dig deep into their reserves of courage and self-belief to see off the Mourne men.

Down led by 0-08 to 0-05 at half-time, but the Rebels turned on the style in the second period. An eight-point tally from Daniel Goulding and five from Donncha O'Connor helped them over the finish line as they inflicted a first ever All-Ireland Senior Football final defeat on Down.

Cork suffered a pre-match blow when injured skipper Graham Canty was withdrawn from the starting fifteen, but they made an explosive start, and Down goalkeeper Brendan McVeigh had to produce a brilliant save to deny Ciaran Sheehan inside the opening minute.

Goulding converted a free, providing the first of just two points for the Rebels in the opening half-hour.

In the meantime, the Mourne men settled in to perform with style and purpose, with Mark Poland and Martin Clarke providing the clever passes and inside duo John Clarke and Paul McComiskey providing the finishing power.

The hard-working Daniel Hughes also contributed a couple of scores as the Ulster men opened up a 0-07 to 0-02 lead by the 27th minute.

Aidan Walsh garnered plenty of possession around the midfield area, but too often found himself closed down by the eager Down men, with half-backs Declan Rooney, Kevin McKernan and Conor Garvey responsible for a handful of vital turnovers.

Conor Counihan's men struggled to deliver long ball to test the Down full-back line and it wasn't until the 32nd minute that Cork got their first point from play.

Goulding latched on to a Pearse O'Neill pass to strike sweetly over the bar for his 100th

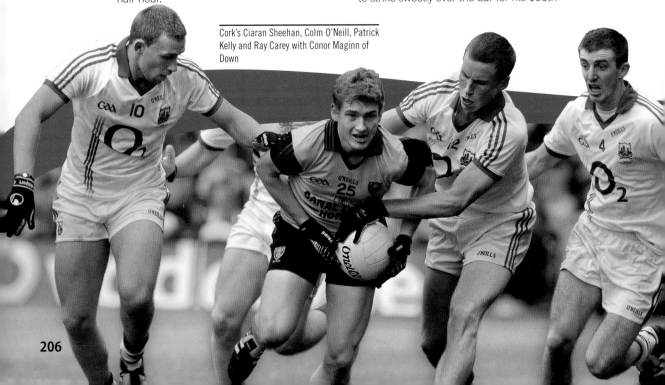

Cork's Ciaran Sheehan, Colm O'Neill, Patrick Kelly and Ray Carey with Conor Maginn of Down

championship point. That was soon followed by a superb score from O'Connor, but Down went in at the break three points ahead.

Counihan introduced the experienced Nicholas Murphy to his midfield at half-time, and while he made an immediate impact, it was Down who stretched the advantage with a delightful angled effort from McComiskey.

Canty joined the action six minutes into the second half with his side still trailing by three, after Goulding had narrowed the deficit from a free.

With a couple of seasoned campaigners now on the field to guide them, Cork enjoyed their best spell of the game, using possession more wisely.

Goulding and O'Connor swept over splendid scores, and it was the flying Paul Kerrigan who sprinted through on 56 minutes to give the Leesiders the lead for the first time since the fifth minute.

Goulding steered over three '45's to open up a three-point lead for a Cork side now performing with fluency and conviction.

Down refused to give up, and late scores from Benny Coulter and Hughes narrowed the gap to a single point, but Cork held on to reach the Promised Land.

CORK: A Quirke; E Cadogan, M Shields, R Carey; N O'Leary, J Miskella, P Kissane; A O'Connor, A Walsh; C Sheehan (0-01); P O'Neill, P Kelly, D Goulding (0-09); D O'Connor (0-05), P Kerrigan (0 01)
Subs: N Murphy for A O'Connor; G Canty for P Kissane; C O'Neill for P O'Neill; J Hayes for P Kerrigan

DOWN: B McVeigh; D McCartan, D Gordon, D Rafferty; D Rooney, K McKernan (0-01), C Garvey; P Fitzpatrick (0-01), K King; D Hughes (0-03), M Poland (0-01), B Coulter (0-01); P McComiskey (0-03), J Clarke (0-01), M Clarke (0-03)
Subs: C Maginn for J Clarke; R Murtagh (0-01) for P McComiskey; B McArdle for D Rafferty; C Laverty for M Poland

REFEREE: D Coldrick (Meath)

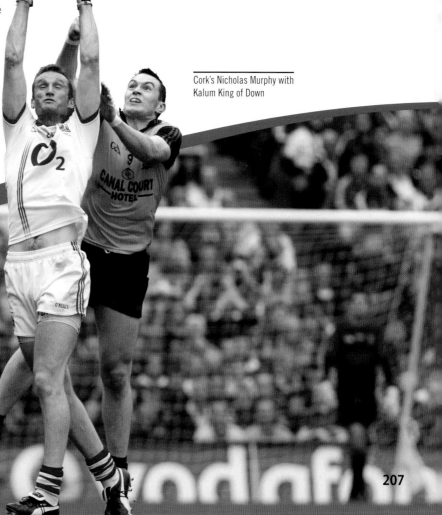

Cork's Nicholas Murphy with Kalum King of Down

Graham Canty
lifts the Sam
Maguire

Cork players celebrate at the end of the game

Cork's Graham
Canty lifts the
Sam Maguire Cup

Ambrose Rogers
of Down dejected
at the end of the
game

211

DES CAHILL

Hurling

10. Carlow make the step up

Every genuine hurling fan was thrilled with Carlow's performance this year. After a very good league campaign in division 2, they were beaten by Laois in the preliminary round of the Leinster championship.

But when the sides were drawn again in the qualifiers, Carlow scored a famous victory, winning with an injury-time point from Denis Murphy. It finished Carlow 1-19 Laois 3-12.

Carlow then travelled to Casement Park, and performed heroically again – it was only a controversial decision for an Antrim goal that saw them lose by 2-18 to 3-12.

Here's hoping they can build on it for next year!

9. Antrim beat the Dubs

It's an ongoing battle for Antrim hurlers to keep the game strong in Ulster.

They were complete underdogs when they travelled to Croke Park to take on Anthony Daly's side. In the previous round, Antrim had scraped past Carlow, while Dublin had a hugely impressive win over Clare.

But Antrim produced a brilliant display that saw them stay in touch with the Dubs throughout, and finish the stronger to score a memorable win and earn a clash with Cork in the quarter-final.

8. Henry Shefflin's standing ovation

It was the most high profile GAA injury for years. We were told Henry Shefflin would DEFINITELY miss the final after his cruciate knee injury in the semi-final. Then we heard how much hard work he was doing with physio Ger Hartmann to beat the odds and make an appearance. Then we had a crowd of 8,000 cheering at Nowlan Park as he took part in a training session.

Then he's named in the starting line-up for the final. Incredible! But how long would he last?

Sadly, he only lasted 12 minutes before his knee gave in.

But it was really emotional to watch both sets of supporters give him a standing ovation – in recognition of an incredible effort to make the final. A rare and special moment!

7. Kilkenny show they can be classy in defeat

It is easy to win graciously. When you have the trophy in your hands you can heap praise on all of your opponents and all the officials.

But this year Kilkenny's management and players deserve great credit for the manner in which they overcame the massive pain of failing to win the five in a row.

There were no complaints or excuses about losing their star man Henry Shefflin so early in the game, or decisions going against them. They simply praised and congratulated Tipperary graciously for being the better team and deserving their win.

It just added to our respect for this great squad.

6. Offaly on the way back

Wasn't it great to see Offaly making a mark again in the Leinster Championship?

Their two semi-final clashes with Galway produced great drama and excitement, but more importantly seemed to restore their supporters' pride.

Having drawn the original game in Croke Park (Offaly 3-16 Galway 2-19), it was generally felt that Galway had got off the hook and would win the replay comfortably.

Galway cruised into a big lead in Portlaoise, but Offaly showed great pride and grit as they battled back in a real thriller, before eventually being pipped by 3-17 to 2-18.

5. Cork v Tipp in the Munster quarter-final
Cork 3-15 Tipperary 0-14

What a fantastic way to get the championship underway! A massive shock as Tipperary were torn apart by a brilliant Cork display.

There were so many elements to Cork's stunning win – notably, Donal Óg Cusack's puck-outs, Eoin Cadogan at full-back, the peerless display from the Cork half-back line, and Aisake Ó hAilpín's stunning performance at full-forward.

And we all wondered if Tipperary were gone after this defeat!

4. Tipp v Galway: A quarter-final to bring the championship alive

The Hurling Championship needed a boost by the time these sides met in the quarter-final. Both sides had previously underperformed in big games, but not on this occasion.

It was a real thriller, and Tipp fans will admit they were relieved to come away with a 3-17 to 3-16 victory.

But as the summer progressed, it was clear that we were watching Tipp's youngsters learning and maturing and growing in stature.

Spare a thought for Galway, though – they did little wrong and in September they must have been wondering about what might have been!

3. Tony Browne's free

It may not have been a classic Munster final but it was dramatic. After a dull start the game sparked to life in the second half when Cork hit two goals in under two minutes.

It appeared Cork were coasting to victory but Waterford began to eat into their lead. Three minutes into injury-time, Waterford were three points behind when they were awarded a 20-metre free. Like any free-taker worth their salt Eoin Kelly went for the jugular but Donal Óg Cusack and his defenders stood firm.

But cometh the hour (or the 74th minute in this case) cometh the man. The evergreen Tony Browne waltzed in, struck a sweet ground stroke on the rebounding ball and the net shook. At 37 years of age, the oldest man playing in the championship had given Waterford a second chance!

2. The Munster Final replay: Waterford win under the lights

A fantastic win for Waterford, and a great team display - but the setting added to the occasion. The replay needed extra time, and that meant the floodlights were on for the thrilling finale in Thurles. The great Dan Shanahan came on as a sub to score a tremendous winning goal for Waterford, and it will be a long time before I forget the amazing sight of the wild celebrations amongst the Waterford supporters who were soaked to the skin by the driving rain. They couldn't have been happier if they were basking on a beach in Hawaii!

1. Tipp v Kilkenny: The classic final
Tipperary 4-17 Kilkenny 1-18

This final will be remembered for years. It was a fast flowing thriller that saw Tipp's young tigers overcoming one of the greatest sides in the history of the game.

Lar Corbett gets the plaudits for a magnificent hat-trick of goals, but this was very much a team performance. Tipp played with courage, skill, tenacity and a coolness that won universal praise.

But it takes two teams to provide a thriller and, as ever, Kilkenny battled to the end, and on several occasions when it looked like the match was gone from them, they came back into contention.

I'm looking forward to next season already!

Football

10. Kildare's battling qualities

Yes, it looked like a disaster for the Lillies when they lost to Louth in Leinster. But Kieran McGeeney has moulded a team that showed fantastic mental strength and resilience to continually defy the odds in the qualifiers.

Their victories in Antrim and Derry brought them to Croke Park where they played some fantastic football as they beat Monaghan, then Meath in an absolute thriller, before being edged out by Down in the semi-final, in a breathtaking game!

9. Sligo beat Galway and Mayo

Sligo were the star turn in the early part of the championship. They showed remarkable skill and courage as they overcame both Mayo and Galway in thrilling encounters. Their fans felt the team didn't do themselves justice in the Connacht final, but there is the compensation of recalling the famous wins over Connacht's big two!

8. Dublin's newcomers convince the Hill

The narrow one-point defeat to eventual winners Cork masks a remarkable year for the Dubs. Pat Gilroy and his management team deserve massive credit for developing a new team and staying loyal to them when their supporters deserted them. Crowds dwindled for Dublin's games in the qualifiers; there was even a 'Gilroy Out!' banner on display. But they stuck to their principles and the young Dublin side finished as one of the most impressive teams of the 2010 championship.

7. Kerry v Cork replay in Killarney
Kerry 1-15 Cork 1-14

A repeat of last year's All-Ireland final. The first game in Páirc Uí Chaoimh the previous week couldn't separate them and this needed extra-time!

It was pulsating stuff. Intense rivalry and neither side prepared to concede anything to the other. Colm Cooper inspired a Kerry win and lots of experts were quick to say that Kerry wouldn't be beaten...and that Cork were gone!

6. Roscommon win the Connacht title
Roscommon 0-14 Sligo 0-13

Boy did the Roscommon supporters show how much a Connacht title meant to them at the final whistle! Fantastic scenes after a memorable win for the young Roscommon team.

Donie Shine was the individual star with 10 fantastic points, but credit must be shared all over the pitch for the Roscommon lads who built up an impressive lead and then hung on with great tenacity to earn their first Connacht title since 2001.

5. Bernard Brogan

In a team game it's not always fair to pick out an individual, because a lot of others have to do a lot of dirty work to help the 'stars' shine. However, Bernard Brogan's scoring exploits were quite outstanding and definitely one of the memories of the football year. He was double marked in most games, but that never stopped him gaining possession.

Even more impressively, he then maintained the poise, strength and balance required to get his scores despite the close attention of so many defenders.

A class year for the St Oliver Plunkett's man.

4. Dermot Earley plays on the night of his dad's funeral

The death of Lieutenant-General Dermot Earley brought great sadness to the GAA family which was immensely proud of his achievements – both on and off the pitch.

Many fantastic tributes were paid to him at every level of society. But surely the greatest tribute came from his son, Dermot, who lined out for Kildare against Antrim on the evening of his funeral.

It must have been so difficult for him, but he knew that would be exactly what his Dad would have wanted.

A great moment.

3. Down beat Kerry and Kildare in Croke Park

Despite their defeat to Tyrone in the Ulster semi-final, this talented young Down team continued to blossom under James McCartan and his management team. They progressed impressively through the qualifiers, and then lit up when they got to Croke Park.

Surely it was the performance of the year when they beat champions Kerry in the quarter-final by 1-16 to 1-10!

They followed that up with an equally exciting victory over Kildare, by 1-16 to 1-14, in the semi-final.

Yes, they were beaten in the final, but their first-half display against Cork showed they are capable of going all the way in the future.

2. Cork end the heartache

Nobody can begrudge Cork their victory in the 2010 championship. Having been in the previous six semi-finals, and having lost three finals, they earned their title the hard way.

Lots of people were writing them off after their defeat to Kerry and what they considered an unimpressive run in the qualifiers.

But they stayed focused, and enjoyed a thrilling win over Dublin in the semi-final. They trailed badly against Down during the final, but yet again that Rebel spirit emerged, and they were quite brilliant in the second half and deservedly took the title.

Who will be good enough to topple them next year?

1. Louth v Meath

This is certainly not my favourite moment from the year – quite the opposite, but I think it will be the most memorable. In 20 years time anyone who saw it will remember how Meath's Joe Sheridan was incorrectly awarded a goal in stoppage time to take the title.

There is no other way of saying it: Louth were robbed of a first provincial title in 50 years by a dreadful decision from the team of officials.

It certainly wasn't satisfactory for Meath, but it's hard to put into words the sense of injustice felt by the Louth squad.

They had played heroically to be on the cusp of one of the greatest GAA achievements for years. A cruel, cruel moment.

Here's hoping they come battling back next year!